Optimize
Equity and Trusts

D1368843

OPTIMIZE LAW REVISION

Titles in the series:
Contract Law
Criminal Law
The English Legal System
Equity and Trusts
EU Law
Land Law
Public Law
Tort Law

The Optimize series' academic advisors are:

— **Michael Bromby**, Higher Education Academy Discipline Lead for Law 2011–2013, Reader in Law, GCU.

'The use of visualisation in Optimize will help students to focus on the key issues when revising.'

— **Emily Allbon**, Law Librarian and creator of Lawbore, City University.

'Partnering well-explained, comprehensive content with visual tools like maps and flowcharts is what makes the Optimize series so unique. These books help students take their learning up a notch; offering support in grappling with the subject, as well as insight into what will help make their work stand out.'

— **Sanmeet Kaur Dua**, Lecturer in Law, co-creator of Lawbore, City University.

'This series sets out the essential concepts and principles that students need to grasp in a logical way by combining memorable visual diagrams and text. Students will find that they will not easily forget what they read in this series as the unique aim higher and interaction points will leave a blueprint in their minds.'

— **Zoe Swan**, Senior Lecturer in Law, University of Brighton.

'The wide range of visual material includes diagrams, charts, tables and maps enable students to check their knowledge and understanding on each topic area, every step of the way... When combined with carefully explained legal principles and solid, understandable examples, students will find this series provides them with a win- win solution to the study of law and developing revision techniques.'

Optimize
Equity and Trusts

Judith Riches

Routledge
Taylor & Francis Group

LONDON AND NEW YORK

First published 2014
by Routledge
2 Park Square, Milton Park, Abingdon, Oxon OX14 4RN

and by Routledge
711 Third Avenue, New York, NY 10017

Routledge is an imprint of the Taylor & Francis Group, an informa business
© 2014 Judith Riches

British Library Cataloguing in Publication Data
A catalogue record for this book is available from the British Library

Library of Congress Cataloging in Publication Data
A catalog record for this book has been requested

ISBN: 978-0-415-83373-8 (pbk)
ISBN: 978-1-315-84900-3 (ebk)

Typeset in TheSans
by RefineCatch Limited, Bungay, Suffolk

MIX
Paper from
responsible sources
FSC   FSC® C013604
www.fsc.org

Printed and bound by CPI Group (UK) Ltd, Croydon, CR0 4YY

Contents

Optimize – Your Blueprint for Exam Success

Why Optimize?

In developing the *Optimize* format, Routledge have spent a lot of time talking to law students like you, and to your lecturers and examiners, about assessment, about teaching and learning, and about exam preparation. The aim of our series is to help you make the most of your knowledge to gain good marks – to optimize your revision.

Students

Students told us that there was a huge amount to learn, and that visual features such as diagrams, tables and flowcharts made the law easier to follow. Learning and remembering cases was an area of difficulty, as was applying them in problem questions. Revision guides could make this easier by presenting the law succinctly, showing concepts in a visual format and highlighting how important cases can be applied in assessment.

Lecturers

Lecturers agreed that visual features were effective to aid learning, but were concerned that students learned by rote when using revision guides. To succeed in assessment, they wanted to encourage them to get their teeth into arguments, to support their answers with authority, and show they had truly understood the principles underlying their questions. In short, they wanted students to show that they understood how they were assessed on the law, rather than repeating the basic principles.

Assessment criteria

If you want to do well in exams, it's important to understand how you will be assessed. In order to get the best out of your exam or essay question, your first port of call should be to make yourself familiar with the marking criteria available from your law school; this will help you to identify and recognise the skills and knowledge you will need to succeed. Like course outlines, assessment criteria can differ from school to school, so if you can get hold of a copy of these criteria, this will be invaluable. To give you a clear idea of what these criteria look like, we've collated the most common terms from 64 marking schemes for core curriculum courses in the UK.

research

reading

Evidence

Understanding

Structure Critical Argument

Application Use sources

Analysis

Knowledge

Presentation

Common Assessment Criteria, Routledge Subject Assessment Survey

Optimizing the law

The format of this 'Optimize Law' volume has been developed with these assessment criteria and the learning needs of students firmly in mind.

- ❖ **Visual format:** Our expert series advisors have brought a wealth of knowledge about visual learning to help us to develop the books' visual format.
- ❖ **Tailored coverage:** Each book is tailored to the needs of your core curriculum course and presents all commonly taught topics.
- ❖ **Assessment led-revision:** Our authors are experienced teachers with an interest in how students learn, and they have structured each chapter around revision objectives that relate to the criteria you will be assessed on.
- ❖ **Assessment led-pedagogy:** The 'Aim Higher', 'Common Pitfalls', 'Up for Debate' and 'Case Precedent' features used in these books are closely linked to common assessment criteria – showing you how to gain the best marks, avoid the worst pitfalls, apply the law and think critically about it.
- ❖ **Putting it into practice:** Each chapter presents example essay or problem questions and template answers to show you how to apply what you have learned.

Routledge and the 'Optimize' team wish you the very best of luck in your exams and essays!

Preface

Dear Reader,

This book aims to help you with revision and to gain higher marks but you can also help yourself. One of the best ways to do this is to show that you have read widely (e.g. Law Commission reports, journal articles), and to refer to those articles in your answer, particularly if it is coursework (but remember to reference your sources). 'The Conveyancer' is a particularly useful journal for articles on trusts.

Now for some practical tips on examination technique:

1. Before you go into the examination room, make a mental note of how long you can spend on each question. If it is a three-hour examination and you have to answer four questions, you have 45 minutes for each answer, although this will include reading the examination paper at the beginning and reading through your answers at the end. Try to ensure that you give equal time to each answer.
2. The reason it is important to do this is that it is easier to attain the first 50% of marks on an answer than the second 50% of marks, and it follows that you do not want to run out of time before you can finish that last answer and gain at least those first 50% of marks for it.
3. It is always a good idea, whether it is a problem question or an essay question, to draft a rough answer plan. This can be difficult to do when everyone around you seems to be busy writing an answer but if you can discipline yourself to do this, you will probably produce a far better paper. By giving some preliminary thought to your answer, you are less likely to leave points out and your answer will undoubtedly have a better structure.
4. If you are answering an essay question, remember to keep that question in mind throughout, tailor your knowledge to that question and refer back to the question/statement where you can. This is because it is a common mistake to regurgitate lecture notes on a topic without reference to the wording or niceties of the question.
5. Finally, it is a good idea to answer your favourite question first because it will inspire you.

Guide to Using the Book and the Companion Website

The Routledge 'Optimize' revision series is designed to provide students with a clear overview of the core topics in their course, and to contextualise this overview within a narrative that offers straightforward, practical advice relating to assessment.

Revision objectives

These overviews are a brief introduction of the core themes and issues you will encounter in each chapter.

Chapter Topic Maps

Visually link all of the key topics in each chapter to tie together understanding of key issues.

Illustrative diagrams

A series of diagrams and tables are used to help facilitate the understanding of concepts and interrelationships within key topics.

Up for Debate

'Up for Debate' features help you to critique current law and reflect on how, and in which direction, it may develop in the future.

Case precedent boxes

A variety of landmark cases are highlighted in text boxes for ease of reference. The facts, principle and application for the case are presented to help students understand how these courses are used in legal problems.

Aim Higher and Common Pitfalls

These assessment-focused sections show students how to get the best marks, and how to avoid the most common mistakes.

Table of key cases

Drawing together all of the key cases from each chapter.

Companion Website

www.routledge.com/revision

Visit the Law Revision website to discover a comprehensive range of resources designed to enhance your learning experience.

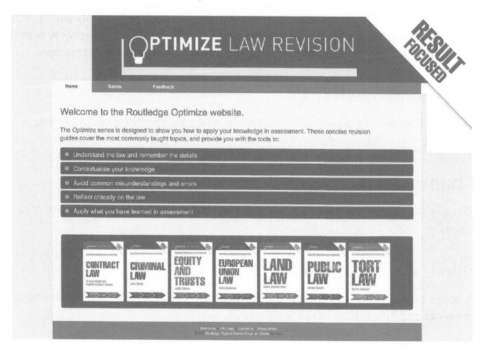

Resources for Optimize Law revision

- ❖ Revision tips podcasts
- ❖ Topic overview podcasts
- ❖ Subject maps for each topic
- ❖ Downloadable versions of Chapter Maps and other diagrams
- ❖ Flashcard Glossary
- ❖ MCQ questions

Table of Cases and Statutes

■ Cases

■ Statutes

■ European Legislation

1

Introduction to Equity and Trusts

Revision objectives

Understand the law
- Can you explain how an *inter vivos* trust is created?
- Are you able to identify the different types of trust?

Remember the details
- Can you describe how the trust developed from the use?
- Are you able to trace the history of equity?

Reflect critically on areas of debate
- Can you state whether the Judicature Acts of 1873 and 1875 fused the rules of equity and the common law?
- Are you able to give examples to back up your statement above?

Contextualise
- What is the difference between a discretionary trust and a power of appointment?
- Why is it important to distinguish between the two?

Apply your skills and knowledge
- Can you define the terms and concepts in the question at the end of this chapter?

Chapter Map

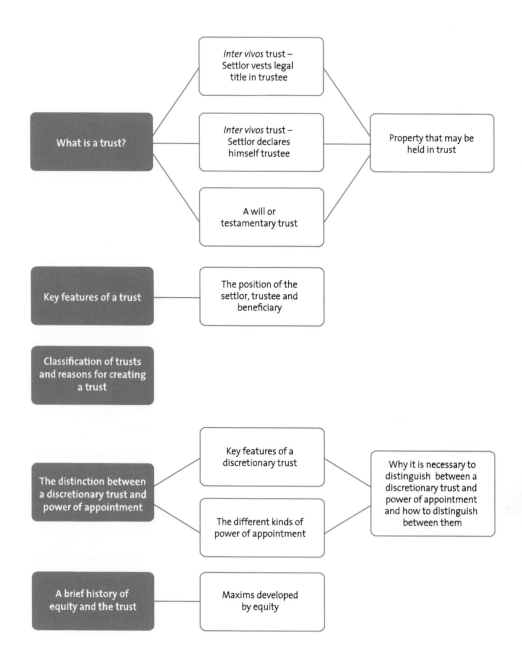

Inter vivos trust –
Settlor vests legal
title in trustee

Inter vivos trust –
Settlor declares
himself trustee

A will or
testamentary trust

Property that may be
held in trust

What is a trust?

Key features of a trust

The position of the
settlor, trustee and
beneficiary

Classification of trusts
and reasons for creating
a trust

The distinction between
a discretionary trust and
power of appointment

Key features of a
discretionary trust

The different kinds of
power of appointment

Why it is necessary to
distinguish between a
discretionary trust and
power of appointment
and how to distinguish
between them

A brief history of
equity and the trust

Maxims developed
by equity

What is a trust?

The trust (or its predecessor, 'the use') has been an important part of English law for over 800 years. As we progress with our revision of trusts in this book, we shall see what a clever and extraordinarily useful device the trust has proved to be, both in commercial situations and in many aspects of our ordinary lives.

We begin our journey into the world of equity and trusts by looking at examples that explain the nature of a trust and how it may be created. The examples are based on the following scenario.

> **The Scenario**
>
> Samuel Stone wishes to provide income for the private education of his granddaughter, Brenda. He decides to do this by creating a trust of his 20,000 shares in Abbott plc, which will generate enough income to pay for Brenda's education. As the following examples illustrate, Sam could create this trust in three ways.

Example 1 – an *inter vivos* trust: Settlor vests legal title in trustees

The trust that Sam is going to create is an *inter vivos* trust, meaning 'between the living', i.e. made between Sam (the settlor) and Tim and Toby (who have agreed to act as his trustees).

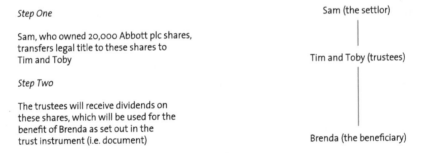

Step One

Sam, who owned 20,000 Abbott plc shares, transfers legal title to these shares to Tim and Toby

Step Two

The trustees will receive dividends on these shares, which will be used for the benefit of Brenda as set out in the trust instrument (i.e. document)

Sam (the settlor)

Tim and Toby (trustees)

Brenda (the beneficiary)

A key feature of a trust is **duality of ownership.** The trustees are the **legal owners** of the shares but they do not enjoy the benefit of the shares. Brenda has the beneficial interest in the shares – she is the **beneficial owner.** The beneficial interest is usually referred to as the equitable interest because a trust is a product of equity, which has always protected the beneficiary's equitable interest.

Example 2 – an *inter vivos* trust: Settlor declares himself trustee

This is a different way of creating a trust in which the settlor declares himself trustee. For example, instead of vesting legal title in trustees, Sam could declare that he was now holding the 20,000 Abbott shares in the capacity of trustee for the benefit of his granddaughter, Brenda.

In the following case, the settlor was taken, by his words and conduct, to have declared himself a trustee of his bank deposit account.

> ### Case precedent – *Paul v Constance* [1977] 1 WLR 527
>
> **Facts:** Mr Constance, who was separated from his wife, began living with Mrs Paul in 1967. He opened a bank deposit account and paid into it £950, which he had received as damages for personal injury. Although the account was in his sole name, he told Mrs Paul on many occasions that 'the money is as much yours as mine'. The account also contained their joint bingo winnings and the only withdrawal ever made was used for the joint benefit of Mr Constance and Mrs Paul. Mr Constance died intestate (i.e. without making a will) and the question arose as to the ownership of the money in the deposit account. The Court of Appeal held that, by his words and conduct, Mr Constance had declared himself trustee of the account during his lifetime, both for himself and Mrs Paul. It followed that when he died intestate, his widow, Mrs Constance was entitled to his half of the account while Mrs Paul was entitled to the other half.
>
> **Principle:** A declaration of trust may be construed from the settlor's words and conduct.
>
> **Application:** This is regarded as a borderline decision but it illustrates the fact that a settlor does not have to use technical words in order to declare himself trustee. This topic of a declaration of trust by the settlor is considered in more detail in Chapter 4.

Example 3 – A will trust/testamentary trust

Sam, the testator, may create the trust for Brenda in his will. On his death, Sam's estate will vest in his executors who are under a duty to transfer legal title to the trust property to his trustees.

Note: the above trusts made by Sam are all **express private trusts** because they have been **expressly** created by him for the benefit of an ascertained **person**.

What kind of property may be held in trust?

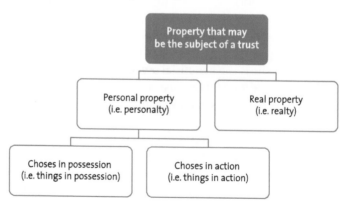

- Real property is freehold land/buildings and leasehold land/buildings.
- Personal property is made up of choses in possession (i.e. tangible property). Common examples of choses in possession that might be held in trust are paintings, antiques and jewellery. A chose in action is intangible property and includes shares, money and copyright.

It is important to know that future property cannot be held in trust. For example, if Sam promised to settle any property that he inherited from his brother, this would not be a valid trust because it refers to future property, and is a mere hope (in Latin – *spes*). If Sam did in fact inherit property from his brother, the inheritance would then become existing property, and at that point, Sam would be expected to carry out his promise and settle the property.

You should also be aware that a beneficiary may create a sub-trust. In other words, his equitable interest may form the subject matter of a sub-trust as illustrated below.

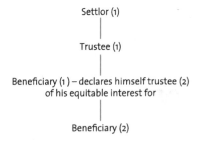

Settlor (1)

Trustee (1)

Beneficiary (1) – declares himself trustee (2)
of his equitable interest for

Beneficiary (2)

Other key features of a trust

These key features are considered below from the perspective of the settlor, the trustees and the beneficiary.

The settlor
In *Paul v Constance* [1977], you may have noticed that Mr Constance was not only the settlor but also the trustee and a beneficiary.

However, as the following case illustrates, once the trust is created, the settlor (in his capacity as settlor) loses his control over the property.

Case precedent – *Re Bowden* [1936] Ch 71

Facts: When becoming a nun, in accordance with her vows of poverty, Catherine Bowden agreed to settle property to which she might become entitled under her father's will. Some years later, when her father died, the property she inherited was transferred to trustees. In 1935, 60 years on, Catherine Bowden left the convent and sought unsuccessfully to recover the property she had settled on trust.

Principle: Once a trust is created, the settlor has no control over the property and cannot undo the trust.

Application: However, as we shall see shortly, the beneficiaries of a trust may, in certain circumstances, terminate the trust under the rule in *Saunders v Vautier*.

The trustees

The trustees hold legal title to the trust property but have no right to enjoy that property, the benefit of which is for the beneficiary. Trustees are under a **mandatory obligation** to carry out the trust and, if they fail to do so, they will be in breach of trust and may be sued by the beneficiary. They are described as fiduciaries and, as such, they must avoid any conflict of interest.

Their appointment, retirement and removal will be considered later in this book, as will their duties and powers and their liability for breach of trust.

The beneficiary

With the exception of charitable purpose trusts and unenforceable trusts, trusts must have a beneficiary who can enforce the trust against the trustees, i.e. who can sue the trustees if they fail to carry out their obligations. In the case of charitable purpose trusts, the Attorney General is charged with enforcement.

The beneficiary has a proprietary interest in the subject matter of the trust, which means that, if necessary, he can recover it from anyone who might acquire it wrongly or innocently, with the one exception of a bona fide purchaser for value who acquires the property without notice of the beneficiary's interest.

As he has a proprietary interest, the beneficiary may, if he wishes, transfer that interest to another.

It is important to know that under the rule in *Saunders v Vautier* [1841], provided all the beneficiaries under a trust are together absolutely entitled, and are of full age and mental capacity (i.e. in Latin *sui juris*), they may join together to terminate the trust and may order the trustees to transfer the legal title to them.

Classification of trusts

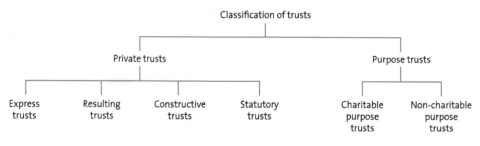

Private trusts

Private trusts are trusts for ascertained beneficiaries and can be subdivided into:

Express trusts – these are trusts expressly created by the settlor and will be studied in more detail in Chapters 2, 3 and 4. At the beginning of this chapter, we noticed that the trusts created by Sam for his granddaughter were express private trusts.

Resulting trusts – these are generally based on the presumed intention of the settlor/ transferor and will be studied in Chapter 6. An example of a resulting trust would be when an express trust fails for some reason, and the property is held on resulting trust for the settlor, i.e. the property results back to him.

Constructive trusts – these arise by operation of the law. For example, where a person is unjustly enriched at the expense of the claimant, he will hold the property on constructive trust for the claimant. Constructive trusts will be studied in Chapter 7.

Statutory trusts – as their name implies, these are created by Parliament and are set out in a statute. An example is the Trusts of Land and Appointment of Trustees Act 1996, which provides that joint legal owners of land hold the legal title on a statutory trust of land. This is covered in land law.

Purpose trusts

Purpose trusts are for purposes rather than for people, and are of two kinds:

Charitable purpose trusts – these are also called public trusts. They are created for charitable purposes as set out in the Charities Act 2011 and are enforced by the Attorney General. They will be studied in Chapter 10.

Non-charitable purpose trusts – also called private purpose trusts. Apart from three exceptions (known as unenforceable trusts), non-charitable purpose trusts are void, the reason being that there is no beneficiary to enforce them. They will be studied in Chapter 9.

Some reasons for creating a trust

Throughout this book, we will see why people create trusts and therefore only a few examples are given at this stage.

- ❖ Land owned by more than one person has to be held on a trust of land, which is governed by the Trusts of Land and Appointment of Trustees Act 1996.
- ❖ A minor cannot hold the legal estate in land and therefore it is necessarily held on trust for him until he reaches his majority.
- ❖ A testator may wish to benefit his family in succession. For example, to achieve this, he could create a trust in his will whereby his widow is entitled to his

house and the income from a fund of £600,000 for her life and, upon her death, the house and the capital fund pass to his children absolutely. This is illustrated in the following diagram.

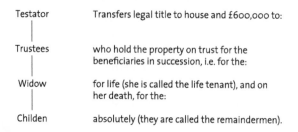

Testator	Transfers legal title to house and £600,000 to:
Trustees	who hold the property on trust for the beneficiaries in succession, i.e. for the:
Widow	for life (she is called the life tenant), and on her death, for the:
Childen	absolutely (they are called the remaindermen).

- ❖ A testator may wish to provide for someone secretly after he dies. He can do this by means of a secret trust, which we will be studying in Chapter 5.
- ❖ A testator may be anxious that his pet dog is cared for after his death and therefore sets up a trust for the care of the animal. Such a trust is called an unenforceable trust (because the dog cannot go to court to enforce it). These trusts will be studied in Chapter 9.
- ❖ Settlors create discretionary trusts for a number of reasons, as we shall see next.

The distinction between a discretionary trust and a power of appointment

Textbooks often compare a trust with other concepts, e.g. a contract, but the comparison most likely to come up in an examination is that between a discretionary trust and a power of appointment. It is a difficult topic and we will approach it by looking at the nature and key features of a discretionary trust, then consider powers of appointment and finally discuss the importance of being able to distinguish between the two concepts.

The nature of a discretionary trust

In a discretionary trust, the trustees have complete discretion as to who, from a class of beneficiaries, should receive a beneficial interest and the size of that beneficial interest. A discretionary trust may relate to the distribution of income as in the example below, but it could relate to the distribution of capital, or income and capital.

> '£500,000 on trust for my trustees to distribute the income amongst such of my children as the trustees in their absolute discretion shall decide.'

There are various reasons why the settlor might want to create a discretionary trust. These include enabling the trustees to provide benefit only to those who might be in need in the future when the settlor is dead, and safeguarding the trust fund from creditors. For example, where one of the class of potential beneficiaries is declared bankrupt, it would not be prudent to distribute the income to him; benefiting only those beneficiaries who prove to be deserving and who will not dissipate the income from the trust; enabling the trustees to pay the income to those who pay no/little income tax as opposed to potential beneficiaries who, for the time being, are subject to higher-rate tax.

Key features of a discretionary trust

A discretionary trust may be exhaustive or non-exhaustive	The rights of individual beneficiaries under a discretionary trust	The rights of beneficiaries as a group under a discretionary trust
An exhaustive discretionary trust is where the trustees **have** to distribute the income each year (or capital within the trust period)	An **individual** beneficiary has no entitlement to the trust fund unless the trustees exercise their discretion in his favour	The beneficiaries as a whole (if they are all of full age and sound mind) may collectively terminate the trust and divide the property between themselves under the rule in *Saunders v Vautier*
With a non-exhaustive discretionary trust, the trustees may decide not to distribute the income but may accumulate it instead (i.e. add it to capital)	However, an individual beneficiary can require the trustees to exercise their discretion bona fides and in a responsible and fair way	Similarly, if the beneficiaries are all of full age and under no disability, they may collectively assign the trust fund to a third party – *Re Smith* [1928]

A key point to remember is that with a discretionary trust, the trustees have **a duty to exercise their discretion** and, in the case of an exhaustive discretionary trust, they must select amongst the beneficiaries, whilst in the case of a non-exhaustive trust, they can exercise their discretion by deciding to accumulate.

The nature of a power of appointment
Here is an example of a power of appointment.

'My residuary estate on trust for my widow for life with power to dispose of it amongst my children and grandchildren as she may think fit and, in default of appointment, to be divided amongst my children equally.'

The main difference between a power of appointment and a discretionary trust is that the donee of the power (i.e. the widow in the above example) has no duty to appoint an object (i.e. the children/grandchildren) and, if she chooses not to do so, the gift over in default will take effect.

Question: Why did the testator (i.e. the donor of the power) give this power of appointment to his widow (i.e. the donee of the power)?

❖ **Answer**: When the widow dies, as she has only a life interest under the trust, someone will be entitled to the remainder. As the widow has survived her spouse, she will be aware of changing circumstances amongst her children and grandchildren and therefore be in a better position than the testator would have been, when he created the trust, to decide who should receive the property on her death, and so she is given this power of appointment. If she does not exercise the power (i.e. does not choose to appoint), then the children will receive the remainder interest equally.

As you can see from the above example, powers often arise behind a trust.

Types of power of appointment

There are three kinds of power of appointment, as follows:

A general power of appointment	A special power of appointment	An intermediate (or hybrid) power of appointment
Example: 'My estate to my wife with power to allocate the estate to anyone she wishes'	The power of appointment in the example we looked at above was a special power of appointment	Example: 'My estate to my wife with power to allocate the estate to anyone except my brothers'
As the testator's widow could appoint the estate to herself, this is tantamount to a gift. General powers of appointment are rare	The power of appointment can only be exercised in favour of a class of people. In the above example, the class was the donor's children and grandchildren	The power of appointment can be exercised in favour of anyone except members of a particular class; in this case, the donor's brothers

Common Pitfall

Confusion can arise with the terminology regarding powers.

Fiduciary power/power collateral – this is when the power of appointment is given to a trustee. Although the trustee does not have to exercise the power, as a fiduciary, he must consider from time to time whether he **should** exercise it in favour of the objects of the power.

Mere power/bare power – this is when the power of appointment is given to someone other than a trustee and we have seen that such a donee has no obligation to do anything.

Trust power – this is another name for a discretionary trust. As it is in fact a trust, the trustees have an imperative obligation to exercise their discretion to allocate the trust property to a beneficiary unless it is a non-exhaustive discretionary trust, in which case they may decide to accumulate the income.

Question: Why is it important to know whether one is dealing with a discretionary trust or a power of appointment?

❖ **Answer**: It is important because there are differences between the two. The main differences are as follows:
  ❖ If a power of appointment is not exercised, then if there is a gift over in default that will take effect. If there is no gift over then the property will return to the donor of the power/his estate.
  ❖ In the case of a discretionary trust, if the trustee does not exercise his discretion as required by the trust, then he is in breach of trust and the court could intervene. In such circumstances, the court would normally order the fund to be divided equally – [1840].
  ❖ As noted earlier, the beneficiaries of a discretionary trust can collectively agree to terminate the trust provided they are all of full age and sound mind. The objects of a power cannot do this as they have no proprietary interest in the property until an appointment is made in their favour.
  ❖ As we shall see in Chapter 2, there must be certainty as to who are beneficiaries and who are objects of a power of appointment in order that the trustee or the donee of a power can exercise their discretion/power. Prior to the House of Lords case of [1971], a list was required of all the beneficiaries of a discretionary trust; this was not required for a power where it was only necessary to be able to say whether any given person was or was not a member of the class of objects. This latter test now also applies to discretionary trusts so there is no longer a distinction between a discretionary trust and a power in this respect.

Question: How can you tell whether it is a power of appointment or a discretionary trust?

❖ **Answer**
  ❖ Look at the language of the gift and remember that a trust is an imperative obligation whereas a power of appointment is not mandatory. Thus, if the gift read 'my widow **may** select . . .', this would infer that it is a power of appointment.
  ❖ Likewise, the existence of a gift over in default is evidence that a selection does not have to be made, i.e. it is not an imperative duty and therefore it is a power of appointment.

A brief history of equity and the trust

The great legal historian, FW Maitland, regarded the trust as 'the greatest and most distinctive achievement performed by Englishmen in the field of jurisprudence'. With that in mind, it is now time to see how equity and the trust, which is a product of equity, came to exist and how they developed through the centuries.

Date	
Thirteenth century	**Emergence of the use** It was during the thirteenth century that the **use** (the forerunner of the trust) emerged in respect of land. There were a number of reasons for its development. Feudal tenants of land were subject to 'incidents' (a form of tax), which were payable, for example, on the death of the tenant when his land passed to his heir, and a further 'incident' if the heir was an infant. Such 'incidents' could be avoided if the land was held by two or more trustees for the use of the heir. As the trustees could be replaced when necessary, the nominal tenant of the land (i.e. the trustee) was always an adult and never died, and the incidents above would not have to be paid. The use also enabled the feudal tenant to avoid the general rule of primogeniture, i.e. that land should pass to the eldest son. Another advantage of the use was that a feudal tenant, who was going on a crusade and might be absent for years, could transfer the land to trustees who would hold it for the benefit of the crusader's family while he was away. You should be aware of the old terminology regarding a use, i.e. the feoffor (the modern day settlor), the feoffee (the trustee) and the *cestui que* use (the beneficiary).
Fourteenth century	**Emergence of equity** A claimant could only bring a case at common law if there was a writ that covered his particular wrong. If such a writ did not exist, then he was left without a remedy. In these circumstances, claimants who were without a remedy began to petition the King for justice. As the petitions grew more numerous, the King passed them to his Chancellor, an ecclesiastic and the so-called keeper of the King's conscience. The Chancellor would make such order as appeared to him fair and 'equitable'. Likewise, the interests of beneficiaries under the use were not recognised by the common law. In the event of a dispute regarding their rights, the beneficiaries would petition the Chancellor to exercise his discretion and do equity. This is how the use and ultimately the trust became a principal feature of equity.

Beginning of the fifteenth century	**Development of a Court of Chancery** The sittings of the Chancellor to hear the petitions became more regular and by the beginning of the fifteenth century had developed into a new Court of Chancery. At first, the Chancellor's jurisdiction was vague – hence the saying 'Equity varies with the length of the Chancellor's foot' – but gradually a doctrine of precedent and principles began to develop.
1535	**The Statute of Uses 1535** The avoidance of the feudal incidents affected the King's coffers and in 1535, during Henry VIII's reign, the Statute of Uses was enacted. This statute executed the use, meaning that in most cases the *cestui que* use (the beneficiary) was regarded as the legal owner of the property, thus restoring the payment of incidents of tenure.
1615	**Conflict between the common law and equity** The conflict had arisen because of Chancery's power to issue injunctions that could prevent a litigant from pursuing his claim at common law, or prevent him enforcing a common law judgment. Things came to a head in the *Earl of Oxford's Case* in 1615. King James I intervened in the dispute that had arisen regarding this case between Chief Justice Coke and the Chancellor, Lord Ellesmere, and, acting on the advice of his Attorney General, Bacon, the King decided in favour of equity. Thereafter, equity and the common law co-existed as parts of a system.
1700	**Development of the trust from the use upon a use** During the seventeenth century, the importance of feudal incidents had diminished and the practice had developed of creating a use upon a use, e.g. land was held to the use of Alfred to the use of Bertram. If the first use was executed in accordance with the Statute of Uses and Alfred was the legal owner, then it could be argued that Alfred was holding the land on use (on trust) for Bertram.
Late seventeenth, eighteenth and early nineteenth centuries	**Development of equity into a system of established rules and precedents** The late seventeenth century through to the eighteenth century saw the transformation of equity into a system of established rules and precedents, largely due to the work of a number of notable Chancellors, including Lord Nottingham (Chancellor from 1673–1682), Lord Hardwicke (Chancellor from 1736–1756) and Lord Eldon (Chancellor from 1801–1827). However, one of the problems of this period was that if a litigant sought both an equitable and legal remedy, he had to bring separate cases in the Court of Chancery and the Common Law courts, which made litigation both expensive and slow and, in those courts, procedure was very different. These problems were resolved during the course of the next 21 years as follows.

Date	
1854	**Common Law Procedure Act 1854** This Act gave the Common Law courts (e.g. the Queen's Bench, the Court of Common Pleas and the Exchequer) the power to grant equitable remedies.
1858	**Chancery Amendment Act 1858** This Act (also known as Lord Cairn's Act) gave the Court of Chancery the power to award the common law remedy of damages.
1873–1875	**Judicature Acts of 1873 and 1875** These Acts created the Supreme Court of Judicature, which replaced the separate courts of Queen's Bench, Common Pleas, Exchequer, Probate and Divorce Court, Court of Admiralty and Court of Chancery by creating the High Court with three divisions: Queen's Bench Division; Probate, Divorce and Admiralty Division; and Chancery Division, all of which could exercise both the common law and equity. See 'Up for Debate' below on the question of whether these Acts fused the principles of equity and common law. Section 25 of the Judicature Act 1873 also enshrined the following principle '. . .in all matters . . . in which there is any conflict or variance between the rules of equity and the rules of the common law with reference to the same matter, the rules of equity shall prevail'.
1981	**Senior Courts Act 1981** This Act assigned certain matters to the Chancery Division of the High Court including trusts, administration of estates of deceased persons and bankruptcy.
1987	**Recognition of Trusts Act 1987** As we have seen, the device of the trust was English in origin. It is used in other common law jurisdictions and, due largely to fiscal advantages, trusts are often set up overseas in states that may not be familiar with the concept of the trust. Accordingly, the Hague Convention on the Law Applicable to Trusts and their Recognition sought to establish common principles and definitions relating to trusts amongst signatory states whose domestic law might not recognise the nature of a trust. This Convention was implemented in the United Kingdom by the Recognition of Trusts Act 1987.

> **Up for Debate**
>
> There is one school of thought which considers that the **Judicature Acts of 1873** and **1875** not only fused the administration of equity and the common law but also fused/merged the rules of equity and the common law, and that, in the words of Denning J in *Central London Property Trust Ltd v High Trees House* [1947] '... at this time of day, when law and equity have been joined together for over 70 years, principles must be reconsidered in the light of their combined effect'.
>
> However, the orthodox view is that the rules of equity and the common law remain distinct and that there are many examples of this. We will encounter some of these examples in this book, notably that legal ownership of property is quite distinct from beneficial ownership, and that equitable remedies are discretionary whereas the common law remedy of damages is available as of right.

Maxims of equity

Over the centuries, broad principles of equity were developed by Chancery. These are called maxims and are still applied today. Some of these maxims are considered below, together with a reference to the relevant chapter where we will see cases in which the particular maxim has been applied.

Equity looks to the intent not the form

Equity is concerned with a party's intentions rather than the formalities/form of words used. For example, in *Paul v Constance* [1977] mentioned earlier in this chapter, the court held that Mr Constance's informal words and conduct inferred that he wanted his bank deposit account to be held on trust. This maxim is considered again in Chapter 2.

Equity is equality

Where property is held for two or more persons but there is no declaration as to their share, this maxim may apply so as to allow equal division – see Chapter 2.

Equity will not perfect an imperfect gift

A donor must comply with the appropriate formalities to transfer legal title and make a perfect gift, otherwise the gift will fail and will not be saved by equity. The exceptions to this maxim are considered in Chapter 4.

Equity will not allow a statute to be used as an instrument of fraud

If a defendant relies on the strict provisions of a statute that enable him to get away with fraud, the court will suspend the operation of that statute. This maxim is considered in Chapter 5 regarding secret trusts.

He who comes to equity must come with clean hands

A litigant who seeks an equitable remedy must have behaved correctly himself. This maxim is considered in Chapter 6 when we study resulting trusts and illegality.

Equity regards as done that which ought to be done

If a party had a duty to do something then, in equity, the parties involved will acquire rights and liabilities as if the duty had been carried out. This maxim was applied in *Attorney General for Hong Kong v Reid* [1994], which we consider in Chapter 7.

Equity follows the law

This maxim illustrates that generally equity and the common law co-exist. The maxim was applied recently by the Supreme Court in *Jones v Kernott* [2011] to the effect that where legal title to land is held jointly, there is a presumption that there is also joint beneficial interest in the land. This topic is considered in Chapter 8.

Putting it into practice

It is important to understand the terminology used in trusts and, as the subject is often linked with wills, you should also be familiar with key terms used in the law of succession. This question therefore requires you to explain the meaning of the following words.

(a) *Cestui que* use
(b) *Inter vivos* trust
(c) Testamentary trust
(d) Personal representative
(e) Executor
(f) Administratrix
(g) Legatee
(h) Devisee
(i) Residuary beneficiary
(j) Absolute interest
(k) Power of appointment
(l) Fiduciary power
(m) Administrative power
(n) Life tenant
(o) Remainderman
(p) Trust instrument
(q) *In personam*
(r) *In rem*
(s) Chose in action
(t) Chose in possession
(u) Disposition

(v)　Proprietary right
(w)　Volunteer
(x)　Joint tenants
(y)　Tenants in common
(z)　Future property

Feedback on putting it into practice

(a)　*Cestui que* use – former name for a beneficiary
(b)　*Inter vivos* trust – a trust made between living persons
(c)　Testamentary trust – a trust in a will
(d)　Personal representative – an executor or an administrator
(e)　Executor – person named in a will whom the testator wishes to administer his estate
(f)　Administratrix – a woman to whom letters of administration have been granted to administer an intestate estate
(g)　Legatee – a person who receives a gift of personal property (a legacy) under a will
(h)　Devisee – a person who receives a gift of real property (a devise) under a will
(i)　Residuary beneficiary – the beneficiary under a will who is entitled to the testator's residuary estate, i.e. property not specifically bequeathed or devised (the residue)
(j)　Absolute interest – complete ownership, legal and equitable
(k)　Power of appointment – a power given to a donee to appoint a person(s) to take property
(l)　Fiduciary power – a power of appointment given to a trustee
(m)　Administrative power – authority given to a trustee to delegate or maintain, etc.
(n)　Life tenant – a beneficiary who is entitled to property for the duration of his life
(o)　Remainderman – a beneficiary who is entitled to take the remainder, e.g. after the death of the life tenant
(p)　Trust instrument – trust document
(q)　*In personam* – rights enforceable against the person
(r)　*In rem* – rights enforceable against the world at large
(s)　Chose in action – intangible property
(t)　Chose in possession – tangible property
(u)　Disposition – a transfer of title by way of gift, sale, assignment
(v)　Proprietary right – right of ownership
(w)　Volunteer – a person who has not given consideration
(x)　Joint tenants – co-ownership where two or more persons are each regarded as being entitled to the whole property: on the death of one joint tenant, the property vests in the survivor

(y)   Tenants in common – co-ownership where two or more persons each have a distinct but undivided share in the property

(z)   Future property – a right to property that has not yet been acquired (after-acquired property)

Table of key cases referred to in this chapter

Case name	Area of law	Principle
Bowden, Re [1936]	Settlor's position	Once a trust is created, the settlor cannot undo it
Burrough v Philcox [1840]	Discretionary trust	If the trustee does not exercise his discretion, court may order equal division amongst the beneficiaries
Paul v Constance [1977]	Creating an inter vivos trust	Declaration of trust by the settlor construed from his words and actions
Saunders v Vautier [1841]	Beneficiary's position	Beneficiaries may terminate the trust if, together, they are absolutely entitled and they are of full age and sound mind

@ Visit the book's companion website to test your knowledge

❖   Resources include a subject map, revision tip podcasts, downloadable diagrams, MCQ quizzes for each chapter, and a flashcard glossary

❖   www.routledge.com/cw/optimizelawrevision

2

The Three Certainties

Revision objectives

Understand the law
- Can you identify the three certainties discussed in this chapter?
- Can you explain the effect of uncertainty?

Remember the details
- Do you remember the cases that illustrate the three certainties?
- Can you recall the tests for certainty of intention and certainty of objects?

Reflect critically on areas of debate
- Are you able to explain the rationale for the three certainties?
- Can you distinguish the cases regarding segregation of property to be held on trust?

Contextualise
- Are you able to explain the inter relationship of certainty of intention and certainty of subject matter?
- Can you distinguish between a fixed trust and a discretionary trust?

Apply your skills and knowledge
- Can you complete all parts of the problem question regarding the three certainties?

Chapter Map

Essential for the formation of a valid express private trust: → The three certainties

- Certainty of intention/words
- Certainty of subject matter
- Certainty of objects

Certainty of intention/words:

- Equity looks to the intent rather than the form
- The problem of precatory words and the test → *Re Steele's Will Trusts*
- Intention in a commercial context
- A sham intention?

Effect of uncertainty of intention

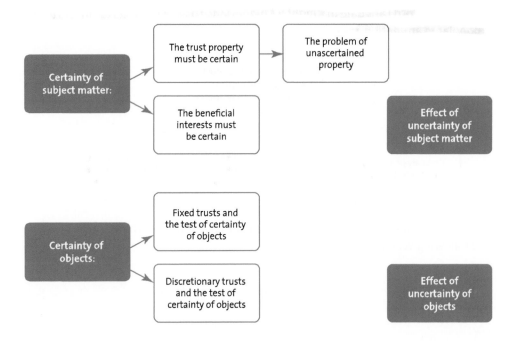

Introduction to the three certainties

In Chapter 1, we saw that an express private trust is one that is created expressly for the benefit of an individual or a class of individuals, e.g. 'for my employees'. In order to create such a trust, there are a number of requirements – the first of these was identified by Lord Langdale in *Knight v Knight* [1840] as the three certainties. This is a popular examination area.

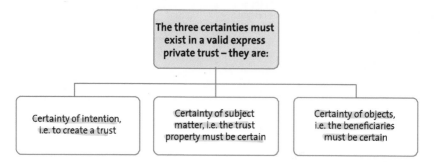

Before we consider these three certainties in detail, let us see whether they exist in the following scenario:

John Smith executes a will that contains the following provision:

£50,000 to my sister, Brenda, hoping that she will use the bulk of the money to benefit my friends.

Brenda seeks your advice as to whether there is a valid trust.

Brenda would need to be advised that, for three separate reasons, there is no trust. Firstly, the words 'hoping that' do not impose a legal obligation on Brenda to act as trustee, i.e. there is no certainty of intention to create a trust; secondly, 'the bulk of the money' is not precise, i.e. there is no certainty of subject matter; and thirdly, the concept of 'friends' is uncertain (what constitutes a friend), so there is no certainty of objects. We shall see later that in this particular scenario, Brenda would take the £50,000 absolutely. Of course, if this were a problem question, you would need to expand your answer by referring to the legal principles and citing relevant cases as discussed in this chapter.

Aim Higher

As you progress through this chapter, also think about the rationale for the three certainties so that you are able to answer an essay question such as the following: *The three certainties ensure that there are obligations which are workable and capable of being policed by the court. Explain this statement with reference to decided cases.*

Certainty of intention/words

Where a trust is drafted by a solicitor, there is generally no problem regarding certainty of intention of the settlor/testator as the property would be stated to be held 'on trust'. When the situation is not so clear, the following points are relevant:

Equity looks to the intent rather than the form

In the first chapter you will have noticed the following equitable maxim:

> Equity looks to the intent rather than the form

Accordingly, when considering whether an express trust has been created, the court will look at the surrounding circumstances to discover whether the settlor/testator intended to create a trust rather than focusing solely on the form of words he used, i.e. it is not essential to use the words 'on trust'.

We saw an example of this in *Paul v Constance* [1977] in the first chapter. Mr Constance did not state that he was creating a trust, but it was possible for the courts to infer this intention from his statements and his conduct. This decision was followed in *Rowe v Prance* [1999], which we consider in Chapter 4.

Another interesting case in which the court had to determine whether there was an intention to create a trust is *Duggan v Governor of Full Sutton Prison* [2004] – see below.

Case precedent – *Duggan v Governor of Full Sutton Prison* [2004] 2 All ER 966 CA

Facts: The claimant was a prisoner serving a life sentence. He claimed that cash taken from him when he arrived at the prison, and money he had earned while in prison, was held by the Prison Governor on trust for him in accordance with prison rules and that the Governor, as trustee, therefore had a duty to invest those monies.

The relevant prison rule that had to be construed by the court provided that 'any cash which a prisoner has at prison shall be paid into an account under the control of the Governor and the prisoner shall be credited with the amount in the books of the prison'.

The Court of Appeal held that the rule did not reveal an intention to create a trust with an accompanying duty on the part of the Governor to invest the 'trust money', but was consistent with a debtor/creditor relationship.

Principle: Intention is deduced from all the circumstances of the case.

Application: This illustrates that the issue of intention is determined by reference to the language and conduct of the parties and the surrounding circumstances of the case. (Imagine how impractical and bureaucratic it would be if every prisoner's money was held on trust and therefore had to be invested – such a result could not have been intended by the draftsman of the prison rules.)

The problem of precatory words – and the test

A problem can arise regarding certainty of intention when a testator drafts his own will and uses precatory words. These are words expressing a hope or desire that something be done, e.g. Tom bequeaths £60,000 to Jane 'trusting that the money will be used to benefit our mother'. Obviously, when the will comes into effect, the testator is not around to explain precisely what he intended when he used these precatory words.

Examples of precatory words and cases in which they appeared. All failed to create a trust.

'feeling confident that...'   – *Mussoorie Bank Ltd v Raynor* [1882]
'specially desire...'   – *Re Connolly* [1910]
'wish them to...'   – *Re Hamilton* [1895]

Let us look again at the provision in Tom's will and consider the questions below:

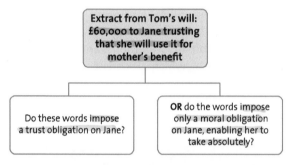

You will notice that Tom has used a precatory word 'trusting'. When considering which question above is correct, it is important to note that the law's attitude to precatory words has changed... The watershed case is said to be *Lambe v Eames* (1871).

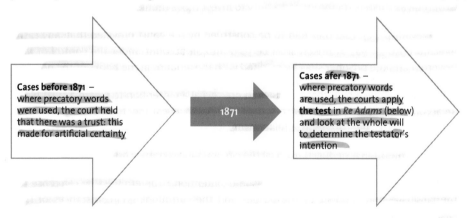

To illustrate the application of this test, it is useful to compare two cases in which the same precatory words 'in full confidence' were used.

Case precedent – *Re Adams and Kensington Vestry* [1884] 27 Ch 394

Facts: The testator gave his estate '... to the absolute use of my dear wife, Harriet ... in full confidence that she will do what is right as to the disposal thereof between my children either in her lifetime or by will'. The court held that Harriet took absolutely. The lack of detailed instructions indicated that the testator did not intend to impose a trust on his widow.

It is also suggested that a mother would have a natural desire to provide for her children without a trust being imposed upon her.

Principle: When precatory words are used, the court should construe the whole of the will to determine whether the testator intended to impose a trust.

Application: This case illustrates the test to determine whether there is a trust or whether the donee can take absolutely, i.e. free of any obligation to act as trustee.

Common Pitfall

Be aware that where the words are held not to create a trust, the donee of the property takes beneficially. It is a common mistake to think that the property results back to the donor.

Case precedent – *Comiskey v Bowring-Hanbury* [1905] AC 84

Facts: The testator gave his estate '... to my very dear wife, Ellen Hanbury ... absolutely in full confidence that she will make use of it ... and that at her death she will devise it to such one or more of my nieces as she may think fit and in default of any disposition by her thereof by her will ... I hereby direct that all my estate and property acquired by her under this my will shall at her death be equally divided among the surviving said nieces'. The detailed instructions and the fact that, in any event, the nieces would obtain an interest in the property indicated that the testator intended to create a trust.

Principle: The will, when construed as a whole, demonstrated that a trust was intended.

Application: Precatory words (such as those above, i.e. 'in full confidence') should not be read in isolation but in the context of the whole will. Therefore, in a problem question regarding a will, look at the whole will in order to ascertain the testator's intention.

Re Steele's Will Trusts

Suppose a testator, intending to create a trust, ill-advisedly uses a pre-1871 precedent when drafting his will. Although with the passing of time this is highly unlikely to occur today, it did arise in *Re Steele's Will Trusts* [1948].

Case precedent – *Re Steele's Will Trusts* [1948] Ch 603

Facts: The testatrix left a diamond necklace to her son in her will 'to be held as an heirloom by him and by his eldest son on his decease . . .' and added the words 'I request my son to do all in his power to give effect to this my wish'. These words had been copied verbatim from a will in the case of *Shelley v Shelley* [1868] in which they had been held to create a trust.

Wynn Parry J held that while the courts' attitude towards precatory words had changed since 1868, the fact that the testatrix had copied the exact language used in the earlier case afforded the strongest indication that the testatrix intended to create a trust.

Principle: Intention may be inferred where a precedent regarding the creation of a trust is exactly copied.

Application: Although this situation is highly unlikely to re-occur, the case could be mentioned in an essay answer on certainty of intention.

Intention in a commercial context

The existence of an express trust can be important when a business becomes insolvent and there are insufficient funds to pay creditors. For example, if a customer who makes pre-payments for goods can prove that he is not in fact a creditor but a beneficiary under a trust of that money, he will be entitled to the return of his money, i.e. it is not part of the business's assets. Of course, he would have to prove that there is a valid trust, i.e. that the three certainties (and other essential requirements) are present.

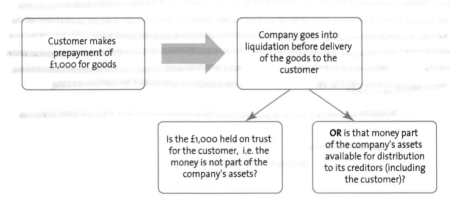

This issue arose in the following case:

Case precedent – *Re Kayford Ltd* [1975] 1 All ER 604

Facts: Kayford Ltd ran a mail order business and customers either paid the full purchase price or a deposit when ordering goods. The company's main supplier ran into financial difficulties, and fearing insolvency as a result, the accountants of Kayford Ltd advised that the company open a separate account to be called the 'Customers Trust Deposit Account' into which all further sums of money paid by customers for goods not yet delivered should be paid. This advice was not precisely followed as a dormant deposit account was used in which there was already a credit balance of £47.80. A fortnight later Kayford Ltd resolved to go into liquidation and it was shortly after this that the words 'Customer Trust Deposit Account' were added to the name of the dormant deposit account. In the liquidation proceedings, the question arose as to whether the money in the account (now amounting to £37,872.45) was held on trust for the customers who had paid it, or whether it formed part of the assets of Kayford Ltd and was thus available to the creditors of the company.

It was held that the steps taken by the company to pay the money into a separate account were evidence of an intention to create a trust and that the company had made it clear that it had no right to use the money itself.

Principle: In the words of Megarry J in *Re Kayford Ltd*, 'the question was whether in substance a sufficient intention to create a trust has been manifested'.

Application: It is important to note that such a trust will not be valid where it constitutes a preference of those who are already legally regarded as creditors. In this respect, see *Re Farepak Food and Gifts Ltd (in administration)* [2006] below.

Case precedent – *Re Farepak Food and Gifts Ltd (in administration)* [2006] EWHC 3272

Facts: Farepak operated a Christmas savings scheme through 26,000 agents to whom customers paid small amounts of money. The agents then passed the money on to Farepak. Just before Christmas 2006, Farepak became insolvent (owing £38 million) and in the three days leading up to administration, the directors sought to set up a trust of the monies received from customers. The court held that for this to be effective, the trust must have existed when the company (including the agents) received the money and very few would fall into this category.

Principle: Money received from pre-payment customers may be held on trust provided they are not already creditors.

Application: When citing this case, you could also mention that the directors' **intention to create the trust** only existed in the last three days.

A sham intention

The court will not uphold a trust where the intention to create the trust was a sham, e.g. merely a ruse to prevent creditors claiming the property.

Case precedent – *Midland Bank v Wyatt* [1995] 1 FLR 696

Facts: A trust deed was executed by a husband in respect of the family home declaring that the property was held on trust for his wife and daughters (who were unaware of these facts). The home was subsequently mortgaged to the Midland Bank from whom the husband continued to borrow. When the bank sought to sell the house to recover the outstanding debt, the husband revealed the existence of the trust deed, claiming that he had no beneficial interest in the home. The court held that the trust was a sham and void, having been created to defeat the claims of the husband's creditors.

Principle: If the intention to create the trust was a sham/fictitious, the trust will not be upheld.

Application: Note that this principle would apply even if the settlor was acting honestly but on poor legal advice.

Effect of uncertainty of intention

Remember to follow a problem question through. Therefore, looking back at the problem at the beginning of this chapter, if you argue that there is no certainty of intention on John Smith's part, then state that no trust is imposed on Brenda, who will take absolutely.

Certainty of subject matter

There are two branches to this certainty – the trust property must be certain – and the beneficial interests of the beneficiaries must be certain.

The trust property must be certain

Example

In his will, Sam states that 'most of his property should be held on trust'.

This trust will fail for uncertainty of subject matter because it is not clear how much property should be held on trust, e.g. it could be from 51% to 99%.

As the following case illustrates, when a trust is attached to a gift, it must be clear how much is an outright gift and how much is held on trust.

Case precedent – *Palmer v Simmonds* [1854] 2 Drew 221

Facts: By her will, the testatrix gave her residuary estate to her friend, Thomas Harrison, adding, *'as I have full confidence in him that if he should die without lawful issue, he will leave the bulk of my estate'* to four named persons.

The question for the court was whether a valid trust had been created for the four named persons. (Remember that pre-1871, the precatory words 'full confidence' would not have posed a problem regarding certainty of intention.) The issue related to certainty of subject matter.

It was held that as it was unclear how much was to be held on trust, the trust failed and Thomas Harrison took absolutely.

Principle: When a trust is attached to a gift, it must be clear how much is held on trust. The same principle applied in *Sprange v Barnard* [1789] 2 Bro CC 585.

Application: You may have noticed that the effect of uncertainty in this case was that Thomas took the property absolutely. This was because the trust was attached to a gift and, when the trust failed, the gift was regarded as absolute. (Compare this with the result in the example regarding Sam where there was simply a failed trust, i.e. it was not attached to a gift.)

Problem questions often ask you to advise whether 'the following dispositions are valid'. The word 'disposition' includes gifts as well as trusts and it is often forgotten that certainty of subject matter applies not only to trusts but also to gifts, e.g. if Sam left 'most of his land' to Brenda in his will, this gift would fail because it would not be certain how much land Brenda should inherit.

Common Pitfall

Confusion sometimes arises with the concept of residuary gifts in a will. If Sam left 'the residue of his estate on trust for Brenda', this trust would be valid because once all the legacies under the will had been distributed, it would be certain what constituted the residue.

The problem of unascertained property (i.e. property that has not been set aside)

The orthodox approach

This is a popular examination area and it is important to be familiar with the main cases below.

Case precedent – *Re London Wine Co (Shippers) Ltd* [1986] PCC 121

Facts: The company held large stocks of wine in its warehouses and customers who placed orders for wine would receive a certificate of title so that they had some assurance that the wine was held on trust for them pending delivery. However, there was no segregation of their bottles from the general stock. The company went into receivership and the question for the court was whether the customers were indeed beneficiaries of the wine under a trust, or whether the wine was part of the company's stock, the proceeds of which would be available to pay its creditors (which in this case would include the customers).

It was held that no trusts had been created as there was no certainty of subject matter.

Principle: There can be no trust of tangible property that has not been segregated, i.e. that is unascertained.

Application: This principle should be applied where the settlor attempts to create a trust of part of a bulk of tangible property, e.g. four of my pictures to be held on trust for Brenda.

The next case is a Privy Council decision and therefore highly persuasive.

Case precedent – *Re Goldcorp Exchange Ltd* [1995] 1 AC 74

Facts: Goldcorp sold gold and precious metals to clients for future delivery. When the company went into receivership, three groups of clients, who had pre-paid, claimed that their orders were held on trust for them, i.e. they were not creditors of the company. The issue for the Privy Council was whether there was certainty of subject matter.

The first group's gold had been physically segregated in vaults from the rest of the stock and therefore the subject matter was certain.

The second group's gold had not been segregated and therefore there was no trust for them.

The third client had ordered 1,000 gold maple leaf coins but the company had purchased a greater number of these coins. Although there was only one client who claimed a trust of the coins, his claim failed for uncertainty of subject matter as his order of 1,000 coins had not been segregated from the rest of the maple leaf coins.

Principle: No client can claim to have a beneficial interest in tangible property they have ordered until that property has been ascertained, i.e. segregated from the stock.

Application: When applying this Privy Council decision, you should mention that the maple leaf coins were identical and yet the strict principle applied.

The third case taking the orthodox approach is *MacJordan* below.

> **Case precedent – *MacJordan Construction Ltd v Brookmount Erostin Ltd* [1994] CLC 581**
>
> **Facts:** Under a building contract between a building contractor and Brookmount (a property developer), it was agreed that Brookmount would retain 3% of the money due to the contractor pending approval of the work. The retention money was to be held on trust and placed in a separate bank account. When the developer went into receivership, the retention monies amounted to £109,247 and the developer owed £2 million to its bank (a secured creditor).
>
> The Court of Appeal held that as the retention monies had not been placed in a separate account (as previously agreed), there were no identifiable assets to form the subject matter of the trust. The contractor could not therefore claim that the monies were held on trust and only had contractual rights against the developer and, as such, was an unsecured creditor.
>
> **Principle:** There must be identifiable assets upon which to impress a trust or it will fail for uncertainty of subject matter.
>
> **Application:** Note that when a company goes into liquidation, its assets are distributed to its creditors in a certain order. Unsecured creditors are at the bottom of that list and it is unlikely that they will receive all/any of the money they are owed. That is why they argue that they are entitled to the assets as beneficiaries under a trust.

The decision in Hunter v Moss

As this case often arises in questions, it is dealt with in some detail. First, see if you can identify the key difference(s) with the three cases above.

> **Case precedent – *Hunter v Moss* [1994] 3 All ER 215**
>
> **Facts:** Moss was the registered holder of 950 shares in Moss Electrical Co Ltd and orally declared that he would hold 50 of these shares on trust for Hunter under Hunter's contract of employment. When Moss subsequently sold the 950 shares and kept all the proceeds, Hunter claimed that he was entitled to a proportion of the proceeds. The issue for the Court of Appeal was whether Hunter had **beneficial rights** in the 50 shares as these had never been segregated from the other shares.
>
> Dillon LJ stated that since the subject matter related to shares of one class in the one company, and were indistinguishable from each other, there was a valid trust of 50 shares even though they had not been separated from the remaining 900 shares. Dillon LJ drew an analogy with a bequest in a will of 50 shares (from a larger holding), which the executors would be able to allocate to the legatee.

Principle: Dillon LJ referred to a distinction between trusts of chattels and shares (which commentators have referred to as a distinction between trusts of tangible and intangible property) with the latter being valid despite the fact that the subject matter of the trust has not been specifically identified.

Application: When applying this decision in a problem question, it is important to mention that whilst the result may be considered fair, the basis for the decision has been criticised. Regarding both these points, see below.

It would have been unconscionable if Moss had been able to renege on his declaration simply by using an equitable principle that there was no certainty of subject matter. Remember the maxim in Chapter 1 that 'He who comes to Equity must come with clean hands'.

A key difference between this case and the three cases where the orthodox approach was adopted is that *Hunter v Moss* did not concern a claim by customers against an insolvent company. Such customers were maintaining that they were not unsecured creditors but had priority over creditors as beneficiaries of the property under a trust.

Up for Debate

The decision in *Hunter v Moss* is criticised for a number of reasons:

❖ Why should there be a distinction between tangible and intangible property, when mass-produced tangible items may be indistinguishable from each other, as was the case with the maple leaf coins in *Re Goldcorp*.
❖ In fact, are shares indistinguishable from each other? A share is a chose in action, which is represented by a number and entry on a register.
❖ The critical distinction should be whether the company is insolvent or solvent, not whether the property is tangible or intangible. If a company is insolvent and it is held that there is a trust for clients, then this could be construed as the preference of a creditor.
❖ Dillon LJ's analogy of a trustee with an executor who acquires legal title to all the deceased's property with power to distribute legacies (see above case) is incorrect because the trustee acquires legal title only to those assets that are subject to the trust and that is the very issue, i.e. what property is subject to the trust?
❖ Problems could arise with the decision in *Hunter v Moss*. Suppose Moss had re-invested the proceeds of the shares and some had been re-invested profitably and some at a loss, the question would arise as to which of the new shares could be claimed by Hunter.

Nevertheless, the decision has been followed in *Harvard Securities Ltd* [1997].

Aim Higher

When you criticise the decision in *Hunter v Moss*, it would be impressive if you could provide an alternative solution by referring to the decision of the Supreme Court of New South Wales in Australia in *White v Shorthall* [2006] NSWSC 1379. The claimant maintained that under a contract, 222,000 shares of a total of 1,500,000 shares were held on trust for him, although the shares had never been segregated from the bulk. The court declined to apply the decision in *Hunter v Moss*, preferring the argument that the defendant held **all** 1,500,000 shares on trust with power to decide which 222,000 shares were held for the claimant.

This avoided the issue of certainty of subject matter as all the shares were held on trust.

The beneficial interests of the beneficiaries must be certain

The following case is an example of a situation where the trust property was certain but the beneficial interests were uncertain, causing the trust to fail.

Case precedent – *Boyce v Boyce* [1849] 16 Sim 476

Facts: A testator left two houses on trust, his trustee 'to convey one, whichever she may think proper to choose to my daughter Maria, and to convey the other to my daughter Charlotte'.

Maria predeceased the testator without choosing and the court held that since it was uncertain which house Charlotte should have, the trust failed for uncertainty of beneficial interest.

Principle: The beneficial interest of the beneficiary must be certain or the trust will fail.

Application: When you apply this decision to a problem, remember to follow your answer through and explain that when such a trust fails, the property is held on resulting trust for the settlor or, if he is dead, for his estate, i.e. for the residuary beneficiary under his will, or if none, for his next of kin under the intestacy rules.

The following is a very useful case as the principle often comes up in questions.

Case precedent – *Re Golay's Will Trusts* [1965] 1 WLR 969

Facts: The testator directed that Tossy (Florence Bridgewater) was 'to enjoy one of my flats during her lifetime and to receive a reasonable income from my other properties'.

The executors were able to choose which flat Tossy should live in but the issue for the court arose over the quantification of a reasonable income.

It was held that the term 'reasonable income' provided a sufficient yardstick to enable the court to calculate the amount – based on the beneficiary's previous standard of living.

Principle: If the court has a yardstick to make an objective assessment of what is reasonable with respect to the beneficial interest, the trust or gift will not fail.

Application: If the word 'reasonable' arises in isolation, e.g. a reasonable amount to be held on trust, there would be no yardstick to calculate the amount and the gift/trust would fail.

The effect of uncertainty of subject matter

Remember to follow your answers through. If you have decided there is uncertainty of subject matter, state the effect of this. Although the different effects have been stated in the cases above, they are summarised below.

If the trust property is uncertain, then the trust will fail as there is nothing for the trust to attach to. However, if the trust was attached to an outright gift as in *Palmer v Simmonds*, then the gift will take effect absolutely.

If the trust property is certain but the beneficial interest is uncertain, then unless the trustees have been given a discretion regarding the amount of the beneficial interest, the trust will fail and the property will be held on resulting trust for the settlor or, if he is dead, for his estate, i.e. for the residuary beneficiary under his will, or if none, for his next of kin under the intestacy rules.

The interrelationship between certainty of intention and certainty of subject matter

Notice that there is an inter relationship between the first two certainties. Sir Arthur Hobhouse stated in the Privy Council case *Mussoorie Bank v Raynor* [1882] 7 App Cas 321, 'Uncertainty in the subject of the gift has a reflex action upon the previous words, and throws doubt upon the intention of the testator, and seems to show that he could not possibly have intended his words of confidence, hope, or whatever they may be . . . to be imperative words.'

Certainty of objects

On this topic, it is important to distinguish between fixed trusts/gifts and discretionary trusts/gifts as the following diagrams illustrate.

A fixed trust

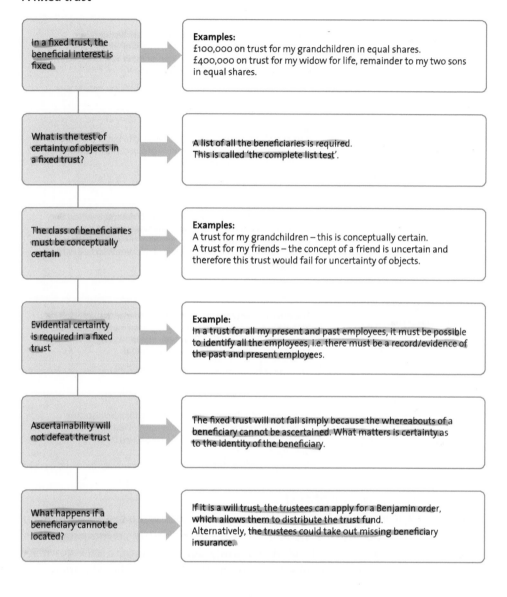

In a fixed trust, the beneficial interest is fixed

Examples:
£100,000 on trust for my grandchildren in equal shares.
£400,000 on trust for my widow for life, remainder to my two sons in equal shares.

What is the test of certainty of objects in a fixed trust?

A list of all the beneficiaries is required.
This is called 'the complete list test'.

The class of beneficiaries must be conceptually certain

Examples:
A trust for my grandchildren – this is conceptually certain.
A trust for my friends – the concept of a friend is uncertain and therefore this trust would fail for uncertainty of objects.

Evidential certainty is required in a fixed trust

Example:
In a trust for all my present and past employees, it must be possible to identify all the employees, i.e. there must be a record/evidence of the past and present employees.

Ascertainability will not defeat the trust

The fixed trust will not fail simply because the whereabouts of a beneficiary cannot be ascertained. What matters is certainty as to the identity of the beneficiary.

What happens if a beneficiary cannot be located?

If it is a will trust, the trustees can apply for a Benjamin order, which allows them to distribute the trust fund.
Alternatively, the trustees could take out missing beneficiary insurance.

A discretionary trust

In a discretionary trust, the beneficial interest is in the absolute discretion of the trustees

Example:
£200,000 on trust for such of my employees as my trustees shall consider most deserving.

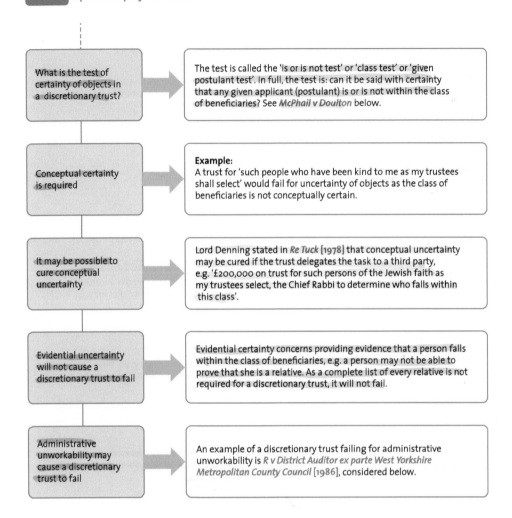

What is the test of certainty of objects in a discretionary trust?	The test is called the 'is or is not test' or 'class test' or 'given postulant test'. In full, the test is: can it be said with certainty that any given applicant (postulant) is or is not within the class of beneficiaries? See *McPhail v Doulton* below.
Conceptual certainty is required	**Example:** A trust for 'such people who have been kind to me as my trustees shall select' would fail for uncertainty of objects as the class of beneficiaries is not conceptually certain.
It may be possible to cure conceptual uncertainty	Lord Denning stated in *Re Tuck* [1978] that conceptual uncertainty may be cured if the trust delegates the task to a third party, e.g. '£200,000 on trust for such persons of the Jewish faith as my trustees select, the Chief Rabbi to determine who falls within this class'.
Evidential uncertainty will not cause a discretionary trust to fail	Evidential certainty concerns providing evidence that a person falls within the class of beneficiaries, e.g. a person may not be able to prove that she is a relative. As a complete list of every relative is not required for a discretionary trust, it will not fail.
Administrative unworkability may cause a discretionary trust to fail	An example of a discretionary trust failing for administrative unworkability is *R v District Auditor ex parte West Yorkshire Metropolitan County Council* [1986], considered below.

More on the 'is or is not test'

Prior to *McPhail v Doulton* [1971], which is explained below, the test for certainty of objects in a discretionary trust was the same as for fixed trusts, i.e. the complete list test. The discretionary trust in *IRC v Broadway Cottages* [1955] 2 WLR 552 failed because it was not possible to draw up a complete list of all the beneficiaries.

Case precedent – *McPhail v Doulton* [1971] AC 424

Facts: In 1941, the settlor, Bertram Baden, executed a deed which stated that a fund was to be held on trust in favour of the staff of Matthew Hall & Co Ltd and their dependants and relatives.

Clause 9 of the deed provided that 'the trustees shall apply the net income of the fund in making at their absolute discretion grants to or for the benefit of any of the officers and employees or ex-officers or ex-employees of the company or to any relatives or dependants of any such persons in such amounts and at such times and on such conditions (if any) as they think fit . . .'

The executors of Mr Baden's will challenged the validity of the trust on the ground of uncertainty of objects. Note that prior to this case, the test of certainty of objects for a discretionary trust was the complete list test.

However, in *McPhail v Doulton*, the House of Lords adopted the 'is or is not test', which applied to powers of appointment. The case was then remitted to the High Court to apply the test to the facts and from there it went to the Court of Appeal – see *Re Baden*, discussed below in the 'Aim Higher' box.

Principle: The 'is or is not test' for certainty of objects in a discretionary trust is 'whether it can be said with certainty that any given individual is or is not a member of the class of beneficiaries'.

Application: You need to be able to apply this test to a problem question concerning certainty of objects in a discretionary trust. Imagine that you are the trustee of a discretionary trust where the class of beneficiaries are residents of Blackstone parish. Unlike a fixed trust, you do not need to be able to make a complete list of all the residents of the parish. However, when any person comes forward as an applicant, it must be possible to say whether he or she is or is not a resident of the parish. For further details regarding the test – see the 'Aim Higher' box below.

Common Pitfall

You will notice that the House of Lords adopted the 'is or is not test', which applied to powers of appointment. Powers of appointment should not be confused with discretionary trusts although they are very similar – in fact, discretionary trusts are sometimes called trust powers. You may find it helpful to look back at Chapter 1, which explained the nature of powers of appointment.

Aim Higher

You will gain higher marks if you are able to discuss the different interpretations given to the 'is or is not test' by the three Court of Appeal judges in *Re Baden* [1972] 3 WLR 250.

Stamp LJ interpreted the test literally and said that a category of 'don't know' regarding any given applicant should not be permitted.

Sachs LJ stated that it was up to an applicant to prove that he was within the class of beneficiaries, and if he could not do so, then he was outside the class. Note that he put the burden of proof on the applicant.

> Megaw LJ permitted a category of 'don't knows', provided a substantial number of claimants fell within the class. (Remember it is the basis of a discretionary trust that there are a number of beneficiaries to choose from.)

Each interpretation may be criticised. Stamp LJ's strict approach, which does not permit a class of 'don't knows', could be regarded as a retreat to the list test. Sachs LJ's approach could result in only one applicant being able to prove positively that he was within the class of beneficiaries. And whilst Megaw LJ's approach avoids this problem, it could still mean that the class of beneficiaries is narrow. Also, what is meant by 'a substantial number of claimants'?

As it is not clear which interpretation would be preferred by a future court, you should mention all three approaches.

Administrative unworkability

In the discretionary trust diagram above, we saw that a discretionary trust will fail if it is administratively unworkable. This issue was considered in the following first instance case.

Case precedent – *R v District Auditor ex parte West Yorkshire Metropolitan County Council* [1986] RVR 24

Facts: The Metropolitan County Council was threatened with abolition by the Government. It had a fund of approximately £400,000 and decided to create a trust for the benefit of 'any or all or some of the inhabitants of the County of West Yorkshire'.

Whilst the class of beneficiaries was conceptually certain, the court held that the trust failed for uncertainty of objects as it was administratively unworkable because there were approximately two and a half million inhabitants.

Principle: The trust will fail if the class of beneficiaries is so wide that it is administratively unworkable.

Application: When you apply this decision, you could also cite the *dicta* of Lord Wilberforce in *McPhail v Doulton* that 'a trust for the residents of Greater London' would fail for administrative unworkability. Such a trust would probably also be regarded as capricious as the class of beneficiaries is so wide that it could not be considered sensibly by the trustee who has a duty, according to Lord Wilberforce, 'to survey the class' and 'examine the field, by class and category, . . . make diligent and careful inquiries, depending on how much money he had to give away and the means at his disposal'.

The effect of uncertainty of objects

Remember to follow your answer through. So, if you establish that a trust fails for uncertainty of objects, explain that the fund will be held on resulting trust for the settlor or, if he is dead, for his estate, i.e. it will be held for the residuary beneficiary under his will, or if none, for his next of kin under the intestacy rules.

Putting it into practice

Peter Wood, who has just died, drafted his own will, which contained the following clauses:

(a) £150,000 to my sister, Angela, confident that she will use a reasonable sum for the care of our brother, Simon.
(b) The money in my Barclays Bank savings account to be divided equally amongst my friends.
(c) £300,000 on trust, the capital to be distributed by my trustees, Thomas and Tobias, amongst such of my relatives as they shall select.
(d) The bulk of the residue of my estate to my sister, Angela.

Explain the effect of the above dispositions.

Feedback on putting it into practice

The whole of this question relates to the three certainties, so you could have a short introduction, identifying the three certainties necessary for the creation of a valid express trust/gift and citing the authority – *Knight v Knight*. A suggested answer is outlined in the following diagram.

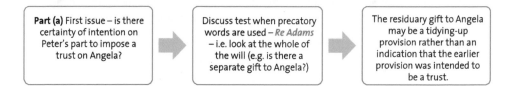

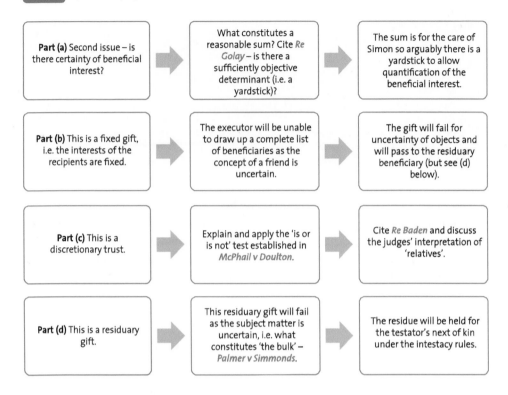

Table of key cases referred to in this chapter

Case name	Area of law	Principle
Adams and Kensington Vestry, Re [1884]	Precatory words	When precatory words are used, the court will look at the whole of the will to determine the testator's intention to create a trust.
Baden, Re [1972]	Discretionary trust – certainty of objects	Sequel to *McPhail v Doulton* in which the 'is or is not' test was applied.
Boyce v Boyce [1849]	Certainty of beneficial interest	The beneficial interest enjoyed by the beneficiary must be certain.
Comiskey v Bowring Hanbury [1905]	Precatory words	Court looked at the whole of the will and decided that despite the use of precatory words, the testator intended to create a trust.
Duggan v Governor of Full Sutton Prison [2004]	Certainty of intention	Intention is deduced from all the circumstances of the case.

Farepak Foods and Gifts Ltd [2007]	Certainty of intention	Money received from pre-payment customers may be held in trust provided they are not already creditors, and provided there was an intention to create a trust.
Golay's Will Trusts, Re [1965]	Certainty of beneficial interest	Trust will be valid if there is a yardstick to determine what is, for example, a reasonable amount.
Goldcorp Exchange Ltd, Re [1995]	Certainty of subject matter	Tangible property (even if identical) must be segregated for there to be certainty of subject matter.
Hunter v Moss [1994]	Certainty of subject matter	A trust for intangible property will be valid even though the property has not been segregated.
Kayford, Re [1975]	Certainty of intention	In substance, there was a sufficient intention to create a trust for the customers.
Lambe v Eames [1871]	Precatory words	Watershed case regarding courts' attitude to precatory words.
Leek, Re [1969]	Discretionary trust – certainty of objects	*Obiter dicta* suggesting that uncertain classes of beneficiaries should be severed from trust instrument.
London Wine Co (Shippers), Re [1986]	Certainty of subject matter	There can be no trust of tangible property that has not been segregated.
MacJordan Construction Ltd v Brookmount Erostin Ltd [1992]	Certainty of subject matter	There must be identifiable assets upon which to impress a trust.
McPhail v Doulton [1971]	Discretionary trust – certainty of objects	Established the 'is or is not' test for certainty of objects in a discretionary trust.
Midland Bank v Wyatt [1995]	Sham intention	If intention to create a trust was a sham/fictitious, the trust will fail.
Mussoorie Bank Ltd v Raynor [1882]	Interrelationship of certainty of intention and certainty of subject matter	Doubt over subject matter will have a reflex action on any doubt over certainty of intention.

Case name	Area of law	Principle
Palmer v Simmonds [1854]	Certainty of subject matter	When the trust is attached to a gift, it must be clear how much is to be held on trust.
Paul v Constance [1977]	Certainty of intention	Intention may be inferred from the settlor's words and conduct.
R v District Auditor ex parte West Yorkshire Metropolitan CC [1986]	Discretionary trust – certainty of objects	Discretionary trust failed as administratively unworkable.
Steele's Will Trusts, Re [1948]	Precatory words	Intention to create a trust may be inferred when a pre-1871 precedent containing precatory words is copied.
White v Shorthall [2006]	Certainty of subject matter	Australian decision providing an alternative solution to *Hunter v Moss* based on a single trust over all the property.

@ Visit the book's companion website to test your knowledge

❖ Resources include a subject map, revision tip podcasts, downloadable diagrams, MCQ quizzes for each chapter, and a flashcard glossary

❖ www.routledge.com/cw/optimizelawrevision

3

The Statutory Formalities

Revision objectives

Understand the law
- Can you describe the statutory formality for the declaration of an express trust of land?
- What is the statutory formality for the disposition of a subsisting equitable interest?

Remember the details
- Do you remember the effect of non-compliance with s 53(1)(b) and s 53(1)(c) Law of Property Act 1925?
- Can you give examples of transactions that constitute a disposition of a subsisting equitable interest?

Reflect critically on areas of debate
- Are you able to critically evaluate the decision in *Vandervell's Trusts (No 2)*?
- Can you explain the decision in *Oughtred v IRC*?

Contextualise
- Can you explain the tax context of *Grey v IRC* and the *Vandervell* cases?
- Would the outcome in *Vandervell's Trusts (No 2)* have been different if it had involved a new declaration of trust of land?

Apply your skills and knowledge
- Can you complete all parts of the problem question regarding the declaration of a trust of land and the disposition of a subsisting equitable interest?

Chapter Map

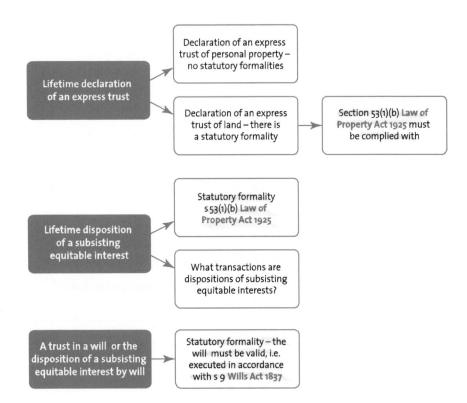

The statutory formalities: a lifetime declaration of an express trust

The Scenario

John **declares** that he is going to create two trusts in favour of his grandchildren, Brenda and Ben.

Firstly, of his 1,000 shares in Abbott Ltd and secondly, of his holiday cottage, Pendrells.

In the above scenario, you will notice that the three certainties (which we considered in Chapter 2) are fulfilled. However, in order to create a valid express trust, John must also vest legal title to the shares and the cottage in the trustees (and this requirement will be considered in Chapter 4). For the present, we are concerned with John's actual declaration of the trusts. **Are there any statutory formalities that John must comply with when declaring these trusts?**

The Answer

There are no statutory formalities regarding the declaration of trust of personal property, although (if the property is valuable or John is declaring **himself** trustee of the 1,000 Abbott shares) it would be advisable for reasons of evidence for the declaration of trust to be in writing.

It is important to note that there **are** statutory formalities when making a declaration of an express trust of land, i.e. regarding the cottage, John must comply with s 53(1)(b) Law of Property Act 1925 – this requirement is examined below.

A declaration of an express trust of land must comply with s 53(1)(b) Law of Property Act 1925

Section 53(1)(b) Law of Property Act 1925 reads as follows:

'A declaration of trust respecting any land or any interest therein must be manifested and proved by some writing signed by some person who is able to declare such trust or by his will.'

We need to analyse this sub-section so that you can apply it to a problem question.

❖ 'manifested and proved by some writing' – this means that the declaration does not have to be contained in a single document, provided there is evidence of the declaration in writing, e.g. in the example above, John could prove his declaration by a number of documents, such as a letter, a memorandum or other writing, provided this evidence revealed the material terms of the trust, i.e. the parties to the trust, the subject matter and how the property was to be dealt with. It seems from *Gardner v Rowe* [1828] that the written evidence may be provided after the declaration, i.e. it need not be contemporaneous with it.

❖ 'signed by some person who is able to declare such trust' – this means that the written evidence would have to contain John's signature.

❖ You will notice that the section does not state the effect of non-compliance. However, it is established by *Gardner v Rowe* that the trust will be unenforceable. This means precisely what it says – so, continuing with the example given above, if anyone contested Ben and Brenda's right to the cottage as beneficiaries under the trust, they would be unable to enforce the trust in court.

Common Pitfall

This statutory formality is often confused with the transfer of legal title of the land to the trustees (which we consider in the next chapter). This confusion may arise from the fact that the vesting of legal title to the land in the trustee and the declaration of trust of the land occur together when the settlor uses a Land Transfer form (Form TR1). It is suggested that you look at this form online – you will see that it is completed by the settlor when he transfers land to the trustees and that part 10 of the TR1 form also allows the settlor to make the declaration of trust.

Note that if a settlor declared himself trustee of the land, he would not vest legal title in himself (as he already holds legal title) and he would have to ensure that there was signed written evidence of his declaration in order to comply with s 53(1)(b) LPA 1925 above.

Section 53(2) Law of Property Act 1925 is also important. It provides:

'This section does not affect the creation or operation of resulting, implied or constructive trusts.'

In other words, resulting trusts and constructive trusts are exempt from s 53(1). This will prove very important when we study trusts of the family home as the following example illustrates.

Sam is Brenda's boyfriend. Five years ago, Brenda moved into his flat and Sam told her on a number of occasions: 'This flat is as much yours as mine.' Brenda relied on these statements and helped Sam to pay the mortgage and also redecorated the rooms at her own expense.

Sam and Brenda have now split up and Sam argues that Brenda has no beneficial interest in the flat. Notice that Brenda will not be able to argue that the flat is held on express trust for her (because of s 53(1)(b) LPA). However, we shall see in a later chapter that she may be able to argue that she has an interest under a constructive trust (which is exempt from s 53(1) under s 53(2) LPA 1925.

A lifetime disposition of a subsisting equitable interest

A lifetime disposition of a subsisting equitable interest must comply with s 53(1)(c) Law of Property Act 1925 as the following diagram illustrates.

Settlor (James) creates a trust of his Abbott shares

|

Trustees (Tim and Tom)

|

Beneficiary: Ben for life   **Ben disposes of his existing equitable interest to Brenda** →   Beneficiary: Brenda for life

|

Beneficiary: Remainder to Carl

In the above example, Ben is entitled (during his life) to the dividends declared on the Abbott shares, and on his death, the shares will pass to Carl. If Ben decides that he does not want/need the dividends, he can dispose of this existing equitable interest, e.g. to Brenda who will then be entitled to the dividends during Ben's lifetime. However, to achieve this, Ben must comply with s 53(1)(c) Law of Property Act 1925.

Section 53(1)(c) Law of Property Act 1925 reads as follows:

> 'A disposition of an equitable interest or trust subsisting at the time of the disposition must be in writing and signed by the person disposing of the same, or by his agent thereunto lawfully authorised in writing or by his will.'

Question: What is the reason for s 53(1)(c) LPA 1925?

❖ **Answer:** Equitable interests are intangible and s 53(1)(c) enables the trustee to know who has the equitable interest at any given time.

If you look at the wording of s 53(1)(c), you will notice that Ben would have to make sure that the disposition was **in writing** (which includes an electronic document) and was signed either by himself, or his duly authorised agent. If he failed to do this, the disposition would be void and Ben would still hold the equitable interest. Notice also that this formality applies to equitable interests generally, i.e. whether they are equitable interests in land or personal property.

Common Pitfall

It is stressed that this statutory formality concerns an **existing trust**. It is a common mistake to think that it is concerned with the creation of an express trust. So, consider this formality as a digression from our main topic of creating an express trust.

Which transactions are dispositions of subsisting equitable interests?

In order to answer problem questions, it is important to be able to recognise whether a transaction is a disposition of an existing equitable interest so that you can advise the beneficiary whether he must comply with s 53(1)(c) LPA 1925.

It is recommended that you remember the headings in each of the following transactions. You should also be able to explain the key cases that demonstrate the transactions.

A direction by a beneficiary to his trustee to hold his equitable interest on trust for another is caught by s 53(1)(c) LPA 1925

If Ben (the beneficiary) telephoned his trustee and asked him to hold Ben's existing equitable interest on trust for Brenda, then this transaction would be void because Ben must comply with s 53(1)(c), i.e. the transaction must be in writing and signed by Ben or his duly authorised agent.

The key case is *Grey v IRC* below, which is also illustrated by a diagram.

Case precedent – *Grey v Inland Revenue Commissioners* [1960] AC 1

Facts: In 1949, Mr Hunter transferred small sums to his trustees (one of whom was Mr Grey) to hold on six trusts for his grandchildren. Mr Hunter owned 18,000 shares in Sun Engraving Co Ltd and, six years later, he transferred these shares to the same trustees to hold on trust for himself. He then **orally directed the trustees** to hold those shares upon the six trusts of the grandchildren's settlements. He made this direction orally in order to avoid stamp duty. (Stamp duty is payable on documents that transfer property, notably shares/land, to another.) His trustees subsequently executed documents confirming that they were holding the shares on trust for the grandchildren.

The IRC successfully argued before the House of Lords that Mr Hunter's direction to his trustees to hold the shares on trust for the grandchildren was in fact a disposition of a subsisting equitable interest, which was void because it was oral (i.e. it did not comply with s 53(1)(c) LPA 1925) and that the documents executed by the trustees constituted the disposition (i.e. it was the confirmatory documents that transferred the equitable interest) and these documents were subject to stamp duty.

Principle: A direction to trustees to hold an existing equitable interest on trust for another must comply with s 53(1)(c) Law of Property Act 1925 – see diagram below.

Application: Remember the principle but you could point out that Mr Hunter could have avoided stamp duty if he had simply declared himself trustee of the shares for his grandchildren (see earlier in this chapter that a declaration of trust of personal property may be achieved orally).

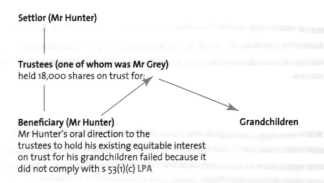

Settlor (Mr Hunter)

Trustees (one of whom was Mr Grey)
held 18,000 shares on trust for:

Beneficiary (Mr Hunter)   Grandchildren
Mr Hunter's oral direction to the
trustees to hold his existing equitable interest
on trust for his grandchildren failed because it
did not comply with s 53(1)(c) LPA

The transfer of the legal interest by the trustee and the equitable interest to a third party is not caught by s 53(1)(c) **LPA 1925**

The case of *Vandervell v IRC*, which illustrates this principle, involved a **bare trust**.

Question: What is a bare trust? ❖ **Answer:** A bare trust is one where the trustee has no duty to perform other than to convey the legal estate to the beneficiary or as the beneficiary directs.

Case precedent – *Vandervell v Inland Revenue Commissioners* [1967] 2AC 291

Facts: These facts relate to the period 1958–1961. The National Provincial Bank held 100,000 shares in Vandervell Products Ltd on bare trust for Mr Vandervell, a wealthy businessman. Mr Vandervell wished to give £150,000 to the Royal College of Surgeons so that it could found a Chair of Pharmacology.

Mr Vandervell decided to do this by orally directing the National Provincial Bank to transfer their legal title and his equitable interest to the shares to the College until dividends amounting to £150,000 had been paid to the College, whereupon it was agreed that Vandervell Trustee Co (a company that acted as trustee for a trust which Mr Vandervell had set up for his children in 1949) could exercise an option to repurchase the shares for £5,000.

The reason why Mr Vandervell chose to benefit the college in this way was that if he received the dividends under the bare trust and then paid the money to the college himself, he would be liable to surtax on that dividend income. Furthermore, the college, as a charity, was not liable to tax on the dividends.

However, the IRC argued that Mr Vandervell had not divested himself of his interest in the shares during the above period and was liable to surtax. They had two arguments:

(1) That his oral direction to the bank to transfer their legal title and his equitable interest to the college was a disposition of a subsisting equitable interest and was void as it was not in writing and signed in accordance with s 53(1)(c) Law of Property Act 1925. This argument failed – see principle below.

(2)   That whilst legal title to the option was held by Vandervell Trustee Co, there had been no declaration as to who was the beneficiary of this option, and therefore, it was held on resulting trust for Mr Vandervell, who accordingly retained an interest in the shares. This argument succeeded. See 'Common Pitfall' below if you are confused on this point. It is important to understand this second argument as it led to *Vandervell's Trusts (No 2)*.

Principle: When the legal title and the equitable interest move together to a third party, this is not a disposition of a subsisting equitable interest and can be achieved orally. Lord Upjohn stated that the object of s 53(1)(c) is to prevent hidden oral dispositions of equitable interests, which does not apply when there is an absolute transfer, i.e. of both the legal and equitable interest.

Application: It is important to recognise the transaction in which both the legal title and equitable interest move to a third party and to remember that it does not get caught by s 53(1)(c) so that you can apply this principle to a problem question. See the diagram below.

Settlor (Mr Vandervell)

Trustee (National Provincial Bank) ———— Legal title to shares transferred to: ————→ **Royal College of Surgeons**

Beneficiary (Mr Vandervell) ———— Equitable interest in shares transferred to:

Common Pitfall

Notice that an option is an item of property and, like all property, is capable of duality of ownership, i.e. the legal title may be held by a trustee, and the equitable/beneficial interest enjoyed by a beneficiary. The option deed in *Vandervell v IRC* was a simple document and the majority of the House of Lords held that whilst the legal title of the option was held by Vandervell Trustee Co., as the deed did not state who the beneficiary of the option was, it followed that the option was held by the trustee company on automatic resulting trust for the person who created the option, namely Mr Vandervell, who therefore retained an interest in the 100,000 shares, which meant that he could be assessed to surtax on the dividend income.

We now consider the **sequel**, *Vandervell's Trusts (No 2)* [1974], which begins where *Vandervell v IRC* ended, with the option to repurchase the shares. Before we look at the case, it may make it more understandable to know the following facts.

Useful preliminary facts about Mr Vandervell:

❖   Mr Vandervell was not aware that he had an interest in the shares (through the option) until 1965, whereupon he executed a deed formally transferring any interest he might have in the option or shares to the Vandervell Trustee Co to hold on trust for his children.

❖ The facts of the sequel, *Vandervell's Trusts (No 2)*, covers the years 1961 to 1965.

❖ Mr Vandervell married his second wife in 1967 and died seven weeks later.

❖ He did not provide for his children (by an earlier marriage) in his will as he believed that they were well provided for by the settlements he had set up for them with the Vandervell Trustee Co acting as trustee.

❖ However, his second wife was the main beneficiary under his will.

Case precedent – *Vandervell's Trusts (No 2)* [1974] 3 WLR 256

Facts: In October 1961, Vandervell Trustee Co exercised the option to purchase the shares from the Royal College of Surgeons, using £5,000 from the children's trust and thereafter paying all the dividends received into the children's settlement with Mr Vandervell's assent. Vandervell Trustee Co also wrote to the Inland Revenue stating that the shares would 'henceforth be held by them for the children's settlement'. This was disputed by the executors of Mr Vandervell's estate as below.

Following Mr Vandervell's death in 1967, the executors of his estate argued that in fact Mr Vandervell had an equitable interest in the repurchased shares under a resulting trust because, when the trust of the shares was declared for the children, this was in fact a disposition of Mr Vandervell's equitable interest (acquired under the option) and it failed because Mr Vandervell had not complied with s 53(1)(c), i.e. it had not been in writing, signed by Mr Vandervell or his duly authorised agent. Therefore, the executors argued, the dividends (amounting to £1 million gross) for the period October 1961 to January 1965 could not be claimed by the children's trust but in fact belonged to Mr Vandervell and therefore passed to his wife under his will.

Lord Denning disagreed and said 'a resulting trust for the settlor is born and dies without any writing at all. It comes into existence whenever there is a gap in the beneficial ownership. It ceases to exist whenever that gap is filled by someone becoming beneficially entitled … In this case, before the option was exercised, there was a gap in the beneficial ownership. So there was a resulting trust for Mr Vandervell. But, as soon as the option was exercised and the shares registered in the trustees' name, there was created a valid trust of the shares in favour of the children's settlement. Not being a trust of land, it could be created without any writing'.

Principle: The termination of a resulting trust upon the declaration of a new trust is not a disposition of a subsisting equitable interest and is not therefore caught by s 53(1)(c) Law of Property Act 1925.

Application: You should be ready to apply this principle to a problem question – see example below – but when you do so, it is important that you should be able to give at least two criticisms of the decision in *Vandervell's Trusts (No 2)* – see 'Up for Debate' box overleaf – and suggest an alternative solution, i.e. the decision in *Grey v IRC* (the facts of which are very similar).

Example: On 1 February David transfers 5,000 shares to his trustees to hold on trust. He tells them he has not yet decided upon the beneficiary but will advise them in a few weeks' time. As noted in *Vandervell v IRC*, equity abhors a vacuum and the shares will be held on resulting trust for David pending his instructions. On 14 February, David telephones his trustees and directs them to hold the shares on trust for his daughter, Anna.

It would seem that David may achieve the transaction above orally. The resulting trust terminated on the declaration of the new trust and does not constitute a disposition of a subsisting equitable interest – *Vandervell's Trusts (No 2)*.

Up for Debate

The decision in *Vandervell's Trusts (No 2)* has been criticised on a number of grounds. It is recommended that you are able to explain at least two of these.

❖ If the equitable interest in the option was held on resulting trust for Mr Vandervell and he was thereby held to retain an interest in the shares in *Vandervell v IRC*, why was there not also a resulting trust of the shares for Mr Vandervell when the option was exercised?

❖ The fact that the £5,000 to repurchase the shares came from the children's trust should not have diverted the benefit of the option (worth far more than £5,000) to the children. Instead, as Megarry J suggested, the children's trust should simply have had a lien over the shares for the repayment of the £5,000.

❖ How could Mr Vandervell **intend** to transfer the benefit of the repurchased shares in 1961 when he did not know that he retained any interest in the shares until the first judgment in *Vandervell v IRC* in 1964, whereupon early in 1965, he executed a deed formally transferring any interest he might have in the shares?

❖ Trustees cannot usually declare a trust either by words or **by conduct** (as in this case).

❖ It was held that the resulting trust of the option terminated when the new trust was declared and this was outside the scope of **s 53(1)(c)**. But this extends **s 53(2)**, which exempts only 'the creation and operation of resulting trusts' from the formality requirements of **s 53(1)** – not the **termination** of resulting trusts.

❖ How can the facts be distinguished from *Grey v IRC* in which Mr Hunter directed the trustees to hold his equitable interest on trust for his grandchildren?

❖ Was the decision in *Vandervell's Trusts (No 2)* based on avoiding a difficult case that would have deprived the children of the dividends?

A declaration by a beneficiary of a genuine sub-trust is not caught by s 53(1)(c) LPA 1925

Example:

In a trust of shares, the equitable/beneficial interest would be the dividends. That equitable interest is property that may form the subject matter of a sub-trust created by the beneficiary. Such a transaction does not constitute a disposition of a subsisting equitable interest and therefore can be achieved orally. See below for a diagram illustrating a sub-trust.

However, note the heading indicates that it must be a declaration of a **genuine sub-trust** to escape s 53(1)(c). The authority for this is *Grainge v Wilberforce* [1889] 5 TLR 436.

Question: What is a genuine sub-trust?	❖ **Answer:** A genuine sub-trust is where the beneficiary who declares himself trustee of his equitable interest has active duties to perform as trustee, e.g. he retains some discretion as trustee regarding the amount of income to be paid to the sub-beneficiary at any one time. Thus if Ben, the beneficiary of a trust of shares, declared himself trustee of his interest in favour of his son, Bobby, but reserved the right to decide how much of that dividend income Bobby should receive each year, this would be a genuine sub-trust.

It follows that if the beneficiary who declares himself trustee has **no** active duties to perform as trustee (i.e. he is giving away all the rights that he enjoyed over the equitable interest and is retaining no control), then this is not a genuine sub-trust. In this situation, the beneficiary is said 'to drop out of the picture' and is in fact disposing of his existing equitable interest, and therefore must comply with s 53(1)(c) if the transaction is to be valid. The difference between the two situations is illustrated in the following diagram.

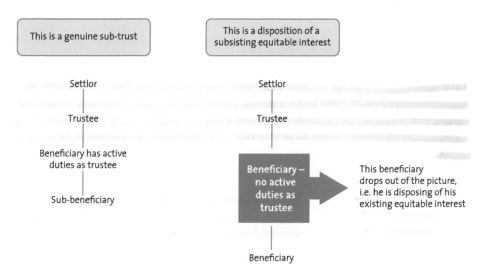

A specifically enforceable contract to transfer an existing equitable interest may be caught by s 53(1)(c) LPA 1925

Two preliminary points need to be understood – firstly, that in a specifically enforceable contract, a constructive trust arises in favour of the purchaser pending the actual *legal* transfer of the property (see box below) and, secondly, that the creation and operation of a constructive trust is exempt from s 53(1)(c) LPA by reason of s 53(2) (see second box below).

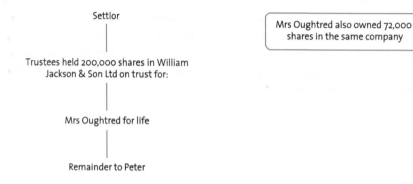

Example of a specifically enforceable contract
Sam makes a contract to sell his shares in a private company to Ben. This contract is specifically enforceable because shares in a private company are not freely available on the market, i.e. they are regarded as unique. Based on the maxim 'Equity regards as done that which ought to be done', pending the legal transfer of the shares, the vendor (Sam) is taken to hold the shares on constructive trust for the purchaser (Ben).

Remember that s 53(2) LPA 1925 provides that s 53(1) does not apply to the creation or operation of resulting or constructive trusts.

These two points were utilised in *Oughtred v Inland Revenue Commissioners* [1960] AC 206. The basic facts were as follows – notice there was a trust of shares but Mrs Oughtred also owned 72,000 shares absolutely in the same company.

Settlor

Mrs Oughtred also owned 72,000 shares in the same company

Trustees held 200,000 shares in William Jackson & Son Ltd on trust for:

Mrs Oughtred for life

Remainder to Peter

If the above trust ran its course, then when Mrs Oughtred (the life tenant) died, inheritance tax would have to be paid. To avoid this, Mrs Oughtred and Peter **orally agreed** that Peter would surrender his remainder interest to Mrs Oughtred so that she became the absolute owner and, in return, she would transfer her 72,000 shares to him.

Question: Why did they make an *oral agreement?* ❖ **Answer:** To avoid paying stamp duty, which you will remember is payable on a document transferring the beneficial interest in shares.

Documents were **subsequently** executed reciting the oral agreement and transferring the 200,000 shares to Mrs Oughtred absolutely. The Inland Revenue claimed that this transfer document constituted a disposition of Peter's existing equitable interest, which complied with s 53(1)(c) but, as it was a document transferring the beneficial interest, it attracted stamp duty.

Question: How did Mrs Oughtred and Peter respond to the IRC's claim?

❖ **Answer:** They argued that the document only transferred the bare legal title – **not the beneficial interest.** They claimed that Peter's beneficial interest had already been transferred because the oral agreement was specifically enforceable and therefore Peter held his interest under a constructive trust for Mrs Oughtred and, by reason of s 53(2), this constructive trust was exempt from s 53(1), i.e. it was not required to be in writing.

This clever argument failed before three of the Law Lords on the basis that whilst a proprietary interest of a sort arose under the oral agreement, it did not transfer the **entire** beneficial interest.

However, the minority in the House of Lords accepted the Oughtred's argument and their reasoning has been followed in the following case.

Case precedent – *Neville v Wilson* [1996] 3 All ER 171

Facts: 120 shares in Universal Engineering Co Ltd were held on trust for a family company called JE Neville Ltd. The shareholders of JE Neville claimed in individual oral agreements with each other to liquidate the defunct JE Neville company and to divide the company's equitable interest in the 120 Universal shares amongst themselves, proportionate to their shareholdings. The question was whether these oral agreements relating to the disposition of JE Neville's equitable interest in the Universal shares were void for failure to comply with s 53(1)(c), in which case the shares would pass to the Crown as *bona vacantia* **OR** whether the oral agreements, being specifically enforceable, gave rise to constructive trusts between the shareholders, which were exempt from s 53(1)(c). The Court of Appeal accepted the second argument.

Principle: Per Nourse LJ – Just as in *Oughtred v IRC*, the son's oral agreement created a constructive trust in favour of the mother, so here each shareholder's oral agreement created a constructive trust in favour of the other shareholders that was exempt from s 53(1)(c).

Application: Note that the principle has limited application because the oral agreement must be specifically enforceable for a constructive trust to arise, i.e. the subject matter of the agreement must be unique, such as an oral agreement for the transfer of shares in a private company.

Up for Debate

Why was the minority view in *Oughtred* followed in *Neville?*

❖ *Neville* was not a tax case. Perhaps *Oughtred* was a policy decision to avoid the use of a possible tax loophole.

❖ If *Oughtred* had not been followed, the shares in Universal would have passed as *bona vacantia* to the Crown, which is not an ideal solution. (*Bona vacantia* is property without any apparent owner.)

A *disclaimer of an equitable interest is not caught by* s 53(1)(c)

If a beneficiary does not accept an equitable interest but disclaims it, then this may be achieved orally because it is not regarded as a disposition of a subsisting equitable interest. The authority is *Re Paradise Motor Co Ltd* below.

Case precedent – *Re Paradise Motor Co Ltd* [1968] 3 WLR 1125

Facts: A stepfather gave an equitable interest in shares to his stepson, who orally rejected the gift. He later changed his mind and argued that his disclaimer was ineffective because it was not in writing as required by s 53(1)(c) LPA. This argument failed.

Principle: A disclaimer of an equitable interest by a beneficiary does not constitute the disposition of a subsisting equitable interest so s 53(1)(c) does not apply.

Application: Note that the above is not a surrender of an equitable interest but a disclaimer by a beneficiary who has not accepted the interest.

A trust in a will or the disposition of a subsisting equitable interest by will

When the testator creates a will trust, or disposes of his subsisting equitable interest by will, the will must be valid under s 9 Wills Act 1837. Briefly, the will must be in writing, signed by the testator in the presence of two witnesses who also sign the will.

Putting it into practice

Explain, with reasons, the statutory formalities (if any) that must be fulfilled in the following situations:

(a) Adam, the freehold owner of Alwood House, orally declares that henceforth he holds the property on trust for his son, Ben.

(b) Carl is the sole beneficial owner of 200,000 shares in Cread Co Ltd, which are held on trust for him by his bank. Carl instructs his bank over the telephone to transfer the shares absolutely to his wife, Denise.

(c) Edward is a beneficiary for life of a trust fund set up by his father, with remainder to Edward's son, George. Edward orally directs the trustees to assign his life interest to his sister, Helen, to whom the trustees should henceforth pay all the income.

(d) Ian decides to set up trusts in favour of some of his grandchildren and to this end, he transfers 2,000 shares in Intell plc to his solicitors, who agree to act as trustees. Ian says he will decide on the beneficiaries in a week's time. The following week, he telephones his solicitors and asks them to hold the shares on trust for his two youngest grandchildren, Jane and Keith.

Aim Higher

Quite apart from explaining the statutory formality (if any), remember that if there is a relevant case, you will gain higher marks if you can cite it.

Feedback on putting it into practice

(a) This part is concerned with s 53(1)(b) Law of Property Act 1925, which requires a declaration of an express trust of land to be evidenced in writing and signed by the settlor. You should explain what is meant by 'evidenced in writing'. Non-compliance by Adam will render the trust unenforceable by the beneficiary. However, evidence in writing signed by the settlor may, it seems, be provided some time after the declaration – *Gardner v Rowe*.

(b) This scenario is concerned with s 53(1)(c) Law of Property Act 1925, which requires a disposition of a subsisting equitable interest to be in writing and signed by the disponer or his duly authorised agent. Carl is clearly the beneficiary under a bare trust and has instructed the bank, which holds the legal title as nominee, to transfer both his equitable interest and their legal title to his wife, Denise. In *Vandervell v IRC*, it was held that when the equitable interest and legal interest pass together to a third party, this is not caught by s 53(1)(c) above and can therefore be achieved orally.

(c) Edward is a beneficiary with a life interest in a trust set up by his father. He has directed his trustees to transfer his subsisting equitable interest to his sister, Helen. This transaction is clearly a disposition of a subsisting equitable interest – *Grey v IRC* – and will be void unless Edward complies with s 53(1)(c) Law of Property Act 1925.

(d) When Ian transferred the shares to his solicitors to hold on trust, he did not identify the beneficiaries, therefore the solicitors held the shares on resulting trust for Ian – just as the beneficial interest in the option was held on resulting trust for Mr Vandervell in *Vandervell v IRC*. When, a week later, Ian asked his solicitors to hold the shares on trust for his youngest grandchildren, Jane and Keith, it has to be considered whether Ian is disposing of a subsisting equitable interest, in which case he will have to comply with s 53(1)(c) Law of Property Act 1925. You should cite the Court of Appeal decision in *Vandervell's Trusts (No 2)* that the termination of a resulting trust upon the declaration of a new trust does not constitute a disposition of a subsisting equitable interest. Remember to mention why this decision has been criticised and that the facts of the scenario bear a strong similarity to *Grey v IRC*. If this latter decision were followed, then the shares would still be held on resulting trust for Ian. (Also be aware that if the question had concerned land as opposed to shares, then even if *Vandervell Trusts (No 2)* were followed, thus escaping s 53(1)(c),the declaration of the new trust would have to comply with s 53(1)(b) LPA.)

Table of key cases referred to in this chapter

Case name	Area of law	Principle
Gardner v Rowe [1828]	Declaration of a trust of land – s 53(1)(b) LPA 1925	Non-compliance renders the trust unenforceable. Also seems from this case that the written evidence need not be contemporaneous with the declaration.
Grainge v Wilberforce [1889]	Section 53(1)(c) LPA 1925	The declaration of a genuine sub-trust by the beneficiary is not caught by s 53(1)(c).
Grey v Inland Revenue Commissioners [1960]	Disposition of a subsisting equitable interest – s 53(1)(c) LPA 1925	A direction to trustees to hold an existing equitable interest on trust for another is caught by s 53(1)(c).
Neville v Wilson [1996]	Section 53(1)(c) LPA 1925	Specifically enforceable agreements transferring an equitable interest and giving rise to constructive trusts that were exempt from s 53(1)(c).
Oughtred v Inland Revenue Commissioners [1960]	Section 53(1)(c) LPA 1925	A specifically enforceable agreement transferring an equitable interest was caught by s 53(1)(c) – a policy decision?
Paradise Motor Co Ltd, Re [1968]	Section 53(1)(c) LPA 1925	A disclaimer of an equitable interest is not caught by s 53(1)(c).
Vandervell v Inland Revenue Commissioners [1967]	Section 53(1)(c) LPA 1925	The transfer of the legal title by the trustee along with the equitable interest to a third party is not caught by s 53(1)(c).
Vandervell's Trusts (No 2) [1974]	Section 53(1)(c) LPA 1925	The termination of a resulting trust upon the declaration of a new trust with the consent of the beneficial owner is not caught by s 53(1)(c).

@ Visit the book's companion website to test your knowledge

❖ Resources include a subject map, revision tip podcasts, downloadable diagrams, MCQ quizzes for each chapter, and a flashcard glossary

❖ www.routledge.com/cw/optimizelawrevision

4

The Constitution of Express Trusts

Revision objectives

Understand the law
- Can you explain the ways in which a trust may be completely constituted?
- Do you remember how legal title to shares and land is vested in trustees?

Remember the details
- Do you remember the cases that illustrate the 'every effort' rule?
- Can you explain the exceptions to the maxim that equity will not perfect an imperfect gift?

Reflect critically on areas of debate
- Are you able to evaluate the solutions available to a beneficiary when a trust is incompletely constituted?
- Can you criticise the development of the rule in *Strong v Bird*?

Contextualise
- Do the common law and equity have the same regard for a specialty contract?
- Can you explain what constitutes consideration in equity?

Apply your skills and knowledge
- Can you answer the problem question involving an incompletely constituted trust?

Chapter Map

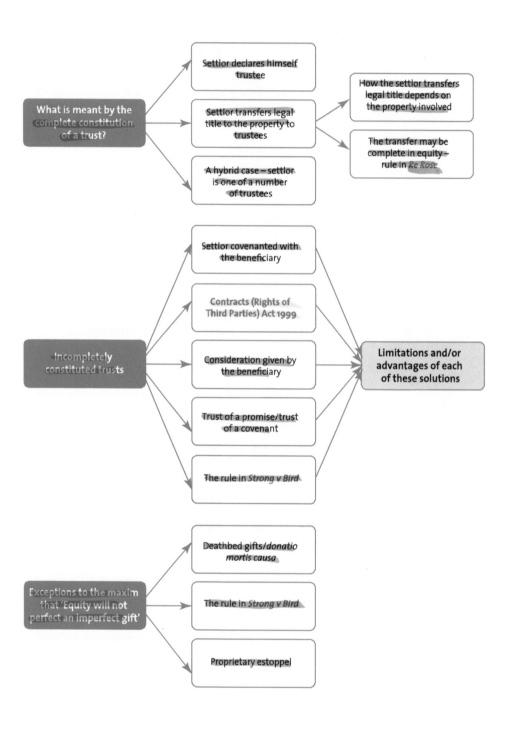

What is meant by the complete constitution of a trust?

Settlor declares himself trustee

Settlor transfers legal title to the property to trustees

A hybrid case – settlor is one of a number of trustees

How the settlor transfers legal title depends on the property involved

The transfer may be complete in equity – rule in *Re Rose*

Incompletely constituted trusts

Settlor covenanted with the beneficiary

Contracts (Rights of Third Parties) Act 1999

Consideration given by the beneficiary

Trust of a promise/trust of a covenant

The rule in *Strong v Bird*

Limitations and/or advantages of each of these solutions

Exceptions to the maxim that 'Equity will not perfect an imperfect gift'

Deathbed gifts/*donatio mortis causa*

The rule in *Strong v Bird*

Proprietary estoppel

What is meant by the complete constitution of an express trust?

The complete constitution of a trust is explained by looking at examples based on the following scenario.

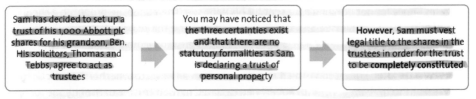

Sam has decided to set up a trust of his 1,000 Abbott plc shares for his grandson, Ben. His solicitors, Thomas and Tebbs, agree to act as trustees	You may have noticed that the three certainties exist and that there are no statutory formalities as Sam is declaring a trust of personal property	However, Sam must vest legal title to the shares in the trustees in order for the trust to be **completely constituted**

In fact, there are two ways of completely constituting a trust. The usual way is stated in the above example, i.e. Sam, the settlor, vests legal title to the trust property in the trustees. The other way is for the settlor to declare himself trustee. Both these methods are considered in greater detail below.

Settlor declares himself trustee

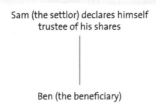

Sam (the settlor) declares himself
trustee of his shares

|

Ben (the beneficiary)

This way of completely constituting a trust can only be used for *inter vivos* trusts as the settlor must obviously be alive to declare himself trustee.

Sam does not have to do anything to vest legal title in himself as trustee, as he already has legal title. However, **it must be clear that he has declared himself trustee** and therefore is now holding the property in a different capacity. The diagram below indicates what will, and what will not, be a valid declaration of trust.

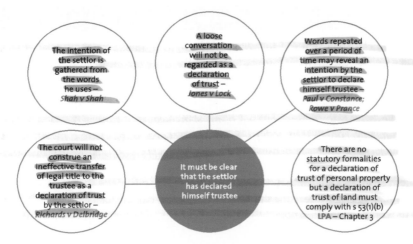

The key cases mentioned in this diagram are considered below.

Case precedent – *Jones v Lock* [1865] 1 Ch App 25

Facts: When Robert Jones returned from a business trip to Birmingham, he was reprimanded by his family for not bringing a present for his baby son. Thereupon, he produced a cheque for £900 payable to himself and said, 'Look you here. I give this to baby. It is for himself and I am going to put it away for him, and will give him a great deal more along with it.'

A few days later, Robert Jones died and the question arose as to whether (a) the cheque was a gift to his baby son; or (b) Robert had declared himself trustee of the cheque for his son; or (c) it belonged to Robert Jones and therefore formed part of his estate.

The court held that the cheque was not a gift to the son since it was payable to Robert Jones, nor could his loose conversation be construed as a declaration of trust. Therefore, the cheque formed part of his estate.

Principle: A loose conversation will not be regarded as a declaration of trust.

Application: It is useful to compare this case with *Paul v Constance* (mentioned in Chapter 1) in which the settlor repeated the same words over a period of time and the court held that a declaration of trust could be inferred.

In *Rowe v Prance* [1999] 2 FLR 787, Mr Prance purchased a yacht and told Mrs Rowe that it was in his name because she did not have an Ocean Master's certificate. Over a period of time, he referred to it as 'our yacht' on which they would live and sail the world. When the relationship broke down, the court followed *Paul v Constance* and held that Mr Prance had effectively declared himself trustee of the yacht for himself and Mrs Rowe.

Case precedent – *Shah v Shah* [2010] EWCA Civ 1408

Facts: Dinesh Shah sent the following letter to his brother, Mahendra Shah, together with a signed stock transfer form but without the share certificate.

Re: Mister Dee International Ltd

This letter is to confirm that out of my shareholding of current 12,500 in the above company, I am as from today holding 4,000 shares in the above company for you – subject to you being responsible for all tax consequences . . . arising from this declaration.

Dinesh Shah later argued that this was not an effective gift of the shares. He said that he had not vested legal title to the shares in his brother as the transfer has not been registered by the company and therefore the gift was imperfect and he still owned the shares.

The Court of Appeal held that the words used by Dinesh – 'I am holding' and 'this declaration' – indicated that the letter was a declaration of trust by Dinesh for the benefit of Mahendra and was not a gift.

Principle: The intention of the settlor to declare himself trustee is gathered from the words he uses rather than his subjective intention.

Application: Be aware of the words which indicate that the settlor is declaring himself trustee.

Compare the words used by John Delbridge in the following case.

Case precedent – *Richards v Delbridge* [1874] LR 18 Eq 11

Facts: John Delbridge had a number of leasehold premises where he carried on his business as a bone manure merchant with the assistance of his grandson (a minor), Edward Richards.

Shortly before he died, John wrote on a lease: 'The deed and all thereto belonging, I give to Edward Benetto Richards … with all the stock in trade.' John gave the deed to Edward's mother to hold for Edward. When John Delbridge died, the question arose as to whether the lease was held on trust for Edward. However, John had not vested legal title in Edward's mother as trustee, which would have required an assignment of the lease under seal. Could John's words be interpreted instead as John declaring himself trustee?

The Court held that his words were inappropriate for a declaration of trust and therefore the lease still belonged to John when he died and formed part of his estate.

Principle: An ineffective transfer of legal title to a trustee will not be construed as a declaration of the settlor as trustee.

Application: Just as we saw in *Shah v Shah*, the settlor's intention will be gathered from the words he uses on the document.

Settlor transfers legal title to the property to the trustee
This is the second and more usual way of completely constituting a trust.

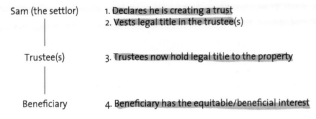

Sam (the settlor)
   1. Declares he is creating a trust
   2. Vests legal title in the trustee(s)

Trustee(s)
   3. Trustees now hold legal title to the property

Beneficiary
   4. Beneficiary has the equitable/beneficial interest

In the section below, we consider how the settlor goes about vesting legal title in the trustees.

The way in which the settlor vests legal title in the trustees depends on the property involved

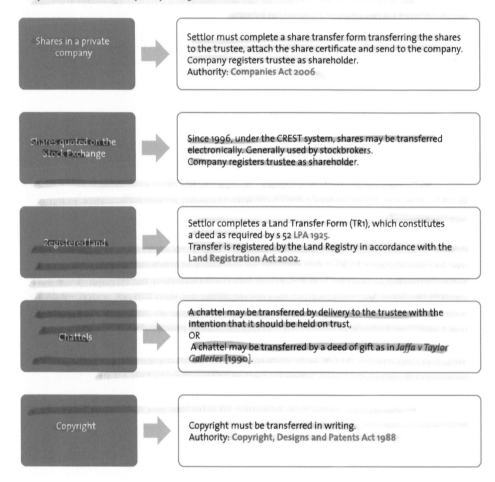

Shares in a private company → Settlor must complete a share transfer form transferring the shares to the trustee, attach the share certificate and send to the company. Company registers trustee as shareholder. **Authority: Companies Act 2006**

Shares quoted on the Stock Exchange → Since 1996, under the CREST system, shares may be transferred electronically. Generally used by stockbrokers. Company registers trustee as shareholder.

Registered land → Settlor completes a Land Transfer Form (TR1), which constitutes a deed as required by s 52 LPA 1925. Transfer is registered by the Land Registry in accordance with the Land Registration Act 2002.

Chattels → A chattel may be transferred by delivery to the trustee with the intention that it should be held on trust, OR A chattel may be transferred by a deed of gift as in *Jaffa v Taylor Galleries* [1990].

Copyright → Copyright must be transferred in writing. **Authority: Copyright, Designs and Patents Act 1988**

The every effort rule of *Re Rose*

You may have noticed from the diagram above that the transfer of shares and the transfer of land to the trustees are both two-stage processes, and the question may arise as to the legal position when the settlor has made every effort to complete the first stage but the transfer remains to be registered by the company/Land Registry, i.e. the second stage. The courts' changing attitude to this question is reflected in the following diagram and the cases below.

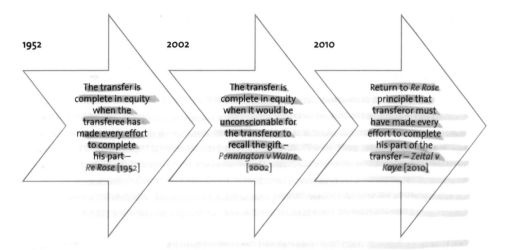

1952	2002	2010
The transfer is complete in equity when the transferee has made every effort to complete his part – *Re Rose* [1952]	The transfer is complete in equity when it would be unconscionable for the transferor to recall the gift – *Pennington v Waine* [2002]	Return to *Re Rose* principle that transferor must have made every effort to complete his part of the transfer – *Zeital v Kaye* [2010]

The dates are relevant in the following case.

Case precedent – *Re Rose (Deceased)* [1952] All ER 1217 CA

Facts: On 30 March 1943, Rose completed his part of two transfers of shares to members of his family. When Rose died on 10 April 1948, the question arose as to whether estate duty applied to the transfers that had been registered by the company involved on 30 June 1943. At that time, estate duty was payable on gifts on death and within five years of death and so appeared to catch the two transfers. However, Rose had completed his part of the transfers on 30 March 1943 (outside the five-year period).

The Court of Appeal held that the transfer was complete in equity when Rose had completed his part on 30 March 1943 and was not therefore liable to estate duty.

Principle: A gift or trust will not fail where the donor or settlor has done everything necessary for him to do, but before registration by the company of the new shareholder has taken place. The transfer will be complete in equity.

Application: This rule is known as the Rule in *Re Rose* or the 'every effort' rule and also applies to the transfer of land.

In *Mascall v Mascall* [1984], a father, having completed his part of a transfer of his house to his son, quarrelled with his son and sought to withdraw from the transfer before it had been registered. However, following the *Re Rose* principle, the court held that the transfer was complete in equity and could not be declared void. Compare *Re Fry* [1946], in which the settlor failed to obtain the necessary consent forms to transfer the shares (a requirement under Defence Regulations at the time). Clearly he had not done everything he was required to do and the trust failed.

The following decision went even further than the 'every effort' rule in an attempt to save the trust.

Case precedent – *Pennington v Waine* [2002] 1 WLR 2075

Facts: Ada Crampton owned 1,500 of 2,000 shares in a private family company. She wanted her nephew, Harold, to become a director of the company but, for this, he would need shares in the company. At a meeting with her auditor (and agent) Mr Pennington, Ada agreed to transfer 400 of her shares to Harold. Harold signed the appropriate consent form agreeing to be a director but the share transfer form regarding the 400 shares, which had been signed by Ada, was placed on a file by Mr Pennington, i.e. it was not sent for registration by the company. When Ada died, the question arose as to whether the 400 shares formed part of her residuary estate or were held on trust for Harold.

The Court of Appeal held that there could be circumstances (as in this case) that made it unconscionable for a donor to change his/her mind regarding a gift, in which case the transfer would be complete in equity. The relevant circumstances here were that Ada had made the gift of her own free will and delivered the share transfer form to her agent for him to secure registration. Mr Pennington had told Harold that he need take no further action. Further, Harold had agreed to become director, which he could not do without the shares being transferred to him. Accordingly, the transfer was complete in equity.

Principle: A transfer may be complete in equity when it would be unconscionable for the transferor to recall the gift.

Application: When applying this decision, it is important to mention that it has been criticised – see 'Up for Debate' below, and to refer to the later decision of *Zeital v Kaye* [2010].

Up for Debate

The decision in *Pennington v Waine* has been criticised for a number of reasons:

❖ The concept of 'unconscionability' is essentially subjective. It is unlikely that criteria could be drawn up to provide a workable test of what is unconscionable.
❖ This subjectivity leads to uncertainty in the law.
❖ The Court adopted the concept of 'unconscionability' from the Privy Council decision in *T Choithram International S A v Pagarani* [2001], which related to a completely different situation, namely a declaration of trust by the settlor.

The more recent case of *Zeital v Kaye* [2010] EWCA Civ 159 indicates that the Court of Appeal has returned to the more orthodox principle of *Re Rose*. In *Zeital v Kaye*, Stefka Appostolova, the long-term partner of Raymond Zeital, alleged that before his death, he had transferred the two shares of Dalmar Ltd to her. However, he had not completed a share transfer form, nor provided the share certificate in respect of the second share, and the Court of Appeal held that as he had failed to do all that was required of him, that second share passed to his widow and daughter upon his intestacy.

A hybrid case – settlor is one of a number of trustees

T Choithram International SA v Pagarani [2001] was an appeal from the British Virgin Islands to the Privy Council. You will see from the facts below that it did not fall within either of the two methods for constituting a trust considered above (i.e. settlor declaring himself trustee or settlor vesting legal title in the trustees).

Case precedent – *T Choithram International SA v Pagarani* [2001] 1 WLR 1

Facts: The settlor, known as TCP, having made provision for his family, wished to establish a charitable foundation to which he would leave the balance of his wealth. A short time before he died, he created the foundation by deed, which named himself as one of nine trustees. He then orally declared that he was giving 'all his wealth to the foundation'. However, he never formally transferred the money or shares to the trustees, nor could his words be deemed to be a declaration of himself as trustee. On his death, it was argued that the trust was incompletely constituted and therefore his wealth should pass to his next of kin under the intestacy rules.

Lord Browne-Wilkinson in the Privy Council stated 'the foundation has no legal existence . . . therefore the words "I give to the foundation" can only mean "I give to the trustees of the foundation deed to be held by them on the trusts of the foundation"'. He continued, 'there can be no distinction between the case where the donor declares himself to be sole trustee . . . and the cases where he declares himself to be one of the trustees . . . In both cases, his conscience is affected and it would be unconscionable . . . to allow such a donor to resile from his gift'. Accordingly, the trust was completely constituted.

Principle: The settlor was one of a number of trustees and had done enough to declare himself trustee. It would be unconscionable for him to recall the gift.

Application: When applying this decision, make the point that it departs from the normal strict rules in inferring that TCP was declaring himself trustee (as the language he used would not indicate such an interpretation) and appears to be based partly on the concept of unconscionability.

Automatic/indirect constitution of a trust

In the following case, *Re Ralli's Will Trusts* [1964], the trust was completely constituted indirectly by a lucky coincidence rather than as the result of a deliberate act of vesting by the settlor. The diagram below helps to explain the complicated facts.

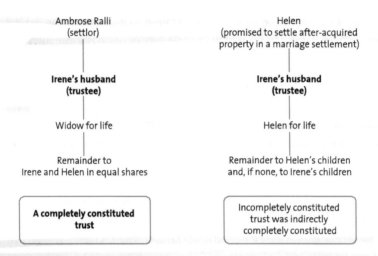

Facts: In 1899, Ambrose Ralli died, leaving his residuary estate on trust for his widow for life, remainder in equal shares to his two daughters, Irene and Helen. The trustee was Irene's husband. In 1924, Helen covenanted in her marriage settlement to settle '…any after acquired property' on trust for herself for life, remainder to any children she might have and, if none, to Irene's children'. Irene's husband was also the trustee of this settlement. So far as the after-acquired property was concerned (which would include the remainder interest under the Ambrose Ralli trust), as this was future property, the trust was incompletely constituted.

Helen died in 1956 without children. Her mother died in 1961. The question then arose as to whether Helen's remainder interest was held on trust for Irene's children under Helen's marriage settlement, or whether it passed under Helen's will. The court held that Helen's settlement had been automatically constituted as Irene's husband already held legal title to the remainder interest as trustee of the Ambrose Ralli trust, and therefore the remainder interest under the marriage settlement was held for Irene's children.

Principle: A trust may be indirectly completely constituted where legal title to the property is already vested in the trustee albeit in a different capacity.

Application: This decision has limited application and should not be confused with the rule in *Strong v Bird*, which we consider later in this chapter.

Incompletely constituted trusts

This is a favourite area for examination questions and therefore the explanations that follow are based on the following problem question.

This problem concerns an incompletely constituted trust as legal title to the shares has not been vested in Sam's trustees. Therefore, the would-be beneficiaries, Ben and Brenda, cannot enforce it as a trust. However, all is not lost – when a trust is incompletely constituted, there are five possible solutions, as indicated in the diagram below, some of which may help Ben and Brenda (and the grandchildren).

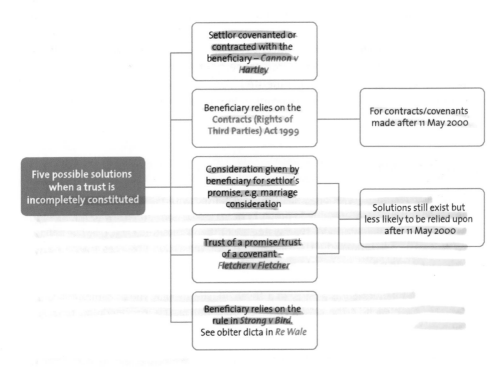

In order to apply these solutions to the problem question, you obviously need to understand **precisely** when they can be used. Therefore, each solution is considered in turn below, together with a relevant authority and the limitations and/or advantages of that solution.

Settlor covenanted with the beneficiary

It is important to know that 'covenanted' means that the settlor 'promised in a deed'. A deed is a signed and witnessed document. When the settlor covenants, he is making what is called a **specialty contract**. This is different to a simple contract (which you will have studied in contract law) because at common law, with a specialty contract, no consideration is required from the promisee. The common law recognises a specialty contract and, if the settlor is in breach of his covenant with the promisee, i.e. in breach of the specialty contract, the promisee may sue him/his estate for damages.

Equity is different. It accepts that a covenant is a promise but, unless that promise is supported by consideration, equity will not enforce the promise. This is in accordance with the maxim 'Equity will not assist a volunteer', a volunteer being a person who has not given consideration. In other words, equity does not recognise that the covenant is a specialty contract, which means that in the event of a breach of the covenant, the equitable remedy of specific performance will not be available.

Relating all this to our sample problem question, you will see that the wording is vague because it does not say whether Sam's promise was contained in a covenant, nor does it say precisely whom he promised. Therefore, for the purpose of this particular solution, let us assume that the question reads: **Sam covenanted with Ben and Brenda to settle his after-acquired property on them for life**. In this case, when Sam failed to settle the shares he inherited from his brother, Ben and Brenda could sue Sam's estate for damages at common law for breach of the covenant (i.e. the specialty contract). The following case is a useful authority for this particular solution.

Case precedent – *Cannon v Hartley* [1949] Ch 213

Facts: By a deed of separation, a husband **covenanted** with his wife and daughter that he would settle any after-acquired property of £1,000 or above on his wife for life with remainder to his daughter. Some years later, the husband inherited £12,500 but he did not settle it as he had promised. After the wife's death, the daughter successfully sued her father for damages for breach of the covenant.

Principle: If a beneficiary is a party to a covenant, she/he may sue at common law for damages for breach of the covenant which does not require consideration from the promisee.

Application: If you apply this decision to a problem, make sure that the beneficiary is the other party to the covenant, not merely a third party who is mentioned in the covenant. So, you are looking for words such as 'Sam covenanted with Ben and Brenda, the beneficiaries'.

Notice the limitations and advantages of this solution in the following diagram. The limitations may mean that it cannot be applied to a problem question, but even if it can be applied, there is nothing lost by mentioning its advantages/limitations in your answer.

Limitations of this solution	Advantages of this solution
A specialty contract is not recognised by equity and therefore the equitable remedy of specific performance is not available	A beneficiary who is a volunteer (i.e. who has not given consideration) may nevertheless sue for breach of the specialty contract at common law provided he is a party to the covenant
Only the common law remedy of damages is available. As this will be an action on a deed, there is a limitation period of 12 years from the date of the breach	

Common Pitfall

If the settlor covenanted with the trustees (as opposed to the beneficiary) to settle property on the beneficiaries, and subsequently failed to keep to that promise, it would be reasonable to suppose that the trustees (acting on behalf of the beneficiaries) could sue the settlor for breach of that covenant.

However, this is not the case. In *Re Pryce* [1917] and *Re Kay's Settlement* [1939], the trustees sought directions from the court on this point and were instructed by the court not to sue the settlor on the covenant, ostensibly because the beneficiaries should not obtain indirectly what they could not obtain directly. Even if the trustees had gone ahead and sued without asking for directions, there are differing opinions as to whether they would have received only nominal damages (as they had personally suffered no loss from the breach of covenant) or whether the damages would represent the value of the property promised by the settlor. In any event, it is argued that as the trust set up by the settlor had failed because it was incompletely constituted, the trustees would in fact hold the damages on resulting trust for the settlor, rendering the whole exercise useless.

So, to recap, the trustees, even though parties to the covenant, would not sue in respect of its breach. Nevertheless, you will see that the existence of a covenant between the settlor and trustees has an important part to play in the next solution.

Beneficiary relies on the **Contracts (Rights of Third Parties) Act 1999**

For our purposes, the key provisions of this Act are as follows:

s 1(1)   Subject to the provisions of this Act, a person who is not a party to a contract (a third party) may in his own right enforce a term of the contract if:

(a) the contract expressly provides that he may, or
(b) subject to subsection (2) below, the term purports to confer a benefit on him.

s 1(2)   Subsection (1)(b) does not apply if on a proper construction of the contract it appears that the parties did not intend the term to be enforceable by the third party.

s 1(3)   The third party must be expressly identified in the contract by name, as a member of a class or as answering a particular description, but need not be in existence when the contract is entered into . . .

s 1(5)   For the purposes of exercising his right to enforce a term of the contract, there shall be available to the third party any remedy that would have been available to him in an action for breach of contract if he had been a party to the contract (and the rules relating to damages, injunctions, specific performance and other relief shall apply accordingly).

This Act came into force on 11 May 2000.

As mentioned earlier, the sample question is vague as we do not know whether Sam's promise was in a covenant or whom he promised. Let us therefore assume for the purposes of this particular solution that the question reads: **Sam covenanted with his trustees to settle any after-acquired property on his children, Ben and Brenda, for life, remainder to his grandchildren**. Note that he is covenanting with the trustees. Now let us relate this to the provisions in s 1 of the Act. The word 'covenanted' indicates that there is a specialty contract between Sam and his trustees and this contract confers a benefit on Ben and Brenda for life (who are third parties identified by name) and his grandchildren (who are third parties as members of a class and who may not yet exist). Therefore, the third parties may rely on the Contracts (Rights of Third Parties) Act 1999.

It is likely that they could only sue for damages and not the equitable remedy of specific performance. The reason is that s 1(5) provides that the third parties would be entitled to the remedy that would have been available if they had been a party to the contract. As a party to a specialty contract, they would only be entitled to the common law remedy of damages and not specific performance as equity does not recognise a specialty contract.

Now notice the limitations and advantages of this solution in the following diagram.

Limitations of this solution	Advantages of this solution
Firstly, there must be a contract or covenant between the settlor and trustee, and secondly, this must have been made on or after 11 May 2000.	Beneficiary can sue even though he is not a party to the contract/covenant and has not given consideration, provided the contract/covenant between the settlor and trustee confers a benefit on the beneficiary
In the case of a covenant between the settlor and trustee, the beneficiaries as third parties would be entitled to damages only – see s 1(5) above.	Whilst there cannot be a valid trust of future property, it is possible for a beneficiary to sue under the Act as a third party in respect of a contract to create a trust of future property

Consideration given by the beneficiary for the settlor's promise – notably marriage consideration

We have already noticed the maxim 'Equity will not assist a volunteer', which means that equity will not help someone who has not given consideration. It follows that if a beneficiary has given consideration for the settlor's promise to settle property on him, then he is not a volunteer and can seek specific performance of this **simple contract**, i.e. equity will assist him.

However, you should be aware that equity requires valuable consideration (unlike the common law where consideration must be sufficient but need not be adequate) and, more to the point, equity recognises the concept of marriage consideration. Marriage consideration arises in a marriage settlement, i.e. a trust made 'before or in consideration of marriage' or as a result of an ante-nuptial agreement. These are relatively rare nowadays but would exist if, for example, a prospective husband promised that, in consideration of marriage, he would settle any property he inherited on trust for himself and his prospective wife and issue. This would be a marriage settlement and **all** those parties (i.e. husband, wife and issue) are regarded as having given consideration for the promise, i.e. they are said to be 'within the marriage consideration'. Only a husband, wife and issue fall within the marriage consideration – **not** other members of the family.

The following case illustrates this concept of marriage consideration.

Case precedent – *Pullan v Koe* [1913] 1 Ch 9

Facts: In a marriage settlement made in 1859, a wife had covenanted with trustees to settle any after-acquired property of £100 and above. In 1879, her mother gave her £285 but instead of settling it as she had promised, the wife paid the money into her husband's bank account and part of it was then invested in bonds. When the husband died, the trustees of the marriage settlement, acting on behalf of the wife and children, claimed the bonds from the husband's personal representatives.

The court held that the wife and children were all within the marriage consideration and could enforce the promise to settle the £285, which was now represented by the bonds.

Principle: Provided he/she is within the marriage consideration, a beneficiary of an incompletely constituted marriage settlement can compel the settlor/his personal representatives to settle the property on trust.

Application: When applying this decision, it is worth mentioning *Re Plumptre's Marriage Settlement* [1910]. In a marriage settlement, a wife covenanted to settle any after-acquired property on trust for her husband and herself for life, with remainder to her children and, if none, for her next of kin. She failed to transfer stock bought in her name and after the death of the husband and wife, there being no children, the next of kin sought to enforce the wife's promise. They were unsuccessful as they were not within the marriage consideration.

If these two cases occurred today, all the would-be beneficiaries could rely on the Contracts (Rights of Third Parties) Act 1999 – but they would not be awarded specific performance as they would be suing as third parties to a covenant, i.e. specialty contract, which is not recognised by equity. So, there could be an advantage in using this solution.

Common Pitfall

The above principle of marriage consideration would **NOT** help Ben and Brenda in our sample question. It is a common mistake to think that just because the would-be beneficiaries are the settlor's children, they can argue that they are within the marriage consideration. In our sample question, the incompletely constituted trust is **NOT** a marriage settlement. Sam did not make the promise 'in consideration of marriage' or in pursuance of an ante-nuptial agreement, so Ben and Brenda cannot plead that they are within the marriage consideration.

Of course, if Ben and Brenda had provided some **OTHER** valuable consideration for Sam's promise (which is unlikely), then we would be dealing with a straightforward simple contract between Sam and his children, and if Sam failed to keep to his promise to settle property, the children could sue for breach of this simple contract claiming the equitable remedy of specific performance.

The following diagram states the limitations and advantages of this particular solution.

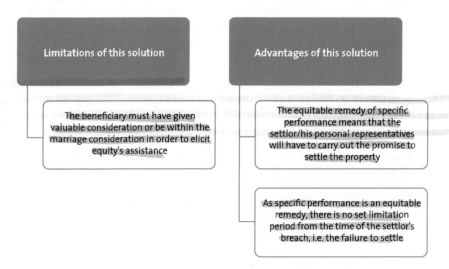

Limitations of this solution

The beneficiary must have given valuable consideration or be within the marriage consideration in order to elicit equity's assistance

Advantages of this solution

The equitable remedy of specific performance means that the settlor/his personal representatives will have to carry out the promise to settle the property

As specific performance is an equitable remedy, there is no set limitation period from the time of the settlor's breach, i.e. the failure to settle

Completely constituted trust of a promise/trust of a covenant

This solution has been superseded by the Contracts (Rights of Third Parties) Act 1999 and would only be worth mentioning briefly in an answer. Essentially, it was a clever device (established in *Fletcher v Fletcher* below) for assisting beneficiaries before the above Act came into force. It was based on the following reasoning.

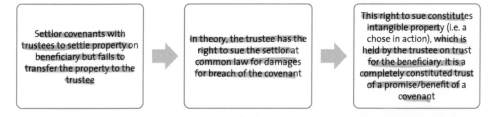

Settlor covenants with trustees to settle property on beneficiary but fails to transfer the property to the trustee

In theory, the trustee has the right to sue the settlor at common law for damages for breach of the covenant

This right to sue constitutes intangible property (i.e. a chose in action), which is held by the trustee on trust for the beneficiary. It is a completely constituted trust of a promise/benefit of a covenant

Case precedent – *Fletcher v Fletcher* [1844] 4 Hare 67

Facts: Ellis Fletcher executed a voluntary covenant with trustees to pay to them £60,000 to hold upon trust for his illegitimate sons, John and Jacob, if they should survive him and attain the age of 21. After Ellis Fletcher's death, this covenant was found amongst his papers. Of the two sons, Jacob had survived and attained the age of 21. He sued the executors of his father's estate to enforce the covenant. The court held that there was a trust of the covenant in favour of Jacob, the beneficiary.

Principle: The covenantees (i.e. the trustees) held the benefit of the covenant (i.e. the right to the money – a chose in action) on trust for Jacob, the beneficiary.

Application: If this arose today, Jacob would be able to rely on the Contracts (Rights of Third Parties) Act 1999. He would be a third party who was intended to benefit under the covenant made between his father and the trustees.

There is some doubt following *obiter dicta* in *Re Cook's Settlement Trust* [1965] as to whether the principle in *Fletcher v Fletcher* is confined to a covenant to settle existing property as opposed to future property. Strictly, this should not be an issue as the subject matter of the trust is the promise itself, not the future property.

One of the main criticisms of the principle is that it is highly unlikely that Ellis Fletcher intended to create a trust of a promise and, in subsequent cases, e.g. *Re Schebsman* [1944], it has been stated that a trust of a promise will only be upheld where it was clear that the settlor (i.e. the covenantor) **intended** to create such a trust.

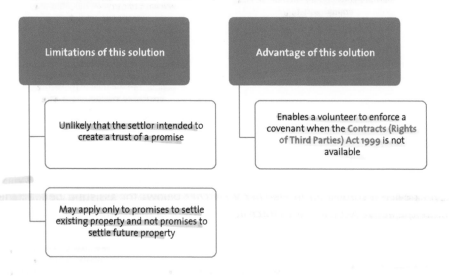

The rule in *Strong v Bird*

What to look out for in a question

If the question concerns an incompletely constituted trust where the settlor died before he could transfer legal title to the trustees, **who are also his executors**, then that question is inviting you to discuss the rule in *Strong v Bird*.

The rule in *Strong v Bird* perfects an imperfect gift (as we shall see later) but *obiter dicta* in *Re Wale* [1956] suggest that it can be used to perfect an incompletely constituted trust. There are two essential requirements for the rule to apply – that the donee/trustee was appointed executor by the donor/settlor, and that the donor/settlor had a continuing intention to give/settle the property. Let us look at its possible application in respect of an incompletely constituted trust in the following scenario.

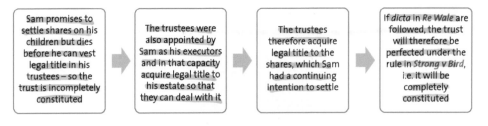

This solution also has its limitations and advantage, as indicated in the following diagram.

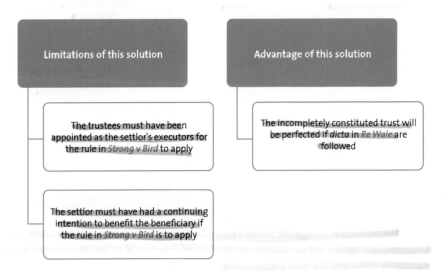

Exceptions to the maxim that equity will not perfect an imperfect gift

Just as the settlor must vest legal title in the trustees in order for a trust to be completely constituted, so the donor of a gift must vest legal title in the donee in order to create a perfect gift. There is a maxim to this effect – 'Equity will not perfect an imperfect gift'. However, there are three exceptions to this maxim, which we consider next.

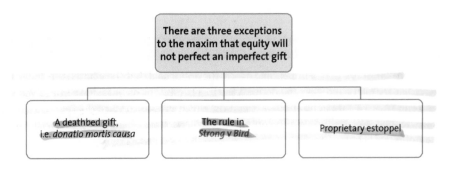

Deathbed gifts/*donations mortis causa*
There are four requirements for a valid deathbed gift.

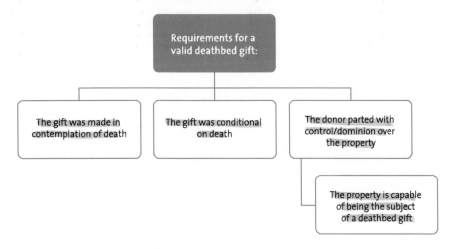

To answer a question on deathbed gifts, you need to be able to cite relevant cases. The following are four useful cases.

Case precedent – *Wilkes v Allington* [1931] 2 Ch 104

Facts: The donor, knowing that he had terminal cancer, made an imperfect transfer of his farm to his nieces. In fact, the donor died, not of cancer, but of pneumonia. The Court held that he had made a valid deathbed gift.

Principle: A deathbed gift must have been made in contemplation of impending death but it does not affect the validity of the gift if the donor died from a cause other than that which he was contemplating.

Application: In a problem question, look for words made by the donor such as 'If anything happens to me, I want you to have . . .' These words will satisfy the second requirement for a deathbed gift, which is that the gift is intended to be conditional on death. If the donor recovers, the gift will be automatically revoked. Of course, the donor could always expressly revoke the gift before he died.

Case precedent – *Re Lillingston* [1952] 2 All ER 184

Facts: In contemplation of impending death, the donor said that she wanted the donee to have her jewellery and gave the donee a key to a trunk, which contained some jewellery and the key to a safe deposit box at Harrods, which in turn contained a key to another safe deposit box, both of which contained jewellery. It was held that there were valid deathbed gifts of the jewellery in the trunk and the safe deposit boxes.

Principle: The donor must deliver or part with control or dominion over the property that is the subject of the deathbed gift. This can be achieved by physically handing over the property or the means of controlling it, for example, by handing over a key as in this case.

Application: This is a useful case on keys and when the facts refer to a box leading to another box.

Case precedent – *Woodard v Woodard* [1995] 3 All ER 980

Facts: In the presence of his wife, the donor, who was terminally ill in hospital, told his son that he could keep the donor's car as he would not be driving it again. The donor died three days later and his subsequently sold the car. The donor's wife, who was the sole beneficiary under the donor's will, claimed the proceeds of the car as part of her husband's estate. The Court of Appeal held that the gift of the car to the son had been made in contemplation of death, that it was conditional on death, and that it would be unrealistic in the circumstances to allege that the son had not been given dominion of the car by his father simply because the donor had a second set of keys at home. Accordingly, the car was a valid deathbed gift.

Principle: The donor's circumstances (i.e. that he was dying in hospital) indicated that he intended to give up his rights to the car.

Application: This case can be contrasted with *Re Craven's Estate* [1937] where it was considered that the retention of a second set of keys by the donor indicated that he had not given up control of the property.

Case precedent – *Birch v Treasury Solicitor* [1951] 1 Ch 298

Facts: In contemplation of death, the donor gave the donee her Post Office savings account book and three other account pass books, intending the money in these accounts should belong to the donee on the donor's death. The court held that delivery of these books constituted valid deathbed gifts of the money in the accounts.

Principle: The savings and pass books were essential indicia or evidence of title, which entitled the possessor to the money in the accounts.

Application: Intangible property cannot be delivered to the donee by the donor, but the above case establishes that if the donor delivers essential evidence of title, this will suffice to prove that the donor has given up control or dominion over the property.

Finally, the property involved must be capable of being the subject matter of a deathbed gift. There are conflicting High Court decisions regarding whether shares can form a valid deathbed gift. (Remember that the High Court does not have to follow its past decisions). *Staniland v Willott* [1850] would indicate that shares can be the subject matter of a deathbed gift, while *Moore v Moore* [1874] and *Re Weston* [1902] would indicate that they cannot.

Until 1991, it was considered that land could not be the subject of a deathbed gift but, in *Sen v Headley* [1991], the Court of Appeal held that the delivery of a key to a steel box containing the title deeds of an unregistered house, together with the dying donor's words to the claimant that the house was hers, constituted a valid deathbed gift. There has been no case regarding a deathbed gift of registered land and it is therefore unknown whether copies of entries on the Land Register would provide the necessary evidence of title.

Common Pitfall

Let us suppose that Stephen, who is terminally ill in hospital, makes a valid deathbed gift of his Rolls Royce to his friend, Jane. Stephen dies two days later and it is discovered that he has left the Rolls Royce in his will to his brother, Daniel. It is a common mistake to believe that Daniel will inherit the car under the will, whereas in fact the deathbed gift will **prevail**. The reason is simple – the deathbed gift takes effect immediately on Stephen's death, whereas the will takes effect only when the executors have obtained probate and distribute the legacies, which may be many months later.

The rule in *Strong v Bird*

Aim Higher

As you read the key cases below, notice how the rule in *Strong v Bird* has developed since it was first applied in relation to the release of a debt to an executor, and consider whether such an extension of the rule is justified. For criticism of the rule, see *'Problems in the Rule in Strong v Bird'* by Joseph Jaconelli – The Conveyancer (2006) 432.

Strong v Bird – *imperfect release of a debt*

Case precedent – *Strong v Bird* [1874] LR 18 Eq 315

Facts: The defendant's stepmother was a lodger in his house and paid rent of £212.50 per quarter. She lent the defendant £1,000 and it was agreed that this would be paid off by the defendant, reducing each quarter's rent. The stepmother paid £100 for two quarters and then decided to release the defendant from his debt and began to pay the full rent. To be legally binding, this release should have been contained in a deed. The stepmother died four years later and, by her will, appointed the defendant as her executor. One of the stepmother's residuary beneficiaries claimed that the defendant owed the balance of the debt to the estate as there had been no formal release of the debt. The court held that, in accordance with the following principle, the defendant was not liable to repay the debt.

Principle: The stepmother had a continuing intention to release the defendant from the debt and his appointment as executor, whereby he received temporary legal title to all his stepmother's estate, perfected the imperfect release of the debt.

Application: When citing this case, you could explain that the rationale for the rule is that the executor is the person who would sue those owing money to the estate and cannot sue himself. The rule in *Strong v Bird* was extended to an imperfect **gift** made to an executor in *Re Stewart* [1908], an extension that has been followed many times since 1908.

Re James – *rule in* Strong v Bird *extended to administrators*

> ### Case precedent – *Re James* [1935] Ch 449
>
> **Facts:** A son who inherited his father's house made an imperfect transfer of the house to his father's housekeeper by simply giving her the title deeds. The son died intestate nine years later and the housekeeper was appointed administratrix of the son's estate, thus acquiring legal title to the house which perfected the imperfect gift.
>
> **Principle:** The rule in *Strong v Bird* extends to a person who applies for, and is granted, letters of administration.
>
> **Application:** You should be aware that this extension to administrators was highly criticised in *obiter dicta* by Walton J in *Re Gonin* below because an administrator (unlike an executor) is not appointed by the deceased and the appointment could be regarded as somewhat fortuitous – as it was in *Re James*.

Re Gonin – *the testatrix must have a continuing intention to give the property*

> ### Case precedent – *Re Gonin* [1964] Ch 288
>
> **Facts:** Lucy Gonin devoted over 20 years to caring for her parents who promised that she would receive their house when they died. Her mother mistakenly believed that she could not leave the house to Lucy in her will because Lucy had been born illegitimate. So instead, she left Lucy a cheque for £33,000 representing the value of the house. This cheque was found in an envelope after the mother died intestate. Lucy's mother had not realised that a cheque is a revocable mandate that ceases to exist once the bank is informed of the drawer's death whereupon the bank account is frozen – as was the case here. Lucy, who was appointed her mother's administratrix, therefore claimed that her mother had always wanted to leave her the house, and that there was an imperfect gift

of the house that was perfected when Lucy acquired legal title to her mother's estate as her administratrix. Walton J held that the rule in *Strong v Bird* could not be applied as the mother had not had a continuing intention to give Lucy the house, having drawn a cheque in her favour instead.

Principle: For the rule in *Strong v Bird* to apply, the deceased must have a continuing intention to give the specific existing property to the donee.

Application: Note that the judge, Walton J, criticised the extension of the rule to an administrator.

Re Wale – *possible extension of the rule in* Strong v Bird *to incompletely constituted trusts*

Case Precedent – *Re Wale* [1956] 1 WLR 1346

Facts: During her lifetime, Elizabeth Wale created a settlement in which she declared her intention to transfer shares to trustees to hold on trust for her daughter. She never transferred legal title to the shares to the trustees but treated the shares as her own until her death. The trustees were appointed her executors in her will and claimed that the incompletely constituted trust of the shares was perfected as they acquired legal title to the shares in their capacity as executors. The claim failed for lack of a continuing intention on the part of the settlor to settle the shares on trust.

Principle: For the rule in *Strong v Bird* to apply, the deceased must have a continuing intention to settle the property.

Application: This is a useful case because it appears that the rule in *Strong v Bird* could be extended to perfect an incompletely constituted trust, provided the settlor maintained a continuing intention to vest legal title in the trustees, who were also appointed as the settlor's executors.

Common Pitfall

It is a frequent mistake to regard *Re Ralli's Will Trusts* [1964] – which we looked at earlier in this chapter – as an application of the rule in *Strong v Bird*. In fact, the two have little in common. The trustee in *Re Ralli* was not an executor or administrator of the deceased settlor, nor did the settlor have a continuing intention to settle her remainder interest. Nor is a remainder interest specific existing property, as required under the rule in *Strong v Bird*.

Proprietary estoppel

The claimant who relies on proprietary estoppel as a way to perfect an imperfect gift must prove three elements.

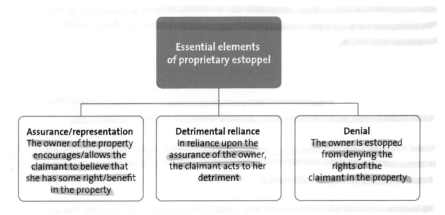

Essential elements of proprietary estoppel

Assurance/representation	**Detrimental reliance**	**Denial**
The owner of the property encourages/allows the claimant to believe that she has some right/benefit in the property	In reliance upon the assurance of the owner, the claimant acts to her detriment	The owner is estopped from denying the rights of the claimant in the property

Two key cases on proprietary estoppel

Case precedent – *Thorner v Major* [2009] UKHL 18

Facts: By his will made in 1997, Peter Thorner left the residue of his estate, including Steart Farm, to his cousin's son, David Thorner. He later quarrelled with one of the legatees and destroyed his will, intending to make another, but died intestate in 2005. Under the intestacy rules, Steart Farm would pass to Peter's sisters as his next of kin.

David Thorner had worked very long hours on Steart Farm from 1976 until Peter's death in 2005 for no pay but on the understanding that he would inherit the farm on Peter's death. Peter Thorner was a taciturn man and David's expectation arose from various hints over the years by Peter Thorner, in particular two life assurance policies worth £20,000, which Peter had given to David, saying these would cover his death duties.

The House of Lords reversed the decision of the Court of Appeal and held that David Thorner was entitled to Steart Farm on the basis of proprietary estoppel.

Principle: To establish a proprietary estoppel, the claimant must show: (a) that the owner's assurance or conduct regarding the gift of the property were sufficiently clear; (b) that the assurances or conduct would lead the claimant reasonably to rely on them, i.e. in the words of Lord Hoffman, they were 'understood as intended to be taken seriously'; and (c) that having acted to his detriment in reliance on the assurance, it would be unconscionable to deny the claimant a remedy.

Application: When applying this case, you could mention that the extent of Steart Farm fluctuated over the years with land being both sold and bought. The court held that David was entitled to the full extent of Steart Farm as it was when Peter died rather than the extent when the representations were made.

Case precedent – *Yeoman's Row Management Ltd v Cobbe* (2008) 1 WLR 1752

Facts: The claimant, Mr Cobbe, a property developer, entered an oral 'agreement in principle' with a director of Yeoman's under which it was agreed that if the claimant obtained planning permission to develop Yeoman's land, the company would sell the land to him for £12 million.

Mr Cobbe was aware that the oral agreement to sell the land was unenforceable because s 2(1) Law of Property (Miscellaneous Provisions) Act 1989 required contracts relating to land to be in writing. Nevertheless, he spent much time and money in obtaining planning permission before Yeoman's unilaterally withdrew from the oral agreement.

In the case before the House of Lords, Yeoman's were appealing against the decision of the Court of Appeal that a proprietary estoppel arose in favour of Mr Cobbe for the enforcement of the oral agreement.

The House of Lords allowed the appeal. Cobbe had taken a commercial risk on the basis of an agreement that he knew could not be enforced.

Principle: For a claim in proprietary estoppel to succeed, the claimant has first to show that there has been an **assurance** of a right to an interest in land. In a commercial context, this is not fulfilled by a non-binding oral agreement.

Application: This decision may be limited to commercial cases because it is considered that it would introduce too much uncertainty into commercial negotiations if a non-binding agreement was subsequently held to be effectively binding following one of the parties successfully pleading proprietary estoppel.

Capacity to create an express private trust

In order to create a valid express private trust, the following must be complied with:

❖ The three certainties (studied in Chapter 2)
❖ The statutory formalities, if any (studied in Chapter 3)
❖ Complete constitution of the trust (studied in this chapter)
❖ Capacity of the settlor to create a trust.

Regarding the last requirement of capacity, any person over 18, who is not suffering from mental incapacity, may create a trust. We have seen that a minor cannot own a legal estate in land and therefore a minor cannot create a trust of land. With respect to other types of property, any trust created by a minor is voidable by him whilst under the age of 18 or within a reasonable time of attaining 18.

Putting it into practice

In April, shortly after his marriage to his second wife, Jill, Samuel Stone called on his solicitors, Thompson and Trent, to sign a new will. At the same time, Thompson and Trent agreed to act as his trustees and, as part of his estate planning, Samuel covenanted with them to settle 20,000 shares in Stone Builders Ltd on Bobby, his 12-year-old son by his first marriage.

Two days later, Samuel suffered a fatal heart attack. His brother, Stephen, was helping Jill to go through Samuel's papers and found a partly completed share transfer form in respect of the 20,000 shares, and a copy of Samuel's newly executed will in which he appointed Thompson and Trent as his executors and left everything to his wife, Jill. Advise Samuel's executors of the legal position regarding the 20,000 shares in Stone Builders Ltd.

Feedback on putting it into practice

An outline approach to answering the question is given in the following diagram.

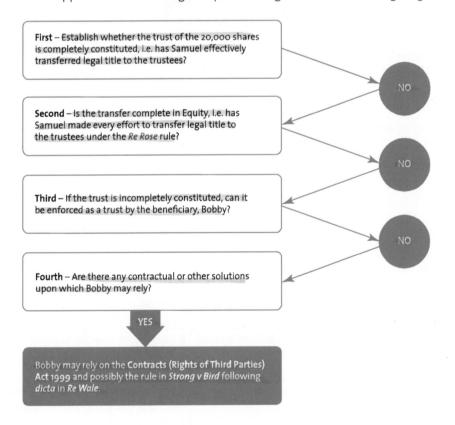

Table of key cases referred to in this chapter

Case name	Area of law	Principle
Birch v Treasury Solicitor [1951]	Deathbed gift	Parting with evidence of title
Cannon v Hartley [1949]	Incompletely constituted trust	Settlor covenanted with beneficiary to settle property
Choithram T, International SA v Pagarani [2001]	Settlor declares himself trustee	Hybrid case where settlor was one of a number of trustees
Fletcher v Fletcher [1844]	Completely constituted trust	Completely constituted trust of a promise/benefit of a covenant
Fry, Re [1946]	The 'every effort' rule	Transfer complete in equity only if donor has made every effort to complete his part
Gonin, Re [1964]	The rule in *Strong v Bird*	Rule did not apply as the donor did not have a continuing intention
James, Re [1935]	The rule in *Strong v Bird*	Rule applied to donee who was appointed administratrix
Jones v Lock [1865]	Settlor declares himself trustee	A loose conversation does not constitute a declaration of trust
Lillingston, Re [1952]	Deathbed gift	Parting with control over the property
Mascall v Mascall [1984]	The 'every effort' rule	Transfer complete in equity if donor has made every effort to complete his part
Paul v Constance [1977]	Settlor declares himself trustee	Words repeated over a period of time may be taken to be a declaration of trust
Pennington v Waine [2002]	Unconscionability	Transfer complete in equity if it would be unconscionable for the settlor to renege on the transaction
Plumptre's Marriage Settlement, Re [1910]	Incompletely constituted trust	Beneficiary was a volunteer
Pullan v Koe [1913]	Incompletely constituted trust	Beneficiary within the marriage consideration
Ralli's Will Trusts, Re [1964]	Method of constitution of trust	Automatic/indirect complete constitution of trust
Richards v Delbridge [1874]	Settlor declares himself trustee	An ineffective transfer to trustees will not be construed as a declaration of trust
Rose, Re [1952]	The 'every effort' rule	Transfer complete in equity if settlor has made every effort to complete his part

Rowe v Prance [1999]	Settlor declares himself trustee	Words repeated over a period of time may be taken to be a declaration of trust
Sen v Headley [1991]	Deathbed gift	Unregistered land the subject of a deathbed gift
Shah v Shah [2010]	Settlor declares himself trustee	The intention of the settlor is gathered from the words he uses
Strong v Bird [1874]	The rule in *Strong v Bird*	Imperfect release of a debt perfected under the rule
Thorner v Major [2009]	Proprietary estoppel	Assurance and detrimental reliance proven
Wale, Re [1956]	The rule in *Strong v Bird*	*Obiter dicta* that the rule in *Strong v Bird* applies to an incompletely constituted trust
Wilkes v Allington [1961]	Deathbed gift	Contemplation of death by the donor
Woodard v Woodard [1995]	Deathbed gift	Parting with control over the property
Yeoman's Row Management Ltd v Cobbe [2008]	Proprietary estoppel	A non-binding agreement did not amount to an assurance in a commercial context
Zeital v Kaye [2010]	The 'every effort' rule	Transfer complete in equity only if donor has made every effort to complete his part

---

@ **Visit the book's companion website to test your knowledge**

❖ Resources include a subject map, revision tip podcasts, downloadable diagrams, MCQ quizzes for each chapter, and a flashcard glossary

❖ www.routledge.com/cw/optimizelawrevision

5 Secret Trusts and Mutual Wills

Revision objectives

Understand the law
- Can you identify the requirements for the creation of a valid fully secret trust?
- Can you remember how the requirements for a valid half-secret trust differ from those for a fully secret trust?

Remember the details
- Can you recall the rules relating to communication of the secret trust to only one of two secret trustees?
- What is the rationale for these rules?

Reflect critically on areas of debate
- What is the theoretical basis for upholding secret trusts?
- Should secret trusts be classified as constructive trusts or express trusts?

Contextualise
- What is the legal position when a fully secret trustee witnesses a will?
- Will the secret trust fail if a fully secret trustee predeceases the testator?

Apply your skills and knowledge
- Can you answer the problem question involving a fully secret and half-secret trust?

Chapter Map

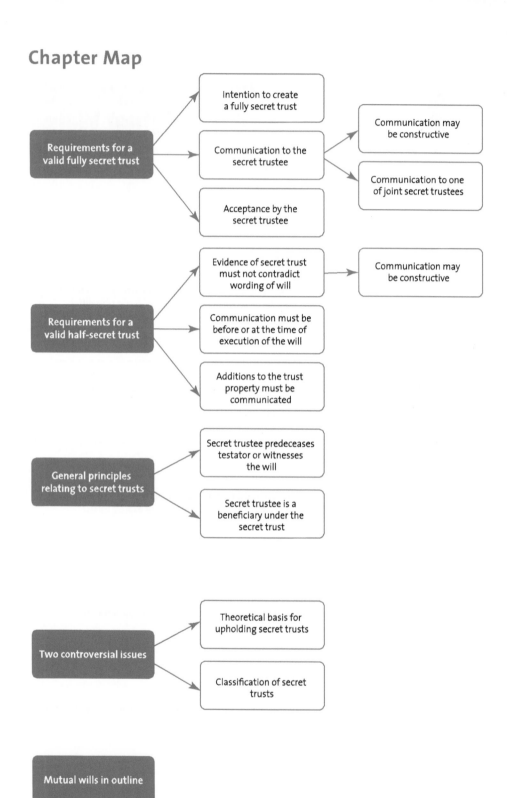

Introduction to secret trusts

Section 9 of the Wills Act 1837 (as amended by the Administration of Justice Act 1982) requires a valid will to be in writing, signed by the testator and attested by two witnesses. When the testator dies, his assets pass to his executors who must obtain probate, after which the will becomes open to public inspection on payment of a small fee. Herein lies the main reason for secret trusts.

The testator may wish to make provision for someone on his death without the public, or his family, knowing about it. For example, he might have a lover or a child about whom his family is unaware, or he may wish to provide for an organisation with which he does not wish to be publicly associated, or the testator may be undecided regarding whom he should benefit under his will and wishes to make up his mind later by means of a secret trust.

There are two kinds of secret trust

Secret trusts may be fully secret trusts or half-secret trusts. Can you work out which is which in the following examples?

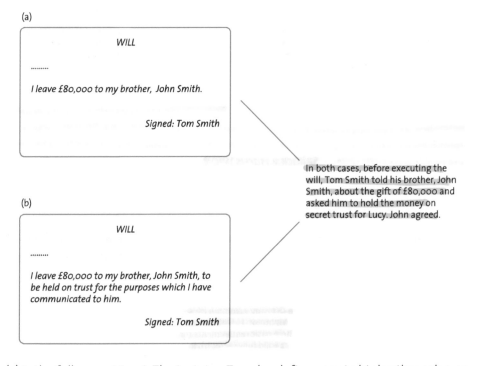

(a)

> **WILL**
>
> ....
>
> I leave £80,000 to my brother, John Smith.
>
> Signed: Tom Smith

In both cases, before executing the will, Tom Smith told his brother, John Smith, about the gift of £80,000 and asked him to hold the money on secret trust for Lucy. John agreed.

(b)

> **WILL**
>
> ....
>
> I leave £80,000 to my brother, John Smith, to be held on trust for the purposes which I have communicated to him.
>
> Signed: Tom Smith

(a) is the fully secret trust. The testator, Tom, has left money to his brother, who, on the face of the will appears to take absolutely as a legatee but who is, in fact, a secret trustee holding the money on secret trust for a secret beneficiary, Lucy. (b) is an example of a half-secret trust. It is evident from the face of the will that John is a trustee but the terms of the trust are not revealed. It is important to know what type of secret trust you are dealing with because the rules governing them are not identical.

Having said that, it is sometimes difficult to know precisely what type of secret trust has been created. In the following example, Tom has used a precatory word 'trusting' and (as explained below) one cannot be sure whether he has created a fully secret trust or a half-secret trust. If this arose in a problem question, it would be necessary to consider the rules relating to **both** kinds of secret trust.

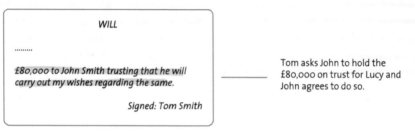

By using the precatory word 'trusting', it could be argued:

That Tom did not intend to create a trust on the face of the will, and therefore the secret trust that exists outside the will is a fully secret trust.	**OR**	That Tom did intend to create a trust on the face of the will, in which case it is a half-secret trust.

Before looking at the rules on secret trusts, it should be noted that a secret trust can arise on an intestacy, as for example if Tom had not made a will but asked his brother John (who as his nearest next of kin would be entitled to his estate) to hold it on secret trust for Lucy – *Sellack v Harris* [1708].

Requirements for a valid fully secret trust

If you identify that the assessment question involves a fully secret trust, you would need to prove that it is valid, i.e. that the following requirements have been fulfilled.

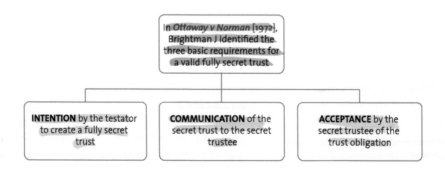

Intention by the testator to create a fully secret trust

Did the testator intend to subject the secret trustee to a **legal obligation** to hold the property for the secret beneficiary?	**OR**	Did the testator simply impose a **moral or family obligation** on the legatee? See *Re Snowden* [1979] below.

Case precedent – *Re Snowden* [1979] Ch 528

Facts: Six days before she died, the testatrix, aged 86, made her will. Apart from her brother, Bert, her nearest relatives were nephews and nieces. She left her residuary estate to Bert and, according to evidence from her solicitors, who witnessed the will, she said she wished to be fair to everyone and **wanted Bert to look after the division for her.** Bert, who died six days after the testatrix, left all his property to his son. The court held that a secret trust had not been imposed on Bert – he was subject only to a family obligation and took absolutely. Therefore, on Bert's death, the testatrix's residuary estate passed to Bert's son under Bert's will.

Principle: It must be shown that the testator/testatrix intended to impose a legal obligation on the legatee to act as secret trustee.

Application: When you apply this decision, you should also mention that in *Re Snowden*, Megarry VC stated that (except where the question of fraud arose) 'the standard of proof is the ordinary civil standard of proof that is required to establish an ordinary trust'.

Communication of the secret trust to the secret trustee
This second requirement for a valid fully secret trust can be sub-divided as follows:

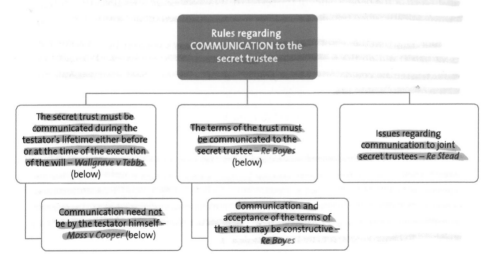

Communication of the secret trust during the testator's lifetime

Case precedent – *Wallgrave v Tebbs* [1855] 2 K & J 313

Facts: In his will, the testator left a legacy of £12,000 to the defendants, Mr Tebbs and Mr Martin. After the will was made, a draft letter was prepared in which the testator asked Tebbs and Martin to use the legacy for the charitable purpose of endowing a church. However, the letter was never sent to Tebbs and Martin and they did not learn of it until **after** the testator's death. The court held that as the testator's intention had not been communicated to Tebbs and Martin during the testator's lifetime, they were entitled to take the property absolutely.

Principle: A fully secret trust must be communicated to the secret trustee before or after the will is executed, provided the communication is during the testator's lifetime.

Application: When you apply this decision, you should mention that when a fully secret trust fails, the intended secret trustee is entitled to take the property absolutely if the secret trust had not been communicated. As we shall see, this is not the case when a half-secret trust fails.

An authorised person may communicate the secret trust to the secret trustee provided this is within the testator's lifetime, i.e. it does not have to be communicated by the testator – see *Moss v Cooper* (below).

The terms of the secret trust must be communicated

Case precedent – *Re Boyes* [1884] 28 Ch 531

Facts: The testator, George Boyes, left his property to his solicitor, Mr Carritt, having previously informed Mr Carritt that he wanted him to hold the property on trust for persons who he would identify by letter. Mr Carritt agreed to hold the property on trust but was not advised of the beneficiaries of the secret trust (a mistress and her child) until **after** the testator's death, when two unattested documents, addressed to Mr Carritt, were found.

The court held that the secret trust failed as the terms of the trust were not communicated to Mr Carritt during the testator's lifetime. As Mr Carritt had accepted the position of secret trustee, he could not take the property beneficially and held it on resulting trust for the testator's next of kin.

Principle: During his lifetime, the testator must communicate the terms of the trust to the secret trustee.

Application: The rationale for this principle seems to be that the secret trustee should have the right to reject the trusteeship when he is told of the terms of the trust. However, against this rationale, there are *obiter dicta* relating to a half-secret trust (which could apply to a fully secret trust) that communication of the terms of the trust and acceptance by the secret trustee may be constructive – *Re Keen* (below), e.g. handed over in a sealed envelope to be opened after the testator's death.

Communication to joint trustees

The next issue regarding communication to joint trustees is best explained by looking at a sample question, considering how to answer it and then debating the reason for the rules that were laid down by Farwell J in *Re Stead* [1900] 1 Ch 231.

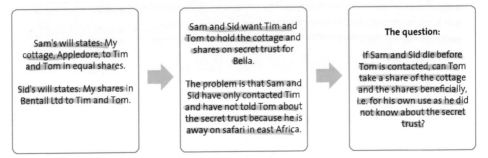

Sam's will states: My cottage, Appledore, to Tim and Tom in equal shares.

Sid's will states: My shares in Bentall Ltd to Tim and Tom.

Sam and Sid want Tim and Tom to hold the cottage and shares on secret trust for Bella.

The problem is that Sam and Sid have only contacted Tim and have not told Tom about the secret trust because he is away on safari in east Africa.

The question:

If Sam and Sid die before Tom is contacted, can Tom take a share of the cottage and the shares beneficially, i.e. for his own use as he did not know about the secret trust?

How to answer the above question

First, you need to decide whether Tim and Tom are tenants in common or joint tenants.

The wording of the gift provides the answer. In the case of the cottage, Tim and Tom are tenants in common because each has a separate share in the property. In the case of the shares, Tim and Tom are joint tenants because they do not have a specified share but are jointly entitled to the whole.

Second, you need to apply the relevant rule as follows:

Where Tim and Tom take as **tenants in common**, only Tim will be bound by the secret trust. Tom is entitled to take his share of the cottage absolutely.

Where Tim and Tom take as **joint tenants**, the timing of the communication to Tim is important:

(i) If Tim was told about the secret trust before the will was made, both Tim and Tom are bound by the secret trust.

(ii) If Tim was told about the secret trust after the will was made, only Tim is bound by the secret trust and Tom can take his share in the Bentall shares absolutely.

Rationale for the above rules

The reason for the rule where Tim and Tom take as tenants in common is said to be that otherwise, Tim, by agreeing to the secret trust, could deprive Tom of his share in the property.

Is there a reason for the differences in (i) and (ii) above? Regarding (i), it is said that no one (i.e. Tom) is allowed to take property beneficially under a fraud committed by another (i.e. Tim), inducing the testator (i.e. Sid) to make the will. In (ii), the testator, Sid, has not been induced by Tim to make the will because he had already made it when he told Tim about the secret trust.

Up for Debate

It is generally considered that these reasons are not convincing and that the rules were a result of a misunderstanding of earlier cases by Farwell J in *Re Stead* [1900].

It is suggested that the only issue should be whether the gift to Tom was induced by Tim's promise to the testator. If it was induced by Tim's promise, then Tom should be bound. If the gift to Tom was not induced by Tim's promise, then Tom should be able to take beneficially.

The above problem only arises with fully secret trusts. In half-secret trusts, the trustees will always take as joint tenants with communication to the one trustee being before the will was made, so both will always be bound.

Acceptance by the secret trustee of the trust obligation

This is the third requirement for a valid fully secret trust. Acceptance by the secret trustee may be express or it may be implied by his silence as the following case illustrates.

Case precedent – *Moss v Cooper* [1861] 1 J & H 352

Facts: The testator left his residuary estate to James Gawthorn, William Sedman and James Owen. Gawthorn prepared a memorandum when the will was made, stating that the testator wished each of the three legatees to keep £25 from the residue for their own use and to divide the remainder for the benefit of various charities. Gawthorn subsequently told Sedman and Owen of the testator's wishes. Sedman informed the testator that he agreed to act as secret trustee but Owen remained silent. It was held that as Gawthorn had been authorised to inform Sedman and Owen of the secret trust, and had done so during the testator's lifetime, the secret trust was valid. Owen's silence implied that he accepted the trusteeship.

Principle: Communication of the secret trust may be by someone authorised by the testator. A secret trustee's silence can be taken as implied acceptance to act as trustee.

Application: When applying this decision, note that, unlike *Re Stead*, all the secret trustees were aware of the secret trust during the testator's lifetime.

Requirements for a valid half-secret trust

Notice from the diagram below that some of the requirements are different to those for a fully secret trust.

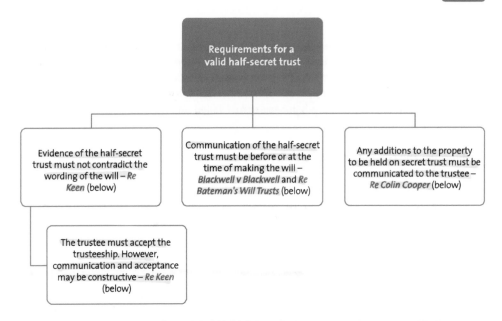

Evidence of the half-secret trust must not contradict the wording of the will

The following very useful case, *Re Keen*, relates to the above principle and also illustrates that a half-secret trust will fail if communication of the trust does not take effect before or at the time of execution of the will. Furthermore, it contains the famous statement by Lord Wright regarding constructive communication and acceptance of a secret trust. He said, 'just as a ship which sails under sealed orders is sailing under orders though the exact terms are not ascertained by the captain till later, so a testator may, during his lifetime, give to the legatee a sealed envelope which is not to be opened until after the testator's death'.

Case precedent – *Re Keen* [1937] 1 All ER 452

Facts: On 31 March 1932, the testator made a will in which he gave the sum of £10,000 to Captain Hazlehurst and Mr Evershed 'to be held upon trust and disposed of by them among such person, persons or charities as may be notified by me to them . . . during my lifetime'.

On the same day, the testator handed to Mr Evershed a sealed envelope containing the name of the intended beneficiary and directed that the envelope was not to be opened until after his death.

On 11 August 1932, the testator made a new will, revoking the will of 31 March 1932. This new will contained an identical clause regarding the sum of £10,000 as that set out above. However, the testator did not give fresh directions to Mr Evershed, who considered himself bound by the earlier communication.

When the testator died, the question arose regarding the validity of the secret trust. The Court of Appeal stated that the delivery of the sealed envelope to Mr Evershed on 31 March 1932 constituted constructive communication of the terms of the trust but this evidence conflicted with the terms of the will of 11 August 1932, which referred to a future communication. Therefore, the half-secret trust failed and the money was part of the testator's residuary estate.

Principle: The communication of the secret trust must not conflict with the wording of the will.

Application: You can also refer to the *dicta* in this case that a half-secret trust must be communicated before or at the time of the execution of the will.

Just as with a fully secret trust, the half-secret trustee must accept the trusteeship.

When answering a question on secret trusts, it is important to follow it through, i.e. to consider what happens to the property if the secret trust fails. In this respect, notice that when a half-secret trust fails, there is no question of the trustee taking the property beneficially. This is because the will identifies him as a trustee so, if the trust fails, he will hold the property on trust for the residuary beneficiary under the testator's will or, if there is no residuary beneficiary, for the testator's next of kin under the intestacy rules.

Communication of the half-secret trust must be before or at the time of the execution of the will

There are *dicta* to the above effect in the following House of Lords case which finally established the validity of half secret trusts. Relating half-secret trusts to fully secret trusts, Viscount Sumner said, 'in both cases, the testator's wishes are incompletely expressed in his will. Why should equity, over a mere matter of words, give effect to them in one case and frustrate them in the other?' In other words, half-secret trusts should also be capable of being valid.

Case precedent – *Blackwell v Blackwell* [1929] AC 318

Facts: In a codicil to his will, the testator, John Blackwell, left a legacy of £12,000 to five trustees 'to apply for the purposes indicated by me to them'. Before he executed the codicil, the testator orally communicated to the five trustees that the money should be held for the testator's mistress and illegitimate son and one of the five trustees made a memorandum of these instructions.

Subsequently, the residuary beneficiaries (the testator's widow and legitimate son) argued that the half-secret trust failed on the ground that parole evidence was inadmissible to establish the trust.

The House of Lords held that as the trustees accepted their obligations under the half-secret trust before the execution of the codicil, oral evidence was admissible of the trust.

Principle: The half-secret trust was communicated before the codicil was executed and was upheld.

Application: Also remember that this case established the validity of half-secret trusts.

To summarise, the House of Lords case, *Blackwell v Blackwell*, contains *dicta* that a half secret trust will fail if it is communicated to the trustees after the execution of the will/codicil. We have noted that there were similar *dicta* in the Court of Appeal case *Re Keen*. These *dicta* were followed in the first instance case *Re Bateman's Will Trusts* [1970] in which trustees were directed by the testator in his will to pay the income from his estate 'to such persons ... as shall be stated by me in a sealed letter ...' This half-secret trust failed because the will referred to a future communication.

Up for Debate

Why do half-secret trusts fail if they are communicated after the execution of the will whereas fully secret trusts are valid provided they are communicated to the secret trustee within the testator's lifetime? This distinction between the two kinds of secret trust is highly criticised. It is thought that it may be due to a misplaced analogy between half-secret trusts and the probate doctrine of incorporation of a document by reference. This doctrine allows an existing document referred to in a will to be admitted to probate, likewise it is argued that the terms of a secret trust referred to in the will must have been communicated, i.e. not in the future. However, there are many differences between the probate doctrine and half-secret trusts; for example, the latter may be communicated orally but the former must exist as a document e.g. a beneficiary under a half-secret trust may witness the will but a beneficiary under the incorporated document will lose his interest if he witnesses the will.

Any additions to the property to be held on secret trust must be communicated to the secret trustee

Case precedent – *Re Colin Cooper* [1939] Ch 811

Facts: The testator left £5,000 to two trustees to hold on a half-secret trust. He later executed a codicil increasing the amount to £10,000 stating 'they knowing my wishes regarding that sum'. However, he did not inform the trustees of the addition. The court held that the additional amount should be held on resulting trust for the testator's residuary estate.

Principle: Any additions to the property to be held on trust must be communicated to the half-secret trustee.

Application: Notice that this case involved a half-secret trust and that any communication would have to be before the codicil was executed. If this situation occurred with a fully secret trust and the testator failed to inform the trustees of the addition during his lifetime, then it could be argued that the trustees could take the additional property beneficially.

General principles relating to secret trusts

Very often, a problem question will contain issues relating to these general principles.

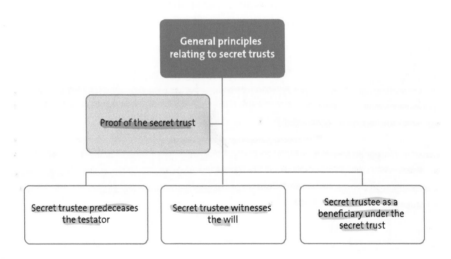

Proof of the secret trust
Consider the following problem:

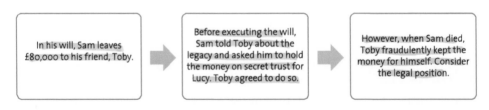

The **burden of proving** a secret trust lies on the secret beneficiary, i.e. Lucy. With a fully secret trust, it is advisable for the testator to provide Lucy with some written evidence of the trust. The problem is not so acute with a half-secret trust because there is evidence of the secret trust on the face of the will.

Regarding the **standard of proof**, in *McCormick v Grogan* [1869], Lord Westbury said 'now, being a jurisdiction founded on personal fraud, it is incumbent on the court to see that a fraud . . . is proved by the clearest and most indisputable evidence'. In other words, the standard of proof is high. However, opinion is divided on this point.

Up for Debate

In *Re Snowden* (see earlier), Megarry VC said '. . . in the present case, there is no question of fraud . . . I therefore hold that in order to establish a secret trust where no question of fraud arises, the standard of proof is the ordinary civil standard of proof that is required to establish an ordinary trust'. This would therefore be on the balance of probabilities.

Some textbook writers consider it incongruous that a higher standard of proof is required where fraud is alleged as this appears to benefit fraudulent trustees. Therefore, it is suggested that the ordinary civil standard of proof should apply in all cases.

Secret trustee predeceases the testator

Under s 25 of the Wills Act 1837, a gift by will to a beneficiary who predeceases the testator lapses, i.e. fails. What is the position if that beneficiary is actually a secret trustee? Look at the will below and imagine that John Smith, who has agreed to hold the £80,000 on a fully secret trust, has predeceased the testator. On the face of the will, John is the beneficiary and when he predeceased Tom, the gift to John would lapse and therefore the fully secret trust would fail – *Re Maddock* [1902] 2 Ch 220.

> WILL
>
> . . . .
>
> *I leave £80,000 to my brother, John Smith.*
>
>   *Signed: Tom Smith*

However, in the case of a half-secret trust (see below), it is clear that John Smith holds the £80,000 as trustee, i.e. he is not a beneficiary under the will, and therefore the secret trust will not fail if he predeceases the testator. Ideally, Tom would need to execute a new will and arrange for someone else to be the half-secret trustee but, if he omitted to do so, the maxim 'Equity will not allow a trust to fail for want of a trustee' would apply and, provided the terms of the half-secret trust could be identified, it is likely that Tom's personal representative (executor) would act as trustee.

> WILL
>
> ....
>
> *I leave £80,000 to my brother, John Smith, to be held on trust for the purposes which I have communicated to him.*
>
> *Signed: Tom Smith*

For the position regarding a secret beneficiary who predeceases the testator, see *Re Gardner* [1923] below.

Secret trustee witnesses the will

Under s 15 of the Wills Act 1837, a gift by will to a beneficiary fails if the beneficiary/ his spouse/his civil partner witnesses the will. This rule ensures that the will is witnessed by independent persons. In a fully secret trust, the secret trustee appears to be the beneficiary under the will and therefore if he witnesses the will, the gift to him will fail and therefore the secret trust will fail.

By contrast, with a half-secret trust, the secret trustee is identified as a trustee on the face of the will, not a beneficiary, and therefore he may witness the will and this will not affect the secret trust.

Regarding a secret beneficiary witnessing the will, see *Re Young* [1951] later.

Secret trustee as a beneficiary under the secret trust

The question of whether a secret trustee may take a benefit under a secret trust depends on whether it is a fully secret trust or a half-secret trust. In *Irvine v Sullivan* [1869], which concerned a fully secret trust, the secret trustee was entitled to keep the surplus after the secret beneficiaries had received their interest under the secret trust. Contrast a half-secret trust in *Re Rees Will Trusts*.

Case precedent – *Re Rees Will Trusts* [1950] Ch 204

Facts: The testator appointed his friend and his solicitor as his executors and trustees and left his entire estate 'to my trustees absolutely, they well knowing my wishes concerning the same'.

When executing his will, the testator had told his trustees that he wanted them to make certain payments from his estate and that they should retain the surplus for themselves. After the payments were made, there was a large surplus but the court held that the trustees could not take this benefit, which therefore passed as on intestacy.

Principle: A secret trustee cannot benefit from the half-secret trust because this would contradict the terms of the will, which states that he takes as trustee.

Application: When you apply this decision, you should mention that the principle has been questioned because secret trusts are regarded as operating outside the will (see later). It is thought that the decision in *Re Rees* may rest on the fact that the solicitor prepared the will and, as Lord Evershed stated, 'the intention of the testator . . . (to benefit the solicitor) . . . should appear plainly in the will and should not be arrived at by the more oblique method of . . . a secret trust'. *Obiter dicta* in *Re Tyler* [1967] suggest that evidence of **all** the terms of the half-secret trust should be admissible although, in respect of a secret trustee claiming a benefit, the evidence would not be 'lightly admitted'.

Two controversial issues regarding secret trusts

These two issues come up in both essay and problem questions.

What is the theoretical basis for upholding secret trusts?

The problem is that a will is governed by the Wills Act 1837 and therefore what is to stop a legatee under the will (who has agreed to be a secret trustee) simply taking the legacy for his own use, and pleading the Wills Act in his defence?

> **In other words, why are secret trusts upheld? There are two theories:**
>
> **The fraud theory:** This is the traditional theory for upholding secret trusts. It is based on the maxim that 'Equity will not allow a statute to be used as an instrument of fraud'. However, see 'Up for Debate' below.
>
> **Dehors the will:** The more modern theory is that the secret trust operates outside (dehors) the will and is therefore not governed by the Wills Act 1837 – see *Re Young* and *Re Gardner* below.

Case precedent – *Re Young* [1951] Ch 344

Facts: Roger Young, the testator, left property to his wife but requested her to make certain bequests on her death, including £2,000 to his chauffeur, Thomas Cobb.

Thomas Cobb had witnessed the testator's will and the question arose whether he could take as a beneficiary under the secret trust. You will remember that s 15 of the Wills Act 1837 prevents a witness of a will taking under that will. The court held that he could receive the gift of £2,000, which arose under the secret trust that took effect outside the will.

Principle: A secret trust arises outside (dehors) the will and therefore is not governed by the provisions of the Wills Act 1837.

Application: Problem questions often involve the secret beneficiary witnessing the will and this is therefore a particularly useful case.

This is another case that illustrates the dehors theory but it is important to note that the reason for the decision has been criticised.

Case precedent – *Re Gardner (No 2)* [1923] 2 Ch 230

Facts: The testatrix left her estate to her husband for life and after his death to be held on secret trust for her nephew and two nieces. One of the nieces predeceased the testatrix and the question arose as to whether the estate of the deceased niece was entitled to her share under the secret trust. You will recall that under s 25 of the Wills Act 1837 a gift to a beneficiary under a will lapses if the beneficiary predeceases the testatrix. The court held that the niece's estate was entitled to her share under the secret trust, which was created when the secret trustee accepted the legal obligation of secret trustee, i.e. during the testatrix's lifetime.

Principle: This controversial decision is often cited to illustrate that a secret trust operates dehors the will and therefore is not governed by the provisions of the Wills Act 1837.

Application: You should mention that this decision has been criticised for a number of reasons; notably, the secret trust was not completely constituted until the trust property vested in the secret trustee, i.e. on the death of the testatrix. Also, a will may be revoked at any time before the testatrix's death but the decision suggests that a will containing a secret trust cannot be altered once the secret trustee has agreed to act as such.

Up for Debate

Commentators find neither of the above theories justifying the enforcement of secret trusts entirely satisfactory. The fraud theory does not explain the enforcement of half secret trusts where there is no possibility of the secret trustee fraudulently keeping the property for his own use. Nor does the theory explain why a fully secret trust for the beneficiary should be upheld. Rather than enforcing the fully secret trust, the trustee could be required to hold the property on resulting trust for the testator's residuary beneficiary—a solution that would not conflict with the Wills Act 1837.

The dehors theory has its critics based primarily on the argument that secret trusts are essentially testamentary dispositions, being both revocable and ambulatory in nature and, as such, should be governed by the Wills Act 1837, which governs 'any testamentary disposition'. For more on this debate, see the article by P Critchley, 'Instruments of Fraud, Testamentary Dispositions and the Doctrine of Secret Trusts' (1999) LQR 631.

Are secret trusts classified as constructive trusts or express trusts?

This is the second controversial issue and would be particularly relevant in a problem question involving an oral secret trust of land.

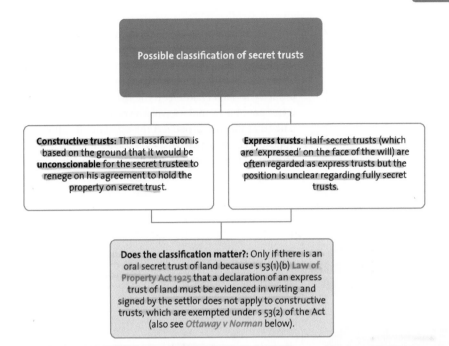

Possible classification of secret trusts

Constructive trusts: This classification is based on the ground that it would be **unconscionable** for the secret trustee to renege on his agreement to hold the property on secret trust.

Express trusts: Half-secret trusts (which are 'expressed' on the face of the will) are often regarded as express trusts but the position is unclear regarding fully secret trusts.

Does the classification matter?: Only if there is an oral secret trust of land because s 53(1)(b) Law of Property Act 1925 that a declaration of an express trust of land must be evidenced in writing and signed by the settlor does not apply to constructive trusts, which are exempted under s 53(2) of the Act (also see *Ottaway v Norman* below).

Case precedent – *Ottaway v Norman* [1972] 2 WLR 50

Facts: Harry Ottaway, the testator, left his bungalow, furniture and £1,500 to his housekeeper, Miss Hodges, with whom he was cohabiting. Miss Hodges (the primary donee) orally agreed with Harry Ottaway that she would leave the bungalow and whatever money remained to the claimants, Mr and Mrs William Ottaway, who were the testator's son and daughter-in-law and referred to as the secondary donees. In fact, by her will, she left the property elsewhere, and this action was brought by the claimants against Miss Hodges' executor that the appropriate parts of Miss Hodges' estate were held on secret trust for them. The court held that the bungalow was held on a valid secret trust for the claimants and had been in suspense during Miss Hodges' lifetime. As there was uncertainty regarding the amount of the money, this was not held on trust.

Principle: Ascertainable property may be held on a secret trust, which may be in suspension during the primary donee's lifetime.

Application: You may have noticed that the fully secret trust of the bungalow was upheld even though there was no compliance with s 53(1)(b) LPA 1925. For this reason, the case is sometimes cited as an authority that fully secret trusts are constructive trusts, although in fact the issue was not addressed by the court.

Mutual wills

Assessment on mutual wills is rare and therefore the topic is covered in outline only. However, the key aspects are indicated below, together with the relevant cases in the event that you need to know more about the subject.

Question: What are mutual wills?

❖ **Answer:** Mutual wills are made by two people (usually spouses) who agree that they will not revoke their wills unilaterally. Frequently, they leave their property to each other with the requirement that the survivor will leave the property to their children on the survivor's death. Whilst it is not possible to make a will irrevocable, when the first party dies having carried out the agreement, equity will impose a constructive trust over the agreed property. Mutual wills are beset by difficulties as the following list reveals, and parties are usually advised not to make them.

Key aspects of mutual wills

There must be an agreement not to revoke the wills

> An agreement not to revoke will not be inferred from identical wills – *Re Goodchild* [1997]. There must be evidence/declaration within the wills that the parties have agreed not to revoke their wills – *Charles v Fraser* [2010], *Olins v Walters* [2008].

The legal position before the first to die

> The agreement not to revoke is contractual. If it is discovered that the first to die did not keep to the agreement, it seems that the survivor could sue the estate for damages.

The legal position of the survivor (i.e. after the first party dies)

> If the first party acted in accordance with the agreement so that the other party received property under the unrevoked will, the survivor becomes a constructive trustee of the property that he/she agreed would be left to the intended beneficiary – *Birmingham v Renfrew* [1936], *Re Hagger* [1930].

To what property does the constructive trust attach?

> **The problem:**
> - The property inherited from the first to die?
> - All the property, including that owned by the survivor at the death of the first party?
> - All property, including that acquired by the survivor after the death of the first party?

Other problems arising with mutual wills

> - Can the survivor dispose of property subject to the constructive trust?
> - Anyway, who will know if he/she is disposing of it?
> - What is the position if the survivor remarries and has other children whom he/she wishes to benefit in his/her will?

Putting it into practice

Philip, who died recently, made the following disposition in his will: 'my house, Oaklands, to my sister, Anne, upon trust for the purposes I will communicate to her'. Shortly before he died, Philip telephoned his sister and told her about the will and asked her to hold the house on trust for his friend, Jane.

(a) Advise Jane, who had witnessed the will, of the legal position.

(b) Would your answer differ if the disposition in the will had read: 'Oaklands to my sister Anne' but the rest of the facts were the same?

Feedback on putting it into practice

You should mention that it is for Jane, the secret beneficiary to prove the validity of the secret trust. You could discuss the standard of proof, citing *McCormick v Grogan* and comparing *Re Snowden*.

The rest of the answer is outlined in the following diagram.

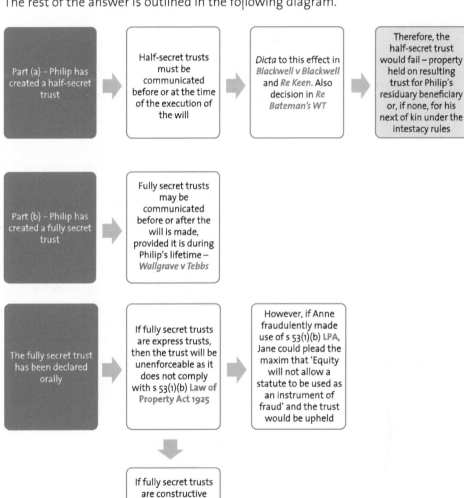

Part (a) – Philip has created a half-secret trust → Half-secret trusts must be communicated before or at the time of the execution of the will → *Dicta* to this effect in *Blackwell v Blackwell* and *Re Keen*. Also decision in *Re Bateman's WT* → Therefore, the half-secret trust would fail – property held on resulting trust for Philip's residuary beneficiary or, if none, for his next of kin under the intestacy rules

Part (b) – Philip has created a fully secret trust → Fully secret trusts may be communicated before or after the will is made, provided it is during Philip's lifetime – *Wallgrave v Tebbs*

The fully secret trust has been declared orally → If fully secret trusts are express trusts, then the trust will be unenforceable as it does not comply with s 53(1)(b) Law of Property Act 1925 → However, if Anne fraudulently made use of s 53(1)(b) LPA, Jane could plead the maxim that 'Equity will not allow a statute to be used as an instrument of fraud' and the trust would be upheld

If fully secret trusts are constructive trusts (as *Ottaway v Norman* suggests), Philip's fully secret trust will be valid as s 53(2) exempts constructive trusts from s 53(1)(b)

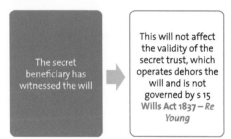

The secret beneficiary has witnessed the will ➡ This will not affect the validity of the secret trust, which operates dehors the will and is not governed by s 15 Wills Act 1837 – *Re Young*

Table of key cases referred to in this chapter

Case name	Area of law	Principle
Bateman's Will Trusts, Re [1970]	Half-secret trusts	Communication of the half-secret trust must be before, or at the same time as, execution of the will
Blackwell v Blackwell [1929]	Half-secret trusts	This case established the validity of half-secret trusts
Boyes, Re [1884]	Fully secret trusts	Testator must communicate the terms of the trust to the secret trustee
Colin Cooper, Re [1939]	Half-secret trusts	Any addition to the property to be held on secret trust must be communicated to the secret trustee
Gardner, Re [1923]	Fully secret trust	Gift to secret beneficiary who predeceases the testator will not lapse
Keen, Re [1937]	Half-secret trust	Evidence of the half-secret trust must not contradict the wording of the will
McCormick v Grogan [1869]	Standard of proof	Clearest and most indisputable evidence required where fraud is alleged
Moss v Cooper [1861]	Fully secret trust	Communication of the secret trust may be by an authorised person. Silence may be taken as acceptance by secret trustee
Ottaway v Norman [1972]	Fully secret trust	Ascertainable property may be held on a secret trust, which is suspended during the primary donee's lifetime
Rees Will Trusts, Re [1950]	Half-secret trust	Half-secret trustee unable to take surplus as a secret beneficiary
Snowden, Re [1979]	Fully secret trust	Testatrix did not intend to create a fully secret trust
Stead, Re [1900]	Fully secret trust	Rules regarding communication to only one of two or more secret trustees
Wallgrave v Tebbs [1855]	Fully secret trust	Communication of the secret trust must be during the testator's lifetime
Young, Re [1951]	Fully secret trust	Secret trust arises dehors the will; secret trustee may witness the will

@ Visit the book's companion website to test your knowledge

❖ Resources include a subject map, revision tip podcasts, downloadable diagrams, MCQ quizzes for each chapter, and a flashcard glossary

❖ www.routledge.com/cw/optimizelawrevision

6

Resulting Trusts

Revision objectives

- Can you explain when an automatic resulting trust and a presumed resulting trust arise?
- When does the presumption of advancement apply?

Remember the details
- Do you remember the cases regarding the transfer of property to another for an illegal reason?
- Can you recall the reliance principle and the withdrawal principle?

Reflect critically on areas of debate
- Do you consider that both types of resulting trust should be based upon presumed intention?
- Do you think that the law regarding transfer of property to another for an illegal reason requires reform?

Contextualise
- Are you able to explain the use of a Quistclose trust in a commercial context?
- Can you discuss the nature of a Quistclose trust?

Apply your skills and knowledge
- Can you complete both parts of the problem question regarding transfer of property to another for an illegal reason?

Chapter Map

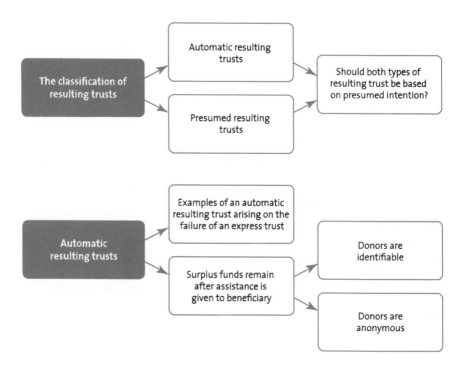

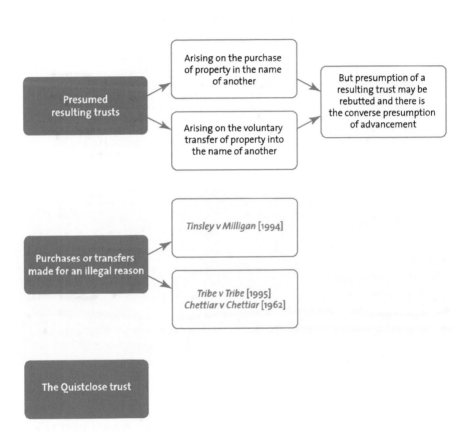

Introduction to resulting trusts

The key characteristic of a resulting trust is that the property returns, i.e. results back, to the settlor/transferor. Megarry J put forward what has become the traditional classification of resulting trusts in *Vandervell's Trusts No 2* [1974].

```
┌─────────────────────────────────┐
│   Traditional classification of │
│        resulting trusts         │
└─────────────────────────────────┘
```

Automatic resulting trusts – Megarry J suggested that these arise automatically when an express trust fails. We have seen this type of resulting trust in Chapter 2, e.g. when an express trust fails for uncertainty of objects, the trust property results back to the settlor. (See below for further examples.)

Presumed resulting trusts – sometimes called a presumption against a gift. Megarry J suggested that these resulting trusts are based on the presumed intention of a transferor of property to a transferee that a gift is not intended, i.e. the transferee holds the property on resulting trust for the transferor (see below).

Up for Debate

Doubt was cast on the above classification by Lord Browne-Wilkinson in *Westdeutsche Landesbank v Islington LBC* [1998], who considered that **both** types of resulting trust are based on presumed intention. Referring to automatic resulting trusts, he suggested that it would be the presumed intention of a settlor (where the express trust he had attempted to set up failed) that the property should return to him. This presumption could be rebutted by evidence that the settlor had abandoned any beneficial interest in the property, in which case the property would pass to the Crown as *bona vacantia* (i.e. ownerless property).

Automatic resulting trusts

As mentioned above, these trusts come about when an express trust fails. This failure may occur for a variety of reasons as you will see from the following diagram.

Examples of the failure of an express trust – with an automatic resulting trust arising

Failure to identify the beneficiary of an express trust

Example:
In Chapter 3, in *Vandervell v IRC* we saw that Mr Vandervell asked Vandervell Trustee Co to hold the option to repurchase the shares but he did not identify the beneficiary. Therefore, Vandervell Trustee Co held the option on automatic resulting trust for Mr Vandervell.

Failure to dispose of the entire beneficial interest	**Example:** Sam, the settlor, transfers £100,000 to his trustees to hold on trust for his son, Alan, for life but does not state what is to happen when Alan dies. As Sam has failed to dispose of the entire beneficial interest, when Allan dies the fund will result back to Sam (or his estate if he is dead).
Trust fails, e.g. for uncertainty of subject matter	**Example:** In Chapter 2, we saw the case of *Boyce v Boyce* [1849] in which the express trust of two houses failed for uncertainty of beneficial interest. The property resulted back to the settlor's estate. The same would apply where a trust fails for uncertainty of objects.
Failure of a specific purpose	**Example:** In *Re Ames's Settlement* [1946], the bridegroom's father created a marriage settlement. The marriage was later declared void and the trust fund was returned to the father under an automatic resulting trust.

Surplus funds and automatic resulting trusts

The issue of surplus funds or unexhausted funds is a popular examination topic and can arise in two situations as follows.

Surplus funds remain after assistance is given to a beneficiary – donors are identifiable

Example
Anna is a final-year student who is finding it difficult to pay her accommodation costs. Her grandparents on both sides of the family decide to create a fund to pay for her accommodation and, between the four of them, donate £7,000. As it happens, Anna obtains a well-paid part-time job and, when she graduates, there is a surplus in the fund of £5,000. What happens to this surplus? There are **two** options:

The donors gave the money for a **particular purpose only** and therefore the surplus funds are held on resulting trust for the donors. See *Re Abbott Fund Trusts* [1900] below.	The donors intended the money as an absolute gift (an out-and-out gift). Payment of accommodation costs was simply a motive for the gift. See *Re Andrews Trust* [1905] below.

Case precedent – *Re Abbott Trust Funds* [1900] 2 Ch 326

Facts: Dr Abbott left funds in his will for the care of his two sisters, who were both deaf and dumb. When the trustee of this fund died, it was discovered that the money had disappeared. Dr Abbott's friends set up a fund inviting subscribers to donate to provide for the sisters' 'very moderate wants'. A large sum was raised and a surplus remained when the sisters died. The fund did not state what was to happen to the surplus and the court held that it was held on resulting trust for the subscribers.

Principle: When the subscribers intend to give for a particular purpose only, then any surplus is held on resulting trust for them.

Application: When applying this decision, compare it with the decision below in *Re Andrew's*. The two decisions are difficult to reconcile and it has been suggested by commentators that the court may have been influenced by the fact that the two sisters in *Re Abbott* were dead whereas in *Re Andrew's* they were still alive. Strictly, this should not have been relevant because the court should be giving effect to the subscribers' intention at the time they contributed the money.

Case precedent – *Re Andrew's Trust* [1905] 2 Ch 48

Facts: The first Bishop of Jerusalem, the Right Reverend Joseph Barclay, died in 1881 leaving seven young children. Friends of the family raised £900, which they gave to trustees with the power to use the funds for the education of the children. The children had all completed their education by 1899, and surplus funds remained. The question for the court was whether the surplus resulted back to the subscribers or whether it could be claimed by the children. The court held that the subscribers had parted with the money out-and-out and the children were entitled to the surplus.

Principle: Where the subscribers intend to part with the money out-and-out and the stated purpose is simply a motive or excuse for the gift, the recipient is entitled to keep the surplus.

Application: As indicated above, this decision may be compared with *Re Abbott*. *Re Andrew's* has been followed in *Re Osoba* [1979] in which a father left money for his daughter's education up to education level. A surplus remained on her graduation from university and it was held that she was entitled to the remaining funds.

Surplus remains in Disaster Appeal Fund – donors are anonymous

Suppose there was an appeal to help refugees and donors gave anonymously, e.g. in street collecting boxes. If a large amount was collected and there was a surplus, what would happen to that surplus, for clearly there would be no way of tracing the donors?

There are three possibilities:		

| If the fund is **charitable** (within the legal meaning, which we will consider later in Chapter 10), then any surplus will be applied *cy-près* (meaning 'so near'), i.e. it will be used for a similar existing charitable purpose. | If the fund is non-charitable, then the surplus will go as *bona vacantia* (ownerless property) to the Crown who will apply it for some worthy purpose. | Alternatively, if the fund is non-charitable, the surplus will be held on resulting trust for the donors – see *Re Gillingham* below. |

Case precedent – *Re Gillingham Bus Disaster Fund* [1958] Ch 62

Facts: In 1951, a bus ran into a squad of Royal Marine cadets marching through Gillingham, killing 24 cadets and injuring many others. A fund was set up to care for the injured cadets and for 'such worthy cause in memory of the boys as should be determined by the mayors of Gillingham, Rochester and Chatham'. Approximately £9,000 was raised, much of it from anonymous donors, but a surplus of about £6,500 remained because the bus company accepted liability.

It was held that the surplus could not be applied for 'such worthy cause' because that was not a charitable purpose as defined by the law and so the question arose as to what should happen to the surplus. Harman J held that it should be held on resulting trust to await claims by the donors.

Principle: Harman J held that the fact that many donors were unidentifiable was no reason to deviate from the general principle of a resulting trust.

Application: When you cite this decision, you should mention that it has been criticised and has not been followed. The surplus was paid into court to await possible claimants and remained there until 1993, when it was decided that it should be withdrawn and used for some worthy memorial to the victims.

Presumed resulting trust – purchase of property in the name of another

This is the other type of resulting trust. When a person (e.g. Alan) purchases property in the name of another (e.g. Ben), equity will assume that the property is held on presumed resulting trust for the person providing the purchase money (i.e. Alan). This is a presumption, not a rule, and like all presumptions, it may be rebutted by evidence to the contrary. It is sometimes referred to as a presumption against a gift.

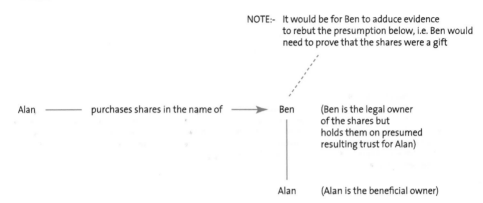

NOTE:- It would be for Ben to adduce evidence
to rebut the presumption below, i.e. Ben would
need to prove that the shares were a gift

Alan ———— purchases shares in the name of ————→ Ben   (Ben is the legal owner
                                                          of the shares but
                                                          holds them on presumed
                                                          resulting trust for Alan)

                                                   Alan   (Alan is the beneficial owner)

This presumption that 'he who pays owns' was first stated in *Dyer v Dyer* [1788]. As we shall see in Chapter 8, it was frequently used by a cohabitant who made a direct contribution to the price of the family home, which was purchased in the other cohabitant's name.

However, since *Stack v Dowden* [2007] the presumed resulting trust has been out of favour regarding a claim of a beneficial interest in the family home, although it is still used for personal property (see *Abrahams* below) and for real property if it is commercial property or property purchased as an investment (see *Laskar v Laskar* below).

Case precedent – *Abrahams v Trustee in Bankruptcy of Abrahams* [1999] BPIR 637

Facts: Mr and Mrs Abrahams joined a lottery syndicate at their local pub 'The Tudor Tavern' in East Preston. There was a list of 15 syndicate members who paid £1 each week. In October 1996, Mrs Abrahams left her husband but continued to pay her own £1 and £1 on behalf of her husband which she used to recover from him. However, after a quarrel, he refused to reimburse her.

The other syndicate members were aware of the situation and did not object when Mrs Abrahams continued to pay £2 with the intention that if the syndicate won a prize, she would be entitled to two shares. In March 1997, Mr Abrahams was declared bankrupt and in May 1997, the syndicate won approximately £3 million. Mrs Abrahams claimed two-fifteenths of the prize money but this was contested by the Trustee in Bankruptcy of Mr Abrahams who claimed one-fifteenth. It was held that in accordance with the presumption of a resulting trust, the ticket purchased in Mr Abrahams' name was held on presumed resulting trust for Mrs Abrahams.

Principle: Where a purchaser provides the money for the purchase of property in the name of another, that other holds the property on presumed resulting trust for the purchaser.

Application: This is a useful case to illustrate the presumption of a resulting trust in respect of personal property.

Presumed resulting trusts – voluntary transfer of property to another

This is very similar to purchasing property in the name of another except that the transferor transfers his own property gratuitously to the transferee, i.e. he does not purchase the property. However, notice that, in this case, a distinction is made between personal property and real property.

Personal property

Case precedent – *Re Vinogradoff* [1935] WN 68

Facts: Mrs Vinogradoff transferred stock worth £800 into the joint names of herself and her granddaughter, Laura Jackson, aged four years. Mrs Vinogradoff continued to receive the dividends until her death and it was unclear from the evidence why she had made the transfer. On her death, she left the stock to another person and the executors sought a declaration as to whether the granddaughter had an interest in the stock.

It was held that Laura held the stock on presumed resulting trust for Mrs Vinogradoff's estate. There was no evidence to rebut the presumption of a resulting trust.

Principle: A gratuitous transfer of personal property into the name of a transferee gives rise to a presumed resulting trust in favour of the transferor.

Application: It may be relevant to note when applying this decision that a resulting trustee may be a minor, as was the case with Laura Jackson.

Real property

Prior to the enactment of s 60(3) Law of Property Act 1925 below, if a transferor intended to transfer land gratuitously to a transferee, he had to use a special form of words in the conveyance. So, if Alan intended to make a voluntary transfer of land to Ben, he had to state that **the property was conveyed for the use or benefit** of Ben. If he failed to use these words, the land would be held by Ben on resulting trust for Alan (despite Alan's intention that it was a gift).

But then s 60(3) Law of Property Act 1925 was enacted as follows:

Section 60(3)

In a voluntary conveyance, a resulting trust for the grantor shall not be implied merely by reason that the property is not expressed to be conveyed for the use or benefit of the grantee.

Up for Debate

There is some uncertainty regarding the effect of s 60(3) **Law of Property Act 1925**.

❖ Has it **completely** removed the presumption of a resulting trust when there is a voluntary transfer of land to another; **or**
❖ Is it simply a word-saving section so that a resulting trust no longer arises **just because** the grantor failed to use the words 'for the use or benefit of the grantee'? In both *Lohia v Lohia* [2001] and *Ali v Khan* [2002] it has been suggested that this is the correct interpretation of s 60(3) and that there is nothing to prevent a resulting trust arising when there is other evidence indicating that the presumption arises. For an example of this, see *Hodgson v Marks* [1971] below.

Case precedent – *Hodgson v Marks* [1971] Ch 892

Facts: Mrs Hodgson, a widow aged 83, was the registered owner of a house. She had a lodger called Mr Evans, aged about 50, of whom she was fond but who was distrusted by her nephew, who also lived in the house. To protect Evans from her nephew, who wanted his aunt to evict Evans, she voluntarily transferred the house to Evans on the oral understanding that she owned the house even though legal title was now in Evans' name. Evans then sold the house to Marks, a bona fide purchaser, and the question arose as to whether Mrs Hodgson was protected against Marks by an overriding interest.

The Court of Appeal held that the voluntary transfer to Evans was not intended as a gift and a resulting trust of the beneficial interest arose in favour of Mrs Hodgson, which acted as an overriding interest because she was in occupation, and protected her against Marks.

Principle: Upon a voluntary transfer of land, a presumed resulting trust may still arise in accordance with the intention of the transferor.

Application: When applying this decision, you should mention that Mrs Hodgson could not argue that there had been a declaration of an **express** trust of land because, under s 53(1)(b) Law of Property Act 1925, such a declaration will be unenforceable unless it is evidenced in writing and signed by the settlor. You may recall from Chapter 3 that 'the creation and operation of **resulting** trusts . . .' are exempt from s 53(1) by reason of s 53(2) Law of Property Act 1925.

Rebutting the presumption of a resulting trust

It is important to remember that we have been looking at a **presumption** of a resulting trust and that a presumption is a standard inference made by the court that may be rebutted by evidence to the contrary. In the following example, Ben would try to rebut the presumption by adducing evidence that a gift was intended by Alan.

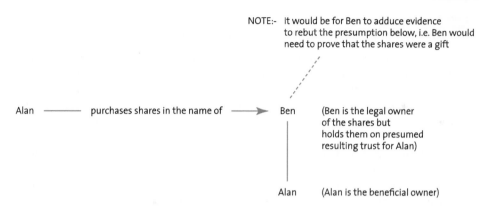

NOTE:- It would be for Ben to adduce evidence to rebut the presumption below, i.e. Ben would need to prove that the shares were a gift

Alan ——— purchases shares in the name of ——→ Ben (Ben is the legal owner of the shares but holds them on presumed resulting trust for Alan)

Alan (Alan is the beneficial owner)

The presumption of advancement

This presumption is the other way round to the presumption of a resulting trust, i.e. it is a presumption of a gift. However, it applies only when property is purchased or property gratuitously transferred in the following relationships:

Husband – to – Wife

Father – to – Child

Person *in loco parentis* – to – Child

So, if a husband purchases property in the name of his wife, it is presumed that this is a gift and it would be for the husband to rebut that presumption by evidence that he intended to retain a beneficial interest in the property, and that his wife therefore holds the property on resulting trust for him – see *Tinker v Tinker* [1970] below. If a wife purchased property in the name of her husband, the presumption of a resulting trust would apply.

As you can imagine, as between husbands and wives, the presumption of advancement has been widely criticised as it discriminates between the sexes. It was famously described by Lord Diplock in *Pettitt v Pettitt* [1970] as based 'on the mores of the propertied classes of the nineteenth century', having little relevance to modern life. It also contravenes Article 5 of the Seventh Protocol to the European Convention on Human Rights that 'spouses shall enjoy equality of rights'. It will eventually be abolished – see below.

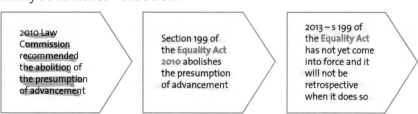

2010 Law Commission recommended the abolition of the presumption of advancement

Section 199 of the Equality Act 2010 abolishes the presumption of advancement

2013 – s 199 of the Equality Act has not yet come into force and it will not be retrospective when it does so

> ### Case precedent – *Tinker v Tinker* [1970] P136
>
> **Facts:** Mr Tinker bought a garage business in Cornwall. It was a new venture for him and, after consulting a solicitor, the house that Mr Tinker subsequently purchased was put in his wife's name to safeguard the house from the claims of creditors, should his garage business fail. However, when his marriage broke up, his wife claimed the house belonged to her. (There was no evidence that the business was in financial difficulty.)
>
> The Court of Appeal held that Mr Tinker was an honest man who, having purchased the house in his wife's name, could not claim as an honest man that he had always intended to retain a beneficial interest in it. Salmon J said, 'in this case, the husband's evidence, far from displacing the presumption has done much to reinforce it'.
>
> **Principle:** When the presumption of advancement arises, the burden of rebutting the presumption is on the transferor to prove that he intended to retain a beneficial interest in the property, i.e. that it was not a gift.
>
> **Application:** When applying this decision, it is useful to compare it with *Tribe v Tribe* [1995] and *Chettiar v Chettiar* [1962] below.

Purchases/transfers made for an illegal reason

We have been considering the situation where a person purchases/transfers property into the name of another, thus raising the presumption of a resulting trust or presumption of advancement depending on the relationship of the parties. Sometimes the purchase/transfer is part of an illegal scheme.

This is a popular area for assessment and a sample question follows.

David transfers his 1,000 shares to his son, Ben. This transaction is to enable David to carry out a tax fraud.

After the fraud has been committed, David asks Ben to return the shares but Ben refuses, relying on the presumption of advancement, i.e. that the shares were a gift.

Advise David of his legal position. How would your answer differ if Ben was David's brother?

To answer such a question, you need to be familiar with the key cases as follows:

> ### Case precedent – *Tinsley v Milligan* [1994] 1 AC 340
>
> **Facts:** Tinsley and Milligan, a lesbian couple, purchased a house, both contributing to the purchase price. However, the house was put into the sole name of Tinsley so that Milligan could pretend to be a lodger and make false claims for social welfare benefits.

After four years, their relationship broke down and Milligan claimed that Tinsley held the house on presumed resulting trust for both of them in equal shares. However, Tinsley claimed that Milligan's evidence of the illegal scheme was inadmissible and therefore Milligan could not claim a beneficial interest in the home.

The House of Lords held that Milligan did not need to rely on her illegal purpose in order to establish her beneficial interest. All she had to prove to raise a presumption of a resulting trust was that she had made a contribution to the purchase price of the property. It would then be up to Tinsley to adduce evidence to rebut the presumption (which she was unable to do).

Principle: When a person purchases property in the name of another/voluntarily transfers property to another, there is a presumption that the property is held on resulting trust for the purchaser/transferor and there is no need for that person to rely on the underlying illegal purpose. This so called 'reliance principle' was also applied in *Silverwood v Silverwood* [1997].

Application: It is important that you are able to contrast this case with the cases below and to evaluate the law in this area – see 'Aim Higher' box below.

Case precedent – *Tribe v Tribe* [1995] 3 WLR 913 CA

Facts: The parties in this case were father and son. The father owned 459 of a total of 500 shares in a family company and was the tenant of two properties where the company carried on business. The landlord of the properties served a notice of alleged dilapidations on the father, which would require him to carry out substantial repairs.

The father was advised that the cost of these repairs could lead to the loss of business assets and his own bankruptcy. In order to avoid his liability to the landlord, the father transferred his shares in the company (worth £78,030) to his son. Although the transfer was said to be made for consideration, it was in fact gratuitous. (Note: safeguarding assets from a creditor is illegal.)

As it happened, the father was not required to carry out the repairs and he sought to recover the shares from his son, who refused, pleading the presumption of advancement.

The Court of Appeal held that as the illegal purpose had not been carried out, the father could give evidence of his dishonest motive **and** that he had intended to retain a beneficial interest in the shares, i.e. he was taken to have withdrawn from the illegal transaction. Accordingly, the son held the shares on resulting trust for the father.

Principle: A transferor can give evidence of an illegal reason for a transfer provided he has withdrawn from the transaction before the illegal purpose has been wholly/partly carried out. This is known as the withdrawal principle.

Application: Note that the withdrawal principle applied although there had been no genuine repentance on the father's part. When citing *Tribe v Tribe*, it is useful to compare it with *Chettiar v Chettiar* [1962] below where the illegal transaction had been carried out.

Case precedent – *Chettiar v Chettiar* [1962] AC 294

Facts: This case between father and son was heard by the Privy Council on appeal from what was then Malaya. The father owned 99 acres of rubber plantation and wanted to purchase more acres. However, upon reaching a threshold of 100 acres, Government regulations would apply, controlling production of rubber. To avoid these regulations, the father purchased 40 more acres in the name of his son, although he intended to retain the beneficial interest in those acres. The Privy Council held that the father could not rebut the presumption of advancement as he would have to rely on his fraudulent intention to avoid the regulations.

Principle: Where property is purchased or transferred into another's name for a fraudulent or illegal purpose and the presumption of advancement applies, the purchaser/transferor cannot rebut the presumption by relying on evidence of his fraudulent/illegal plan if this has been carried out.

Application: It is useful to compare this decision with *Tinsley v Milligan* in which the presumption of a resulting trust applied, which meant that the claimant did not have to rely on her illegality.

The following diagram illustrates how the claimant's success in recovering his property depends on which presumption applies.

Tinsley v Milligan	Chettiar v Chettiar	Tribe v Tribe
Presumption of resulting trust	Presumption of advancement	Presumption of advancement
Illegal plan carried out but claimant recovered property that had been transferred	Illegal plan carried out but claimant could not recover property that had been transferred	Claimant taken to have withdrawn from illegal plan and could recover property that had been transferred

Aim Higher

Firstly, when applying the law in this area, you should mention that the above distinction (which depends on which presumption applies) is clearly arbitrary and unfair.

Secondly, regarding *Tribe v Tribe*, you should mention that the withdrawal principle applied although there was no genuine repentance on the part of the transferor.

Thirdly, be aware of the Law Commission's recommendations for reform, most recently in its 2010 Report No. 320 – *The Illegality Defence*. One of its recommendations was that the presumption of advancement should be abolished and this will take effect when s 199 **Equality Act 2010** eventually comes into force. Although its other recommendation will not be adopted in the foreseeable future, it is worth noting it, i.e. that the courts should be given a **statutory discretion** to decide the effect of illegality when a trust is created in connection with a criminal purpose, and that the discretion should apply whether or not the criminal purpose has been carried out. In exercising the statutory discretion, the Law Commission recommended that the courts should take into account certain factors including:

❖ The conduct and intention of all the parties
❖ The value of the equitable interest at stake
❖ The effect of allowing the claimant to recover the assets.

A Quistclose trust

A Quistclose trust typically arises when an unsecured loan has been made for a specified purpose, as occurred in the case that gave its name to the Quistclose trust, i.e. *Barclays Bank Ltd v Quistclose Investments Ltd* [1970] AC 567.

You need to know the facts and decision of the case, the advantages and disadvantages of a Quistclose trust, and some of the problems regarding the nature of a Quistclose trust as follows:

Fact 1 – Rolls Razor had an overdraft of £484,000 with Barclays Bank (which exceeded their overdraft limit)

Rolls Razor Ltd ←———————————— Quistclose Investments Ltd

Fact 2 – However, Rolls Razor had declared a dividend to be paid to its shareholders

Fact 3 – Quistclose agreed to lend Rolls Razor £209,719 to be used solely for the purpose of paying the dividend

Fact 4 – It was agreed that the loan should be paid into a separate account at Barclays. The bank was aware of the purpose of the loan

Fact 5 – Before the dividend was paid, Rolls Razor went into liquidation

Fact 6 – Quistclose sought to recover the loan but this was opposed by Barclays who claimed a right to set off the money against the overdraft

The House of Lords held that the money had been received by Rolls Razor on a primary trust to use the loan to pay the dividend. As the primary trust had failed, a secondary trust of the money arose in favour of Quistclose, who were therefore entitled as beneficiary to recover the £209,719.

The advantages of a Quistclose trust

- The lender has security until the loan is spent on the specified purpose, whereupon the relationship becomes one of creditor–debtor.

- This security encourages commercial loans to be made for specific purposes and may prevent the bankruptcy/insolvency of the recipient.

- Unlike the normal secured loan (when a charge is registered), the Quistclose trust does not require registration – so there is no public knowledge of the loan transaction.

The disadvantages of a Quistclose trust

- The loan/Quistclose trust (which, as we have seen above, does not require registration) could give a false impression of the borrower's financial situation, leading to the company incurring further liability to creditors.

- If the loan was not used for its proper purpose, the lender would have a proprietary interest in that loan under the Quistclose trust and would enjoy priority over creditors of the borrower. This could be regarded as unfair with respect to those creditors.

Some of the problems relating to the nature of a Quistclose trust are explained in the following question and answer diagrams.

Question: Is the primary trust a purpose trust?

❖ **Answer:** It cannot be a purpose trust because non-charitable purpose trusts are void. Therefore, it must be a private trust.

Question: If it is a private trust, who is the beneficiary?

❖ **Answer:**
❖ The beneficiaries cannot be the shareholders of Rolls Razor because they could have terminated the trust under the rule in *Saunders v Vautier*
❖ Similarly, Rolls Razor could not be the beneficiary because it too could have terminated the trust under the rule in *Saunders v Vautier*
❖ The beneficiary must therefore be the lender, Quistclose, until the borrower uses the money for its proper purpose. The trustee is the borrower. The settlor is Quistclose.

What kind of trust is the primary trust?

Is it an express trust, the borrower having the power to use the money for a specified purpose?	Is it a resulting trust?	Is it a constructive trust?
❖ *Problem: an express trust requires on intention to create such a trust by the settlor (Quistclose), and this was not spelt out in the loan agreement.*	❖ It was stated in *Twinsectra v Yardley* [2002] that a resulting trust exists when the money is lent but is subject to the recipient's power to apply the money for the specified purpose, failing which the money results back to the lender. ❖ *Problem: As the lender, Quistclose is the beneficiary throughout, the money does not 'result back' to it as resulting trusts are supposed to do.*	❖ In *Carreras Rothmans v Freeman Matthews Treasure* [1985] it was suggested that it was a constructive trust. ❖ *Problem: Constructive trusts arise as a result of the inequitable conduct of the borrower. How can there be a constructive trust in this case before the borrower has failed to use the money for the specified purpose?*

The fact remains that the Quistclose trust has been applied in a number of cases including *Carreras Rothmans v Freeman Matthews Treasure* [1985] 1 Ch 207, *Re EVTR Ltd* [1987] BCLC 646 and *Twinsectra Ltd v Yardley* [2002] UKLH 12 (see Chapter 7 for more on *Twinsectra*).

Putting it into practice

David transfers his 1,000 Abbott shares to his son, Ben, solely to enable David to carry out a tax fraud. After the fraud has been committed, David asks Ben to return the shares but Ben refuses, relying on the presumption of advancement.

(a) Advise David of his legal position.
(b) How would your answer differ if Ben was David's brother rather than his son?

Feedback on putting it into practice

When David transferred the shares to his son, the presumption of advancement would apply, i.e. it would be assumed that the shares were a gift		It would be for David to rebut this presumption by proving that he intended to retain the beneficial interest in the shares.		He would be unable to do so because his evidence that he transferred the shares for an illegal reason would be inadmissible. The case to cite is *Chettiar v Chettiar*.

If Ben was David's brother, then the presumption of a resulting trust would apply. All David would have to show was that he gratuitously transferred the shares to Ben		David would not need to rely on evidence of his tax fraud. It would be for Ben to rebut the presumption by evidence that the transfer was a gift. The case to cite is *Tinsley v Milligan*

You could conclude by mentioning that the presumption of advancement will be abolished when s 199 Equality Act 2010 comes into force

After that time, the presumption of a resulting trust will apply to both the son and brother. You could also outline the Law Commission's recommendations

Table of key cases referred to in this chapter

Case name	Area of law	Principle
Abbott Trust Funds, Re [1900]	Surplus funds	Surplus funds held on resulting trust for identifiable donors
Abrahams v Trustee in Bankruptcy of Abrahams [1999]	Presumed resulting trust	Presumed resulting trust for purchaser when lottery ticket purchased in the name of another
Ames's Settlement, Re [1946]	Automatic resulting trust	Purpose of express trust failed and property held on automatic resulting trust for settlor
Barclays Bank Ltd v Quistclose Investments Ltd [1970]	Quistclose trust	Unsecured loan for a specific purpose held on trust for lender until used for stated purpose
Boyce v Boyce [1849]	Automatic resulting trust	Express trust failed for uncertainty of beneficial interest and property held on resulting trust for settlor
Chettiar v Chettiar [1962]	Presumption of advancement	Transferor unable to rely on illegal purpose to rebut the presumption of advancement
Gillingham Bus Disaster Fund, Re [1958]	Surplus funds	Surplus funds held on resulting trust for donors even though many were anonymous
Hodgson v Marks [1971]	Presumed resulting trust	Voluntary transfer of real property gave rise to a presumed resulting trust
Laskar v Laskar [2008]	Resulting trust	Resulting trust still relevant when claiming a beneficial interest in investment property
Tinker v Tinker [1970]	Presumption of advancement	Transferor could not prove that he intended to retain a beneficial interest in the property

Tinsley v Milligan [1994]	Presumed resulting trust	Claimant could claim a beneficial interest under the presumed resulting trust without relying on evidence of illegal scheme
Tribe v Tribe [1995]	Presumption of advancement	Claimant could rebut the presumption by evidence of illegal scheme from which he had withdrawn
Twinsectra Ltd v Yardley [2002]	Quistclose trust	Quistclose trust regarded as a resulting trust subject to the borrower's power to apply loan for specified purpose
Vandervell's Trusts No 2 [1974]	Resulting trusts	Classification of automatic and presumed resulting trusts.
Vinogradoff, Re [1935]	Presumed resulting trust	Presumed resulting trust arising on a voluntary transfer of property
Westdeutsche Landesbank v Islington LBC [1998]	Resulting trusts	*Dicta* that automatic resulting trusts are based on the presumed intention of the settlor

---

@ Visit the book's companion website to test your knowledge

❖ Resources include a subject map, revision tip podcasts, downloadable diagrams, MCQ quizzes for each chapter, and a flashcard glossary

❖ www.routledge.com/cw/optimizelawrevision

7

Constructive Trusts

Revision objectives

Understand the law	• Can you explain the difference between a remedial and institutional constructive trust? • Are you able to identify and explain the cases concerning a fiduciary who makes an unauthorised profit?
Remember the details	• Do you recall the key cases on dishonestly assisting with a breach of trust? • Can you identify the different interpretations of the test of dishonesty in those key cases?
Reflect critically on areas of debate	• Are you able to reflect critically on the decision in *Boardman v Phipps*? • Are you able to evaluate the decision in *Attorney General for Hong Kong v Reid*?
Contextualise	• Can you explain the reason why the law imposes a constructive trust in the context of mutual wills and secret trusts? • Are you able to distinguish between a proprietary remedy and a personal remedy to account?
Apply your skills and knowledge	• Are you able to answer the essay question at the end of this chapter?

Chapter Map

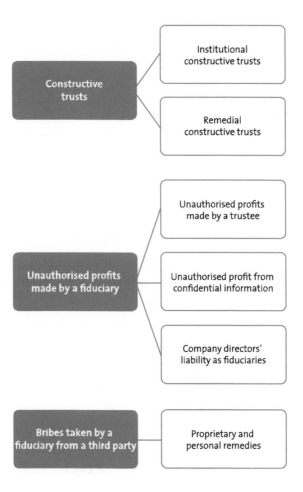

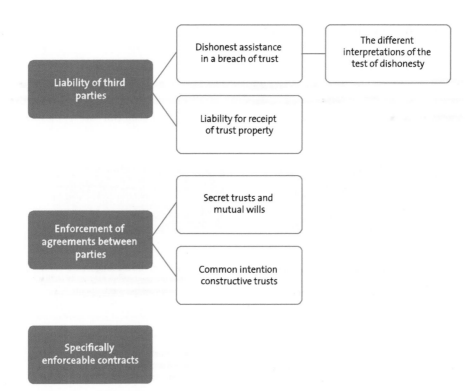

Introduction to constructive trusts

How are constructive trusts created?

Unlike express trusts, constructive trusts are not created expressly but come about by **operation of the law**. In *Westdeutsche Landesbank* [1996], Lord Browne-Wilkinson described a constructive trust as a trust 'which the law imposes on the trustee by reason of his unconscionable conduct'.

Institutional or remedial?

In Canada, Australia and New Zealand, the constructive trust is regarded as remedial, whereas, under English law, the constructive trust is traditionally regarded as institutional. The meaning and implications of this distinction are explained in the diagram below.

Remedial constructive trust	Institutional constructive trust
Meaning: The constructive trust is an equitable remedy awarded in the discretion of the court	**Meaning:** The constructive trust arises from the operation of established legal rules when specific events occur
This remedy is awarded by the court to prevent unjust enrichment by the defendant	The court recognises that the claimant has a pre-existing proprietary right on the occurrence of those specific events
The remedy is awarded as a matter of discretion by the court and is not retrospective	The claimant's proprietary right pre-exists the court's judgment, which simply recognises that proprietary right
As the constructive trust exists from the date of the court order, it does not affect third-party rights acquired before that order	As the court recognises a pre-existing proprietary right, this type of constructive trust does affect third-party interests acquired after the events that gave rise to the claimant's proprietary right

Aim Higher

If you are required to discuss the remedial constructive trust, you could mention that when Lord Denning was sitting in the Court of Appeal in the 1970s, he developed the 'new model constructive trust', which he regarded as remedial. In *Hussey v Palmer* [1972], he said that such a trust would be imposed 'whenever justice and good conscience require it … it is an equitable remedy by which the court can enable an aggrieved party to obtain restitution'.

This new model constructive trust was much criticised at the time because the concept of 'good conscience' is subjective and depends on the moral view of the particular presiding judge, which could lead to uncertainty in the law. In *Springette v Defoe* [1992], Dillon J, referring to the new model constructive trust, said 'The court does not as yet sit, as under a palm tree, to exercise a general discretion to do what the man in the street, on a general overview of the case, might regard as fair.' The new model constructive trust was not invoked after the retirement of Lord Denning in 1982.

Main categories of the institutional constructive trust

We will be revising the main categories as shown in the following diagram.

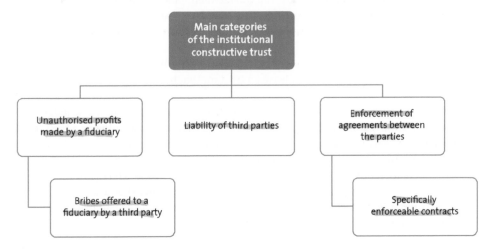

Unauthorised profits made by a fiduciary

There is no comprehensive definition of a fiduciary but, broadly, a fiduciary is someone who undertakes to act in relation to the property of another in a relationship of good faith and trust. It follows that a fiduciary must not put himself in a position where his duty to his principal and his own interests conflict. Nor must he make an unauthorised profit from his position and, if he does, the rule is very strict and he will be liable to account for that profit.

The following diagram gives examples of fiduciary relationships that will be considered in this chapter.

The fiduciary	His principal
Trustee	Beneficiary
Solicitor	Client
Director	Company
Agent	Principal

Unauthorised profits made by a trustee

The classic case is *Keech v Sandford* [1726]. In fact, the rule that a trustee must not make an unauthorised profit is sometimes referred to as the rule in *Keech v Sandford*.

Case precedent – *Keech v Sandford* [1726] Sel.Cas. Ch 61 Ct of Chancery

Facts: A trustee held a lease of the profits of Romford market on trust for an infant. Shortly before the lease expired, the trustee applied to the landlord for its renewal but, whilst the landlord was willing to renew the lease in favour of the trustee, he refused to renew it for the benefit of the infant. The trustee therefore took the lease himself. This was challenged by the infant who successfully sought to have the lease assigned to him together with an account of the profits made by the trustee since its renewal.

Principle: A trustee who renews, in his own favour, a lease that was previously held on trust for a beneficiary will hold that lease on trust for that beneficiary.

Application: When you cite this case, it is useful to remember the words of the judge as these explain the reason for the decision. Lord King LC: 'I must consider this as a trust for the infant, for I very well see, if a trustee, on the refusal to renew, might have a lease to himself, few trust estates would be renewed to *cestui que* use (the beneficiary) … This may seem hard, that the trustee is the only person of all mankind who might not have the lease, but it is very proper that the rule should be strictly pursued, and not in the least relaxed; for it is very obvious what would be the consequences of letting trustees have the lease on refusal to renew to *cestui que* use.'

The same principle applies when a trustee of a lease purchases the freehold for his own benefit. The case that illustrates this is *Protheroe v Protheroe* [1968] below.

Case precedent – *Protheroe v Protheroe* [1968] 1 WLR 519

Facts: The parties married in 1954 and bought a 44-year lease of a house for £1,375 in the husband's name. The wife paid the deposit of £300 and the husband paid the mortgage repayments. Ten years later, the wife filed for divorce. While divorce proceedings were going on, the husband, with the aid of a mortgage, purchased the freehold of the house on his own account.

The husband (as legal owner) held the leasehold on trust jointly with his wife, and the Court of Appeal held that the husband, **being in the position of trustee**, could not claim to be wholly entitled to the difference between the value of the house as a leasehold and as a freehold, although he would be reimbursed for any payment he had made for the freehold.

Principle: The rule in *Keech v Sandford* extends to the purchase by a trustee of the freehold reversion of property, the leasehold of which is held in trust.

Application: This decision may also be useful to know when answering questions on ownership of the family home dealt with in the next chapter.

Unauthorised profit made using confidential information

The next case, *Boardman v Phipps* [1967], involved a solicitor employed by trustees and illustrates the inflexibility and strictness of the rule that a fiduciary should not make an unauthorised profit.

Case precedent – *Boardman v Phipps* [1967] 2 AC 46

Facts: Charles Phipps, the testator, established a trust for his widow for life, remainder to his four children. There were three trustees – his widow, his daughter and a professional trustee – and they employed Thomas Boardman as solicitor.

The trust held 8,000 shares in a private textile company, Lester & Harris Ltd, which had an issued share capital of 30,000 shares. Thomas Boardman and one of the beneficiaries, Tom Phipps, acquired information about the company that was not available to the public and decided that they could increase the profitability of the company if they had a controlling interest. As the trustees had no power under the trust instrument to purchase further shares, after long negotiations with the company, Boardman and Tom Phipps bought the remaining shares themselves and proceeded to reorganise the company. This was done with the knowledge of only two of the trustees, the widow being senile and taking no part in the administration of the trust.

Some of the assets of the company were subsequently sold off at a considerable profit and substantial sums of capital were paid to shareholders, Boardman making a profit of approximately £75,000, and £47,000 for the trust.

Following a claim by the one of the beneficiaries, John Phipps, the House of Lords by a majority of 3:2 held that Boardman was a constructive trustee of the profit he had made and should account for that profit to the trust.

Principle: A fiduciary who makes use of confidential information belonging to the trust or who takes advantage of an opportunity acquired in a fiduciary position will be liable for any profit he makes.

Application: When applying this case you could mention that the House of Lords recognised that Boardman had increased the value of the trust assets and therefore authorised generous remuneration on a *quantum meruit* basis. This case often arises in assessment and you should be aware of the issues raised – see the 'Up for Debate' box below.

Up for Debate

The decision in *Boardman v Phipps* [1966] raised a number of issues that were either not explicitly dealt with by their Lordships or were a matter of dissent between them, and that have since been the subject of much debate by legal commentators.

First – to whom did Boardman owe a fiduciary duty? He was employed as solicitor to the trustees and therefore owed a fiduciary duty to them, yet the claimant who alleged that Boardman was in breach of his fiduciary duty was not a trustee but one of the beneficiaries, John Phipps. It has therefore been suggested that Boardman owed a separate fiduciary duty to the trust (and therefore to the beneficiaries) arising from his attendance at Lester & Harris company meetings when purporting to represent the trust.

Second – what was the basis of Boardman's liability, i.e. how did he breach his fiduciary duty to the beneficiaries? One basis was misuse of trust property, which enabled him to make an unauthorised profit. The majority of their Lordships took the view that the confidential information about Lester & Harris, and the opportunity to acquire that information, had arisen from Boardman's attendance at company meetings when representing the trust. That information was trust property that had subsequently been used by Boardman in his personal capacity to make a private gain. Two of their Lordships dissented and it has been questioned whether information of this sort can in fact be regarded as property. The second possible basis of Boardman's liability was a conflict of interest, i.e. between his duty to the beneficiaries and his personal interest. Against this, it is argued that when Boardman purchased the company shares, the trustees had already made it clear that the trust did not have the power to purchase these shares itself (as Boardman had recommended). This basis of liability seemed to rest on the remote possibility that some time in the future the trustees might seek Boardman's advice regarding the purchase of shares in the company.

Third – who could have authorised the profit made by Boardman? Reference was made by their Lordships to escaping liability by full disclosure and consent by other parties, without clearly identifying whether those other parties were the trustees or the beneficiaries. As it happened, because one of the trustees was senile, only two of the trustees had been informed of Boardman's plan to purchase the shares and reorganise the company, and it transpired that the beneficiaries had not received *detailed* information of Boardman's plan.

Company directors – liability as fiduciaries

Directors are in a fiduciary relationship with their company and, as such, they have a duty of good faith and a duty to avoid a conflict of interest. This fiduciary duty, together with directors' other duties, has now been codified in the Companies Act 2006 in order to make the law more understandable and certain.

Section 175 of the **Companies Act** sets out the duty of a director to avoid a situation in which he has, or could have, an interest that conflicts with the interests of the company, which includes the exploitation of any property, information or opportunity, immaterial of whether the company could take advantage of such property, information or opportunity. The Act confirms that there is no breach of duty if the matter has been authorised by the directors according to the authorisation conditions set out in s 175(4)–(6).

The fiduciary duty as it is appears in the Act is based on former equitable principles and is interpreted having regard to old case law. For that reason, some of the more important cases are considered below.

Case precedent – *Regal (Hastings) Ltd v Gulliver* [1942] 2 AC 134

Facts: Regal owned one cinema in Hastings and wanted to acquire two more with a view to selling the three cinemas together. To that end, they formed a subsidiary company to buy the two cinemas but, as it transpired, had insufficient capital to purchase the cinemas. Four of the directors of Regal bought some of the shares in the subsidiary, thus providing the necessary capital. The cinemas were purchased and Regal and the subsidiary were taken over, with the directors making a substantial profit on the sale of their shares.

The new controllers of Regal brought this action to recover the profits that the directors had made on the sale of the shares, alleging that the directors were in breach of their fiduciary duty to the company.

The House of Lords held that although the directors had acted in good faith and had secured a benefit for Regal when they supplied the capital to purchase the cinemas, the rule that a fiduciary should not make an unauthorised profit was strict, and they were liable to account for the profit they had made.

Principle: Company directors are fiduciaries and should not make an unauthorised profit from their position.

Application: Note that it was irrelevant that the company itself could not provide the capital to buy the shares and that the directors acted in good faith and for the benefit of the company throughout when taking advantage of this opportunity. Note that the four directors had not received formal authorisation from Regal to pursue this opportunity.

Some Commonwealth jurisdictions have not adopted such a strict approach. The British Colombia Court of Appeal heard the case of *Peso Silver Mines Ltd v Cropper* [1966] in which a board of directors bona fides rejected a corporate opportunity to purchase a mine. This opportunity was then taken up by one of the directors personally as a member of a syndicate and proved to be very profitable. The Court held that as the board had rejected the offer to purchase the mine, it was no longer a corporate opportunity and the defendant director was not liable to account for the profit he had made.

A similar decision was reached in Australia in *Queensland Mines Ltd v Hudson* [1978] and now seems to be contained in s 175(4) of the **Companies Act 2006**, which states that there is no breach 'if the situation cannot reasonably be regarded as likely to give rise to a conflict of interest'.

A case in which the director did not act in good faith and took advantage of a corporate opportunity is *IDC v Cooley* [1972] below.

Case precedent – *IDC v Cooley* [1972] 1 WLR 443

Facts: Cooley, the managing director of IDC, was in negotiations (on behalf of IDC) with the Eastern Gas Board regarding a project. The Gas Board subsequently suggested that Cooley bid for the contract personally as the Board did not want to deal with IDC. Cooley pretended to be ill so that he could leave IDC at short notice, took up the contract with the Gas Board and made a large personal profit. The court held that Cooley was liable to account for the profits he had made on the contract. Cooley was in breach of his fiduciary duty as director because, although the opportunity of the contract was offered to him personally, he had acquired information of the opportunity in his capacity as managing director of IDC. He should both have disclosed that information to IDC and endeavoured to obtain the contract for them.

Principle: A fiduciary must not take advantage of an opportunity or information that he receives in his fiduciary capacity and that is of commercial value to his principal.

Application: When applying this decision, you should stress that the principle above applies even when the opportunity is presented to the fiduciary personally, as was the case with Cooley.

We pause now to consider the claimant's remedies as these will be particularly relevant when we come to our last fiduciary – an agent, who, in breach of his fiduciary duty to his principal, accepts a bribe from a third party.

Proprietary and personal remedies available to the claimant

Proprietary remedy	Personal remedy
The Imposition of a constructive trust is a proprietary remedy. The court recognises that the claimant has a pre-existing proprietary interest which the defendant holds on constructive trust.	If no property has been vested in the defendant, the remedy against the defendant is personal, e.g. the fiduciary will be liable to account for any unauthorised profit that he made from his position.
Strictly therefore, a person can only be a constructive trustee if specific property is vested in him.	This order to account both quantifies the profit or loss, and requires the defendant to pay.

As the court is recognising a pre-existing proprietary interest, this gives the claimant priority over third parties who subsequently acquire an interest in the property.	The process of tracing is not applicable.
If the constructive trustee is bankrupt, the property held by him on constructive trust is not available to pay his creditors, i.e. it is not the trustee's personal property.	If the defendant is insolvent, there is no point in the claimant seeking an order to account.
If the property subject to the constructive trust is disposed of by the constructive trustee and is subsequently represented by some other property in the trustee's hands or it has passed to a third-party volunteer (i.e. not a bona fide purchaser for value without notice of the trust), then the claimant may be able to use the tracing process to trace the original property into that for which it has been exchanged. If this is not possible, the claimant will have no option but to pursue a personal action against the trustee.	
The tracing process will enable the claimant to maintain a proprietary interest in the asset acquired by the defendant upon disposal of the property subject to the constructive trust – regardless of its value.	

Unfortunately, in many cases involving fiduciaries, the court has not made it clear whether the case is one of constructive trust or liability to account, and uses the terminology of both. This was particularly evident in *Boardman v Phipps* [1966] where reference was made by the court to Boardman being **a constructive trustee** with **liability to account** for the profit he made.

Bribes taken by a fiduciary from a third party
The following diagram illustrates the situation.

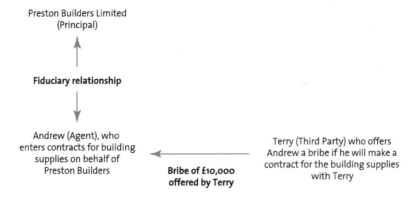

Andrew accepts the bribe and invests the £10,000 in shares that are now worth £20,000. Preston finds out about the bribe and brings an action against Andrew for breach of his fiduciary duty.

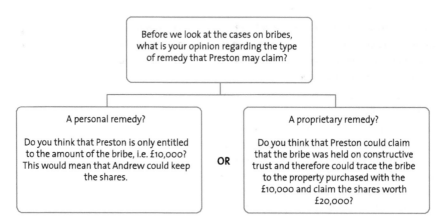

The first case we consider on bribes is *Lister & Co v Stubbs* [1890].

Case precedent – *Lister & Co v Stubbs* [1890] 45 Ch D 1

Facts: Stubbs was employed as a purchasing agent by Lister & Co. He accepted a bribe of £5,500 from a third party with whom he placed business, and then invested the bribe profitably in land and securities. The issue for the court was whether Stubbs was a constructive trustee of the bribe, which would enable Lister & Co to trace the bribe to the investments. The Court of Appeal held that Lister & Co had no proprietary interest in the bribe and therefore could not claim the investments. It stated that the relationship between Lister & Co and Stubbs was one of creditor and debtor, which entitled the claimant to a personal remedy only equivalent to the amount of the bribe.

Principle: A fiduciary who accepts a bribe is liable only to a personal claim by his principal to pay over the amount of the bribe.

Application: You should mention that this decision was highly criticised because the fiduciary benefited from his breach of duty. It is important to note that this was a Court of Appeal decision, which is binding on English courts (excluding the House of Lords/ Supreme Court).

The next case, *Attorney General for Hong Kong v Reid* [1994], was heard by the Privy Council. Its decisions are highly persuasive but are not binding on English courts.

Case precedent – *Attorney General for Hong Kong v Reid* [1994] 1 All ER 1

Facts: Reid was employed as the Director of Public Prosecutions in Hong Kong. In breach of his fiduciary duty to the Crown, he accepted bribes amounting to approximately New Zealand $540,000 to obstruct the prosecution of certain criminals. He invested this money in land in New Zealand, which increased in value to New Zealand $2.4 million. He was subsequently convicted and sentenced to eight years in prison. The Attorney General for Hong Kong claimed the land in New Zealand was held on constructive trust for Reid's employer, the Crown. In the Privy Council, Lord Templeman was able to award such a proprietary remedy on the following basis. Reid was under a fiduciary duty to give the bribes to his employer as soon as he received them. Relying on the maxim 'Equity regards as done that which ought to have been done', Lord Templeman held that it would therefore be deemed that the Crown had acquired an equitable proprietary interest in the bribes, enabling the bribes to be traced to the land in New Zealand.

Principle: The receipt of a bribe by a fiduciary leads to a constructive trust (i.e. a proprietary remedy).

Application: It is important to be able to criticise the decision – see the 'Up for Debate' box below.

Up for Debate

Chief amongst the criticisms of the decision in *Attorney General for Hong Kong v Reid* was its unfair effect if the defendant fiduciary was bankrupt and the principal (the claimant) had a proprietary interest in the bribe. As the claimant could trace the bribe to the fiduciary's assets purchased with the bribe, not only would the claimant become entitled to an unexpected windfall, but unsecured creditors of the defendant would be deprived of assets to satisfy the debts owed to them by the defendant.

For further criticisms of the decision, see A Oakley (1994), 53 Cambridge Law Journal 31.

As mentioned above, Privy Council decisions are persuasive, not binding, whereas the Court of Appeal is bound by its own past decisions unless they were made *per incuriam* (i.e. a decision of the court that is mistaken).

It was therefore significant when, in 2011, the case of *Sinclair Investments (UK) Ltd v Versailles Trade Finance Ltd (In Administration)* came before the Court of Appeal and required the court to decide whether it should follow *Attorney General for Hong Kong v Reid* or *Lister & Co v Stubbs*. The following diagram contains extracts from Lord Neuberger's judgment, explaining some of the reasons why he decided the Court of Appeal should follow *Lister v Stubbs*.

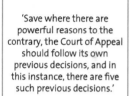

'Save where there are powerful reasons to the contrary, the Court of Appeal should follow its own previous decisions, and in this instance, there are five such previous decisions.'

'It seems to me that there is a real case for saying that the decision in *Reid* is unsound. In cases where a fiduciary takes for himself an asset which ... he was under a duty to take for the beneficiary, it is easy to see why the asset should be treated as the property of the beneficiary. However, a bribe paid to a fiduciary could not possibly be said to be an asset that the fiduciary was under a duty to take for the beneficiary.'

'It seems to me that Lord Templeman may have given insufficient weight to the potentially unfair consequences to the interests of other creditors...'

Lord Neuberger said that 'as a matter of equitable policy, a fiduciary should not be allowed to profit from his breach of duties, even to the extent of retaining any profit from such an asset after compensating a claimant in full. If that is indeed correct, then it seems to me that this should be dealt with by extending, or adjusting, the rules relating to equitable compensation rather than those relating to proprietary interests'. Note that equitable compensation is a personal remedy and would not therefore affect the rights of creditors of the false fiduciary.

Liability of third parties

This category of institutional constructive trust is sometimes referred to as 'Strangers intermeddling with trust property'. There are two sub-divisions to this category, as the following diagram illustrates.

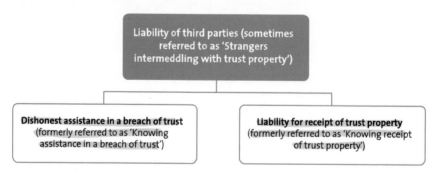

Liability of third parties (sometimes referred to as 'Strangers intermeddling with trust property')

Dishonest assistance in a breach of trust (formerly referred to as 'Knowing assistance in a breach of trust')

Liability for receipt of trust property (formerly referred to as 'Knowing receipt of trust property')

Dishonest assistance in a breach of trust

We are now concerned with a third party who dishonestly assists a trustee in the commission of a breach of trust. The third party does not receive the trust property and it is something of a misnomer to call him a constructive trustee. The beneficiary cannot bring a proprietary claim against the third party because the trust property was never vested in him. However, the beneficiary can bring a personal action against the third party, requiring him to make good any loss he caused to the trust fund.

In *Grupo Torras SA v Al Sabah* [1999], Mance LJ said that four elements must be proved by the claimant:

❖ A breach of trust by the trustee
❖ Assistance in that breach by the third party
❖ Dishonesty on the part of the third party
❖ Resulting loss to the claimant.

We will now look at the facts of the three key cases and then discuss the third element of this action, i.e. the need to prove dishonesty on the part of the third party.

Case precedent – *Royal Brunei Airlines Sdn Bhd v Tan* [1995] 2 AC 378

Facts: The Borneo Leisure Travel Agency (BLT) acted as an agent for Royal Brunei Airlines, selling the airlines' tickets and holding the proceeds on express trust for the airlines until such time as they were paid over.

BLT fell into financial difficulty and used the airlines' ticket money to pay its staff salaries and to reduce its overdraft. This constituted the breach of trust. BLT was insolvent and there was no point in the airlines suing the company. However, the airlines sued Mr Tan, who was the majority shareholder of BLT and its managing director, who had authorised the misuse of the trust funds.

The Privy Council held that Mr Tan was personally liable as a third party dishonestly assisting in BLT's breach of trust.

Principle: A third party who dishonestly assists a trustee in a breach of trust is liable whether or not the trustee is also dishonest.

Application: Remember to mention that this is a Privy Council decision and also to discuss the requirement of dishonesty on the part of the third party – for which, see below. This case clarified that it is not necessary to prove dishonesty on the part of the trustee in order to make the third party liable as *dicta* by Lord Selborne in *Barnes v Addy* [1874] had suggested.

Case precedent – *Twinsectra Ltd v Yardley* [2002] AC 164

Facts: Twinsectra agreed to lend £1 million to Yardley to enable him to purchase land in Bradford. The money was held by Sims (a solicitor associated with Yardley) **on trust** following an undertaking by Sims to Twinsectra that the money would be used solely for the purpose of purchasing the land.

In breach of trust, Sims released the money to Leach (Yardley's solicitor who was dealing with the sale of the land and knew of the above undertaking), who then released the money to Yardley, who used part of the money to pay off a debt.

Yardley failed to repay the loan to Twinsectra, which sued all parties, i.e. including Sims, who it alleged was in breach of trust, and Leach, as a third party who had dishonestly assisted in a breach of trust. The House of Lords held that Leach had not acted dishonestly according to the following principle.

Principle: The claimant has to prove that the defendant was dishonest by the standards of honest and reasonable people and that he himself was aware that his conduct was dishonest by those standards.

Application: Remember to mention that this is a House of Lords decision. We shall see below when we consider the test of dishonesty that the above principle was reinterpreted in the following case – *Barlow Clowes*.

Case precedent – *Barlow Clowes International v Eurotrust International* [2006] 1 WLR 1476

Facts: Through a company based in Gibralter, Peter Clowes operated a fraudulent offshore investment scheme that offered high returns. Many small investors in the UK were attracted by the Barlow Clowes investment scheme but much of the £140 million invested by them was paid into bank accounts of companies on the Isle of Man and dissipated by Peter Clowes and his associates. These associates were directors of the International Trust Corporation that administered the Isle of Man companies through which much of the funds of Barlow Clowes International passed.

In 1987, the fraudulent scheme finally collapsed and Peter Clowes was convicted and sent to prison. An action was brought against two of the directors of International Trust Corporation, Henwood and Sebastian, that they dishonestly assisted Peter Clowes in misappropriating investors' funds.

This appeal to the Privy Council from the Court of Appeal on the Isle of Man related to Henwood's claim that he did not regard his conduct to be dishonest according to the *Twinsectra* test of dishonesty (see principle above). The Privy Council held that by the ordinary standards of reasonable people, the passing of the investment monies through the bank accounts of the companies on the Isle of Man would have been regarded as suspicious and that Henwood had acted dishonestly.

Principle: If, by ordinary standards, a defendant's mental state would be characterised as dishonest, it is irrelevant that the defendant judges it by different standards.

Application: Clearly it is important to discuss the requirement of dishonesty when citing this case and how dishonesty has been interpreted by the courts in the key cases – see below.

The requirement of dishonesty on the part of the third party
In all three cases mentioned above, the courts discussed the test of dishonesty at length and it is important to understand it.

Aim Higher

For higher marks, you should be aware of the tests of dishonesty in the context of third-party liability. As the diagram below illustrates, there are three possible tests of dishonesty: a purely objective test, a purely subjective test and a combined test.

Secondly, you should be aware of how dishonesty has been interpreted in the three key cases *Royal Brunei Airlines v Tan* [1995], *Twinsectra Ltd v Yardley* [2002] and *Barlow Clowes International v Eurotrust International* [2006] – see the second diagram below.

Thirdly, you should be aware that the combined test as stated in *Royal Brunei Airlines v Tan* and endorsed in *Barlow Clowes International v Eurotrust International* represents the current test of dishonesty – see comment below.

The three tests of dishonesty in this context

The purely objective test of dishonesty	The purely subjective test of dishonesty	The combined test of dishonesty
'…acting dishonestly … means simply not acting as an honest person would in the circumstances. This is the objective standard'. Lord Nicholls in *Royal Brunei Airlines v Tan* [1995].	'…a purely subjective standard, whereby a person is only regarded as dishonest if he transgresses his own standard of honesty, even if that standard is contrary to that of reasonable and honest people'. Lord Nicholls in *Royal Brunei Airlines v Tan*. This is sometimes called the Robin Hood defence.	An objective approach, i.e. not acting as an honest person would in the circumstances, and with a subjective element, i.e. taking account of the defendant's intelligence, experience and what he knew of the facts.

In all three of the cases we have looked at, the court rejected the purely subjective test. In *Royal Brunei Airlines v Tan*, Lord Nicholls said 'the standard of what constitutes honest conduct is not subjective. Honesty is not an optional scale, with higher or lower values according to the moral standards of each individual'.

The different interpretations of the test of dishonesty in the three key cases

Royal Brunei Airlines v Tan [1995] – Privy Council

Lord Nicholls regarded the test as being 'not acting as an honest person would act in the circumstances' (objective test). Those circumstances should take account of the facts actually known to the defendant at the time, and his experience and intelligence (a subjective element).

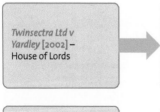

| Twinsectra Ltd v Yardley [2002] – House of Lords | → | Lord Hutton said 'dishonesty requires knowledge by the defendant that what he was doing would be regarded as dishonest by honest people, although he should not escape a finding of dishonesty because he sets his own standards of honesty'. (This interpretation seems to contain a strong subjective element requiring awareness by the defendant that his conduct was dishonest by ordinary standards.) |

| Barlow Clowes International v Eurotrust International [2006] – Privy Council | → | Lord Hoffmann, reinterpreting Lord Hutton's statement above, said it was not necessary for the defendant to be aware that his conduct was dishonest by ordinary standards. If, by ordinary standards, a defendant's mental state would be considered as dishonest, it was irrelevant that the defendant's standards were different. |

Although it is not for the Privy Council to reinterpret the test of dishonesty given by the House of Lords in *Twinsectra*, it is considered that the current test of dishonesty is that enunciated by Lord Nicholls in *Royal Brunei Airlines v Tan* in 1995, and endorsed by Lord Hoffmann on behalf of the Privy Council in *Barlow Clowes International v Eurotrust International* in 2006. Therefore, the test of dishonesty is predominantly objective, while nonetheless considering the defendant's knowledge of the facts at the relevant time and his qualities (e.g. experience and intelligence). He need not be aware of his own wrongdoing. It was this interpretation of the test that was applied in the recent Court of Appeal case – *Starglade v Nash* [2010] EWCA Civ 1314.

Liability for receipt of trust property

We are now concerned with a third party who knowingly receives trust property transferred to him in breach of trust. The third party will be regarded as a constructive trustee and the claimant beneficiary may seek a proprietary or personal remedy against him (see earlier in this chapter for the nature of these remedies).

The key case on liability for receipt of trust property is *Bank of Credit and Commerce International (Overseas) Ltd v Akindele* [2001] below.

Case precedent – *Bank of Credit and Commerce International (Overseas) Ltd v Akindele* [2000] 3 WLR 1423

Facts: A loan agreement was entered into by Chief Akindele with BCCI. Chief Akindele agreed to lend US$10 million to BCCI for a return of 15% on his investment. In breach of their fiduciary duty to BCCI, directors of the company had made this loan agreement for a fraudulent reason of which Chief Akindele was unaware. In due course, in accordance with the loan agreement, Chief Akindele was paid US$16.679 million.

Three years later, BCCI went into liquidation. The liquidator, when investigating the fraudulent loan agreement, held that Chief Akindele was liable to account for the profit he had made (i.e. US$6.679 million) on the basis that he had knowingly received trust property transferred to him in breach of trust.

The Court of Appeal was concerned with the degree of knowledge required to impose liability on the third party, i.e. Chief Akindele. Nourse LJ reviewed the pre-existing law (in particular the five categories of knowledge in *Re Baden* [1993]). He held that dishonesty was not required and formulated a new single test for recipient liability, i.e. 'the recipient's state of knowledge must be such as to make it unconscionable for him to retain the benefit of the receipt'. Applying this test to Chief Akindele, he was found not liable as he had no suspicions regarding the integrity of BCCI when he entered the loan agreement.

Principle: To be liable, the recipient's state of knowledge must be such as to make it unconscionable for him to retain the benefit of the receipt.

Application: You could mention that 'unconscionability' is a nebulous concept. However, in his judgment, Nourse LJ said 'a test in that form, though it cannot, any more than any other, avoid difficulties of application, ought to avoid those of definition and allocation to which the previous categorisations have led. Moreover, it should better enable the courts to give commonsense decisions in the commercial context in which claims in knowing receipt are now frequently made . . .'

Up for Debate

Should an innocent volunteer, who has received misappropriated trust property, be required to restore that property without the need for the claimant to prove fault?

There have been a few cases in which a cause of action has been recognised that requires restitution in equity by the defendant on grounds of unjust enrichment. One such case was *Re Diplock* [1948], which we consider in Chapter 13. This action of unjust enrichment imposes strict liability, i.e. it is not necessary to prove fault, and it is similar to the common law action for money had and received.

A number of judges writing extra-judicially, notably Lord Nicholls in *Restitution – Past, Present and Future*' in Cornish et al (1998), have advocated that this action of unjust enrichment should apply to a third party who receives trust property in breach of trust, and is thus unjustly enriched, i.e. he should be strictly liable to make restitution although the action would be subject to certain specific defences to prevent injustice. Thus it would not apply to a bona fide purchaser for value without notice of the trust, nor where the defence of change of position (which we consider in Chapter 13) was successfully pleaded. For Nourse LJ's view on this, see his *dicta* in *BCCI v Akindele* [2001] 3 WLR 1423.

Enforcement of agreements between parties

This category of institutional constructive trust can be sub-divided as shown in the diagram overleaf. All the sub-categories are based on the principle that the defendant should be prevented from resiling (going back on) an agreement that he has entered into with the claimant and that would result in his unjust enrichment.

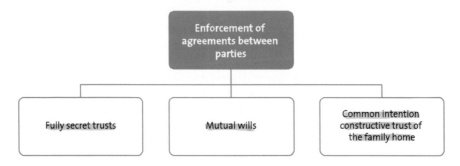

Fully secret trusts

In Chapter 5, we saw that a fully secret trust arises when a testator leaves property to a person in a will and that person *agrees* to hold it on secret trust for a secret beneficiary. There is one school of thought that considers a fully secret trust to be a constructive trust imposed by the law to enforce the **agreement** made between the testator and the secret trustee and thus prevent the secret trustee fraudulently claiming the legacy for himself.

Mutual wills

In Chapter 5, we saw that the doctrine of mutual wills involves two or more testators who execute wills in accordance with an **agreement** not to revoke the wills that are in favour of named beneficiaries. On the death of the first testator, the law will impose a constructive trust on such property of the survivor that it was **agreed** would pass to the named beneficiaries.

Common intention constructive trust of the family home

In Chapter 8, we will be looking at the common intention constructive trust of the family home. We will see that when the legal estate is in the name of one cohabitant, the other cohabitant may be able to claim that the home is held on constructive trust for both of them because there was an express or inferred **agreement** to that effect, which was relied upon to the detriment of the non-legal owner.

Specifically enforceable contracts

Our last category of institutional constructive trust arises when a specifically enforceable contract is made. You will know from contract law that a contract for the purchase of land is specifically enforceable because land is unique and, if the contract is broken, damages would not be an adequate remedy, i.e. the purchaser could seek specific performance.

As soon as contracts for the sale of land are exchanged (and before completion takes place), the vendor becomes a constructive trustee of the land for the purchaser.

One practical effect of this is that he has a duty to take reasonable care to protect and preserve the property for the beneficiary purchaser.

Putting it into practice

There is an important distinction between a personal liability to account and the proprietary remedy of a constructive trust, although that distinction has not always been made clear by the courts in cases involving a fiduciary who makes an unauthorised or secret profit.

Explain this statement with reference to decided cases.

Feedback on putting it into practice

This is a diagram plan for an outline answer.

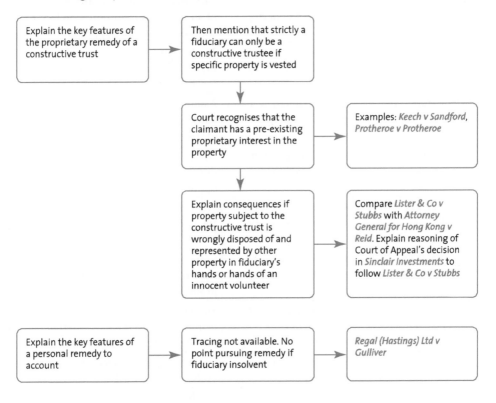

Table of key cases referred to in this chapter

Case name	Area of law	Principle
Attorney General for Hong Kong v Reid [1994]	Bribe accepted by a fiduciary	The receipt of a bribe leads to a constructive trust (i.e. a proprietary remedy)
Barlow Clowes International Ltd v Eurotrust International [2006]	Dishonest assistance in a breach of trust	Defendant liable if by ordinary standards his actions were dishonest
BCCI v Akindele [2008]	Recipient liability	Recipient's state of knowledge is such as to make it unconscionable for him to retain the benefit of the receipt
Boardman v Phipps [1967]	Unauthorised profit made by a fiduciary	Fiduciary who uses confidential information belonging to the trust is liable for any profit he makes
IDC v Cooley [1972]	Unauthorised profit made by a fiduciary	Party must not take advantage of an opportunity/information that he receives in his fiduciary position
Keech v Sandford [1726]	Unauthorised profit made by a fiduciary	Trustee who renews a lease in his favour holds it on constructive trust for the beneficiary
Lister v Stubbs [1890]	Bribe accepted by a fiduciary	A fiduciary who accepts a bribe is liable to account for the amount of the bribe
Peso Silver Mines v Cropper [1966]	Unauthorised profit made by a fiduciary	Opportunity rejected by board of directors is no longer a corporate opportunity
Protheroe v Protheroe [1968]	Unauthorised profit made by a fiduciary	Trustee of a leasehold, who purchases the freehold, holds it on constructive trust
Regal (Hastings) Ltd v Gulliver [1942]	Unauthorised profit made by a fiduciary	Company directors are fiduciaries and should not make an unauthorised profit
Royal Brunei Airlines Sdn Bhd v Tan [1995]	Dishonest assistance in a breach of trust	Third party who dishonestly assists in a breach of trust is liable, whether or not the trustee was dishonest
Sinclair Investments (UK) Ltd v Versailles Trade Finance Ltd (In Administration) [2011]	Bribe accepted by a fiduciary	Court followed the decision in Lister v Stubbs rather than Attorney General for Hong Kong v Reid
Twinsectra Ltd v Yardley [2002]	Dishonest assistance in a breach of trust	Defendant liable if he was aware that he was dishonest by the standards of honest and reasonable people

@ **Visit the book's companion website to test your knowledge**

❖ Resources include a subject map, revision tip podcasts, downloadable diagrams, MCQ quizzes for each chapter, and a flashcard glossary

❖ www.routledge.com/cw/optimizelawrevision

8 Trusts and the Family Home

Revision objectives

Understand the law
- Can you recall how a cohabitant who is not the legal owner can claim a beneficial interest in the family home?
- If so, do you remember how that beneficial interest would be quantified?

Remember the details
- Do you remember the 'excuse cases'?
- Can you explain why the resulting trust is currently out of favour when claiming a beneficial interest in the family home?

Reflect critically on areas of debate
- Why do some commentators regard the 'common intention' constructive trust as a 'fiction'?
- Do you consider that the current law on a cohabitant's rights in the family home should be reformed?

Contextualise
- Are you able to apply the dicta in *Jones v Kernott* to a problem involving a sole legal owner?
- Can you differentiate between an express common intention constructive trust and proprietary estoppel?

Apply your skills and knowledge
- Can you answer the problem question involving a cohabitant who claims a beneficial interest in the family home?

Chapter Map

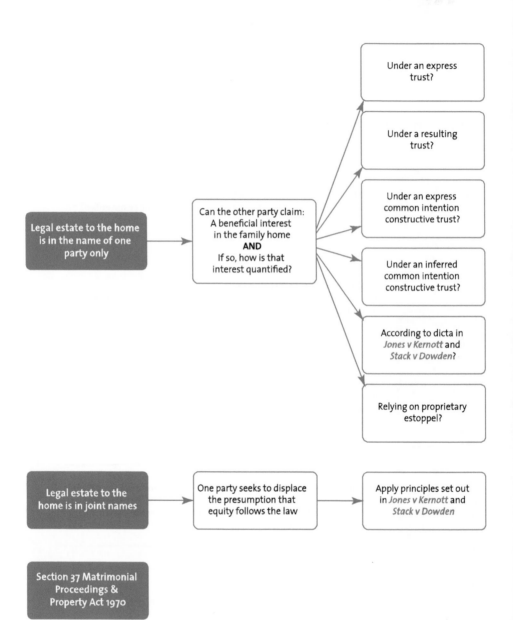

Legal estate to the home is in the name of one party only

Can the other party claim:
A beneficial interest
in the family home
AND
If so, how is that
interest quantified?

Under an express trust?

Under a resulting trust?

Under an express common intention constructive trust?

Under an inferred common intention constructive trust?

According to dicta in *Jones v Kernott* and *Stack v Dowden*?

Relying on proprietary estoppel?

Legal estate to the home is in joint names

One party seeks to displace the presumption that equity follows the law

Apply principles set out in *Jones v Kernott* and *Stack v Dowden*

Section 37 Matrimonial Proceedings & Property Act 1970

Ownership of the family home

This topic is considered under two headings – firstly, where the legal estate is in the name of one party, and secondly, where there are joint legal owners.

The legal estate to the home is in the name of one party only

Example of the problem: In 2005, Jane and Tom decided to live together. They bought a dilapidated cottage for £90,000, which was conveyed into Tom's name alone, although the purchase money was derived as to £30,000 from Tom, £20,000 from Jane and the remaining £40,000 on a mortgage in Tom's name. Jane and Tom have both worked, contributing equally to overheads and living expenses. Tom is a keen DIY enthusiast and has done a lot of renovation work on the cottage. Jane has helped with the decorating and gardening. Tom and Jane have now decided to separate and Tom has received an offer of £400,000 for the cottage.

In *Jones v Kernott* [2011], Lord Walker and Baroness Hale stated: 'The first issue is whether it was intended that the other party has any beneficial interest in the property at all. If he does, the second issue is what that interest is.'

In other words, there is no presumption of joint beneficial interest in the above scenario.

There are two questions:

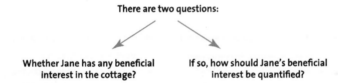

Whether Jane has any beneficial interest in the cottage?

If so, how should Jane's beneficial interest be quantified?

The problem may arise not only where cohabitants separate but, for example, where a cohabitant dies and it is necessary to know what property belongs to the cohabitant's estate.

We need to begin by identifying the area of law with which we are concerned.

Matrimonial proceedings

If Jane and Tom were married but were now divorcing, or seeking judicial separation or nullity of marriage, then the Matrimonial Causes Act 1973 would apply. This Act gives the court discretionary power to make far-reaching property adjustments, notably in the interests of the children.

We are not concerned with matrimonial proceedings.

Dissolution of a civil partnership

If Tom were gay and had a civil partnership with Peter that had broken down, the court has discretionary power under the Civil Partnership Act 2004 to make the same kind of far-reaching property adjustment orders as it can for married couples under matrimonial proceedings.

We are not concerned with this type of action.

Cohabitant seeks a declaration as to his/her beneficial interest in the family home (or more unusually a spouse or civil partner seeks a declaration as to their beneficial interest in the family home).

This is decided in accordance with principles of equity and trusts, and is the area we are concerned with in this chapter.

Does Jane have a beneficial interest in the family home and, if so, how is it quantified?

Jane may be able to prove that she has a beneficial interest by relying on the following:

- ❖ Express trust
- ❖ Resulting trust
- ❖ Constructive trust
- ❖ Proprietary estoppel

An express trust

A legal owner, such as Tom in our example, is always free to declare how the beneficial interests of the property are held. This would normally be done when the property was purchased (see Form TR1 – part 10 – mentioned in Chapter 4). Let us suppose that he did not declare the beneficial interests on that form but that he orally stated to Jane 'this cottage is as much yours as mine'. The problem for Jane would be that unless that declaration of trust of land was evidenced in writing and signed by the settlor (i.e. Tom) in accordance with s 53(1)(b) Law of Property Act 1925, then the express trust of land would be unenforceable. (We covered this topic in Chapter 3.)

In the unlikely event that there was evidence of Tom's declaration in writing that included his signature, Jane would have a beneficial interest in the cottage under an express trust. Her beneficial interest would be easy to quantify, i.e. she would be entitled to half the proceeds of the cottage in accordance with Tom's declaration.

The presumption of a resulting trust

Let us look again at how the purchase of the cottage was financed:

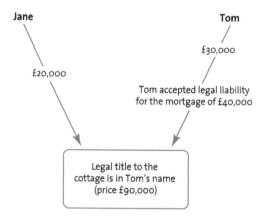

You will remember from Chapter 6 that when one party, e.g. Jane, purchases property in the name of another, there is a presumption that the other party, e.g. Tom, holds that property on resulting trust for Jane in proportion to the **direct contribution** that she made. However, such a presumption may be rebutted by evidence that the money was a gift or a loan and was not intended to be a direct contribution to the purchase price. The following diagram illustrates what constitutes direct contributions and is followed by relevant cases.

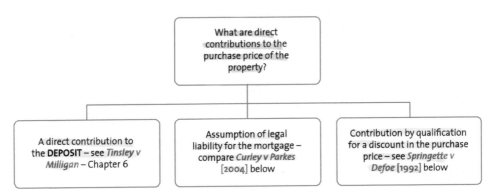

Case precedent – *Curley v Parkes* [2004] EWCA Civ 515

Facts: Miss Parkes and Mr Curley were cohabitants. A house was purchased in the sole name of Miss Parkes. She provided the deposit from the proceeds of sale of a house she had previously owned and a mortgage of £138,000 was taken out in her name. However, in order to help her with her financial commitments, Mr Curley subsequently paid £9,000 into her bank account, which was used to pay later mortgage instalments. When the parties later separated, Mr Curley claimed that this payment entitled him to an 8.5% beneficial interest in the house. In the Court of Appeal, Peter Gibson LJ said, 'The relevant principle is that the resulting trust of a property purchased in the name of another … rises once and for all at the date on which the property is acquired … Subsequent payment of the mortgage instalments are not part of the purchase price paid to the vendor …'

Principle: The parties' rights crystallise at the time of the purchase of the property. Payment of later mortgage instalments are not direct contributions to the purchase price if that party did not accept legal liability for the mortgage at the time of purchase.

Application: When applying this principle to a problem question, it is important to compare the legal position regarding payments of mortgage instalments when an inferred common intention constructive trust is pleaded by the claimant (see later below).

Case precedent – *Springette v Defoe* [1992] 2FLR 388

Facts: Miss Springette and Mr Defoe lived together in a council house in which Miss Springette had been a tenant for 11 years. They decided to purchase the house for £14,445, which represented a discount of 41% because of Miss Springette's former tenancy. They both accepted liability for the mortgage of £12,000 and Miss Springette paid the balance with cash.

When they subsequently split up, it was held that the property was held on a presumed resulting trust that arose from their respective direct contributions. Accordingly, Miss Springette was entitled to 75% of the beneficial interest, which involved crediting her with the 41% discount, her cash contribution and her liability for half of the mortgage.

Principle: A discount in the purchase price of a property is regarded as a direct contribution by the party entitled to the discount.

Application: Remember that only direct contributions give rise to a presumed resulting trust. Miss Springette had made three kinds of direct contribution: the discount, the deposit and liability for the mortgage.

Aim Higher

When you discuss a resulting trust in this context, it is important to mention that following *Stack v Dowden* [2007] (Lord Neuberger dissenting on this point), the resulting trust is out of favour with respect to the family home, although it may be of relevance for commercial property or property bought for investment, as we saw in Chapter 6 in *Laskar v Laskar* [2008].

It would be impressive if you could explain why the resulting trust is out of favour. The following are the key reasons. Note how rigid the resulting trust is.

❖ The parties' rights crystallise at the time of purchase and we saw that this means only direct contributions to the purchase price give rise to the presumption of a resulting trust.

❖ It follows that if a party helps to pay mortgage instalments, this will not give rise to the presumed resulting trust if he/she did not accept legal liability for the mortgage at the time of the purchase.

❖ The beneficial interest is quantified arithmetically, i.e. proportionate to the direct contribution to the purchase price. You could compare quantification under an inferred common intention constructive trust (see below).

In passing, we should note that the **presumption of advancement** would only apply where a husband bought property in the name of his wife. You will remember from Chapter 6 that it is presumed that such a purchase is a gift, although the presumption may be rebutted by evidence from the husband that he did not intend a gift. In

Chapter 6, we noted in *Tinker v Tinker* [1970] that the husband was unable to rebut the presumption. This presumption is very much out of favour because it is unrealistic in the modern world and discriminates between the sexes. It will be abolished once s 199 Equality Act 2010 comes into force.

The common intention constructive trust

Following Lord Bridge's classification in *Lloyds Bank v Rosset* (1991), there are **two types of common intention constructive trust**:

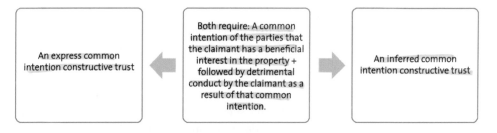

An express common intention constructive trust

Both require: A common intention of the parties that the claimant has a beneficial interest in the property + followed by detrimental conduct by the claimant as a result of that common intention.

An inferred common intention constructive trust

The express common intention constructive trust

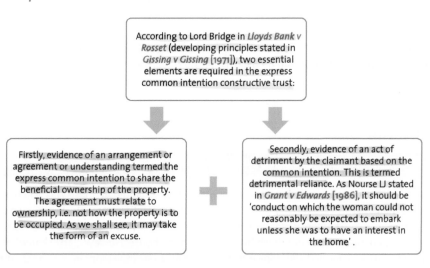

According to Lord Bridge in *Lloyds Bank v Rosset* (developing principles stated in *Gissing v Gissing* [1971]), two essential elements are required in the express common intention constructive trust:

Firstly, evidence of an arrangement or agreement or understanding termed the express common intention to share the beneficial ownership of the property. The agreement must relate to ownership, i.e. not how the property is to be occupied. As we shall see, it may take the form of an excuse.

Secondly, evidence of an act of detriment by the claimant based on the common intention. This is termed detrimental reliance. As Nourse LJ stated in *Grant v Edwards* [1986], it should be 'conduct on which the woman could not reasonably be expected to embark unless she was to have an interest in the home'.

Example

Imagine that Jack and Jill decide to live together in a flat. Jill does not make a direct contribution to the purchase price of the flat but Jack says, 'This flat is as much yours as mine. I have put it in my name merely for tax reasons'.

It would be reasonable for Jill to assume from that conversation that she had a beneficial interest in the flat (see the 'excuse cases' below). In other words, there is an understanding that she shares the equitable interest. The first element of an express common intention constructive trust has been satisfied, i.e. the **common intention**.

Note that it would not be necessary for Jack's declaration to be evidenced in writing and signed by him because s 53(2) Law of Property Act 1925 exempts the creation of constructive trusts (and resulting trusts) from s 53(1)(b) Law of Property Act 1925 (as we saw in Chapter 3).

> **Example (continued)**
>
> Now let us imagine that relying on that understanding, Jill acted to her detriment. Perhaps she helped Jack with the mortgage or she decorated the flat at her own expense or renovated the bathroom and kitchen.

These actions by Jill would satisfy the second element of an express common intention constructive trust, i.e. the **detrimental conduct**. With both elements satisfied, she would be able to claim that Jack held the flat on express common intention constructive trust for himself and her in equal shares in accordance with their common intention.

Where the agreement or understanding is silent regarding the size of the claimant's beneficial interest, then it will be quantified by the court. See later – quantifying the beneficial interest in *Jones v Kernott* [2011], *Stack v Dowden* [2007] and *Oxley v Hiscock* [2005].

The 'excuse cases'

> **Case precedent – *Eves v Eves* [1975] 1 WLR 1338**
>
> **Facts:** An unmarried couple lived together and had two children. A house was purchased in the man's name. He said that he would have put it in joint names if she had been older (i.e. 21 years old). The house was very dilapidated and, believing that she had a beneficial interest in it, the woman did much heavy work on the house. However, after three years the man left and married someone else, then sought to evict the woman and the children from the house. The Court of Appeal held that the woman had a 25% beneficial interest in the home arising from her understanding that she had a share in the home and her detrimental conduct in reliance on that understanding.

> **Case precedent – *Grant v Edwards* [1986] 3 WLR CA (Civ)**
>
> **Facts:** The claimant, who was married with two children, had a relationship with the defendant and had his son. The couple then decided to buy a house but it was put into the name of the defendant who gave the excuse that if it were in their joint names it might prejudice her divorce proceedings. Following a fire at the property, insurance money was

spent on repairs and the balance paid into a joint account. The claimant, believing she had a beneficial interest in the property, made substantial financial contributions to the household without which the defendant would have been unable to pay the mortgage. When the parties subsequently separated and the claimant sought a declaration as to her beneficial interest in the property, the Court of Appeal held that she was entitled to a half share in the party, having regard to the understanding that she was to share the property and her detrimental conduct.

Case precedent – *Hammond v Mitchell* [1992] 1 WLR 1127

Facts: A second-hand car dealer and an ex-Bunny girl lived together with their two children in a house that was bought in the man's name. He gave the excuse that this was best as he was going through divorce proceedings and there were also tax reasons but that she was not to worry as they would soon marry and then half of it would be hers.

In reliance on this understanding, she allowed him to re-mortgage the home as security for a business venture. She also helped him with his business. When the parties subsequently separated, the court held that she was entitled to a half share in the beneficial interest. The judge held that the fact that she had risked her interest in the home by allowing the house to be used as security for a business venture amounted to detrimental conduct on her part. It was not clear from the judgment whether the help she gave with the business was also detrimental conduct.

Principle: The excuse in these three cases could be construed by the claimant as amounting to an assurance that she had a beneficial interest in the property. This understanding had then been acted upon by the claimant to her detriment, which entitled her to a share in the property.

Application: When applying these cases to a problem, you should mention that the common intention appears to be assessed objectively by the court. As we shall see presently, this ties in with the *dicta* of the Supreme Court in *Jones v Kernott* [2011] to the effect that the common intention should be deduced objectively, having regard to a number of factors.

Up for Debate

Some commentators consider that the common intention, notably in the excuse cases, is a fiction. For that reason, other jurisdictions have preferred to find a different basis for the constructive trust in the context of ownership of the family home. Thus in New Zealand (prior to legislation), the constructive trust was imposed on grounds of the reasonable expectation of the claimant – *Gillies v Keogh* [1989]; in Canada, the constructive trust was imposed on the ground of unjust enrichment of the defendant – *Pettkus v Becker* [1980]; and in Australia, on the ground of unconscionability – *Baumgartner v Baumgartner* [1988].

The inferred common intention constructive trust

This is the second type of constructive trust identified by Lord Bridge in *Lloyds Bank v Rosset*. There is no express (even if informal) agreement or understanding between the parties revealing their common intention regarding the claimant's beneficial interest in the home. Instead, the common intention is **inferred** from the conduct of the parties. Again, in theory, two elements are required, i.e. the inferred common intention **and** detrimental conduct on the part of the claimant but, in fact, the claimant's conduct normally fulfils both elements, as you will see from the following example and the questions and answers below.

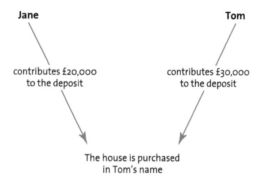

Jane   Tom

contributes £20,000 to the deposit   contributes £30,000 to the deposit

The house is purchased in Tom's name

Question: What can be inferred from Jane's conduct, i.e. direct contribution of £20,000 to the deposit?

❖ **Answer**: From that conduct, it must be inferred that there is a common intention that Jane should have a beneficial interest in the property.

Question: What is Jane's detrimental conduct?

❖ **Answer:** Jane's detrimental conduct is contributing £20,000. In other words, that conduct fulfils both the first element of inferring a common intention and the second element of detrimental conduct.

What conduct has given rise to the inferred common intention constructive trust?

Answer: A DIRECT CONTRIBUTION to the purchase price (as in the above example)	You will notice that this overlaps with the presumed resulting trust – except that here a direct contribution includes help with later mortgage payments	Even a small direct contribution to the purchase price can provide evidence of a common intention – £500 in *Midland Bank v Cooke* [1995]	In 1990 in *Lloyds Bank v Rosset*, Lord Bridge, when referring to direct contributions, said 'it is at least extremely doubtful whether anything less will do'. But in *Stack v Dowden* in 2007, Lord Walker stated 'in my opinion the law has moved on'

So how has the law moved on?

| Answer:
An **INDIRECT FINANCIAL CONTRIBUTION** may give rise to the inference | These are financial contributions to utility bills and other household bills that thereby enable the legal owner to pay the mortgage | As long ago as 1971 in *Gissing v Gissing*, Lord Diplock said 'it may be no more than a matter of convenience which spouse pays particular household expenses' | More recently, in *Le Foe v Le Foe* [2001], Nicholas Mostyn QC said 'the family economy depended for its function on the wife's earnings'. He concluded that the wife contributed indirectly to the mortgage repayments |

But do purely domestic contributions constitute conduct giving rise to the inferred common intention constructive trust?

| Answer:
It seems that purely domestic contributions do not give rise to the inference | In *Burns v Burns* [1984], Ms Burns had lived with the defendant for 16 years and looked after the home and their three children. (She had taken his name although they were not married.) She had made no financial contribution towards the purchase price and had no beneficial interest in the family home | However, now see the possible effect of dicta in *Jones v Kernott* [2011], considered below |

The effect of Jones v Kernott *on the common intention constructive trust*

The difficulty of interpreting the Supreme Court decision in *Jones v Kernott* [2011] UKSC 53 is that the case concerned cohabitants who were joint legal owners and the Court was concerned not with the first question (i.e. did the claimant have a beneficial interest in the property), but with the second question (i.e. how was that beneficial interest to be quantified). Nevertheless, certain key points can be gleaned from extracts from the joint judgment of Lord Walker and Lady Hale, and also from the judgment of Baroness Hale in the House of Lords case *Stack v Dowden* [2007] UKHL 17.

These key points are set out in the diagram below.

Jones v Kernott – *Finding the common intention regarding the beneficial interest*

Lord Walker and Lady Hale at paragraph 52 in their joint judgment in *Jones v Kernott*: 'The common intention has ... to be deduced objectively from (the parties') conduct'

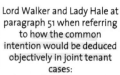

Lord Walker and Lady Hale at paragraph 51 when referring to how the common intention would be deduced objectively in joint tenant cases:
'Examples of the sort of evidence which might be relevant ... are given in *Stack v Dowden* paragraph 69'

Baroness Hale at paragraph 69 in *Stack v Dowden*: 'Many more factors than financial contributions may be relevant to divining the parties' true intentions. These include any advice or discussions at the time of transfer ... the purpose for which the home was acquired; the nature of the parties' relationship; whether they had children for whom they both had responsibility to provide a home; how the purchase was financed, both initially and subsequently; how the parties arranged their finances, whether separately or together or a bit of both; how they discharged the outgoings on the property and their other household expenses ... The parties' individual characters and personalities may also be a factor in deciding where their true intentions lay'

Jones v Kernott – *Quantifying that beneficial interest*

Lord Walker and Lady Hale in their joint judgment in *Jones v Kernott*:
'If the evidence shows a common intention to share the beneficial ownership but does not show what shares were intended, the court will have to proceed as at paragraph 51(4) and 51(5).'

At paragraph 51(4), Lord Walker and Lady Hale referred to Chadwick LJ's judgment in *Oxley v Hiscock* [2005] that each is entitled to that share which the court considers fair having regard to the whole course of dealing between them in relation to the property, and they added:
'In our judgment, the whole course of dealing .. should be given a broad meaning, enabling a similar range of factors to be taken into account as may be relevant to ascertaining the parties actual intentions."

At paragraph 51(5), Lord Walker and Lady Hale continued:
'Each case will turn on its own facts. Financial contributions are relevant but there are many other factors which may enable the court to decide what shares were either intended or fair.'
(See the list of factors mentioned above regarding finding the common intention.)

Note the above quantification would be relevant when assessing the claimant's share under an express common intention constructive trust (when the shares have not been agreed) and also in an inferred common intention constructive trust.

Summary of the effect of Jones v Kernott *and* Stack v Dowden *on sole legal owner cases*

❖ Neither of these cases overrules the previous decisions mentioned under express common intention constructive trusts or inferred common intention constructive trusts.

❖ However, *dicta* in *Jones v Kernott* indicate that the common intention of the parties should be deduced objectively from their conduct.

❖ Factors that are relevant when deducing that common intention are listed in paragraph 69 of *Stack v Dowden*

❖ When quantifying that beneficial interest, the court has regard to the whole course of dealing between the parties (i.e. an holistic approach) and the same factors as those listed in paragraph 69 are relevant.

Proprietary estoppel

The Law Commission stated in its 2007 Report No. 307 on Cohabitation: The Financial Consequences of Relationship Breakdown, '. . . the courts are reluctant to provide an exact definition, preferring to retain the flexibility to develop the jurisdiction'. However, it is accepted that certain elements are essential.

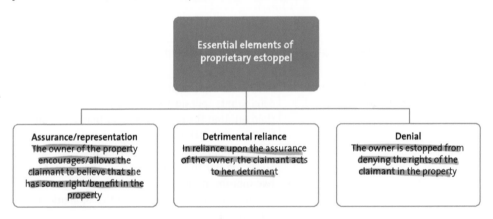

You may have noticed the similarity between the above elements and those required in an express common intention constructive trust. However, as Lord Walker stated in *Stack v Dowden* [2007] 'proprietary estoppel typically consists of asserting an equitable claim against the conscience of the true owner. The claim is to a mere equity. It is to be satisfied by the minimum award necessary to do justice . . . which may sometimes lead to no more than a monetary award. A common intention constructive trust, by contrast, is identifying the true beneficial owner or owners, and the size of their beneficial interests'.

These essential differences are summarised in the table below.

The express common intention constructive trust	Proprietary estoppel
This is imposed on the ground of an express agreement/bargain, and the claimant acquires a beneficial interest in the home, i.e. there is an express common intention.	This is based on an assurance given by the legal owner to the claimant who relies on that assurance to his detriment. The court has a wide discretion regarding the remedy awarded to the claimant (see variety of remedies below).
Unless there was agreement as to the size of the beneficial interest, the court will quantify the claimant's interest having regard to the whole course of dealing between the parties.	The court will balance the expectation of the claimant against the detriment suffered by the claimant and will identify the minimum equity to do justice (see cases below).
The claimant's beneficial interest under the constructive trust arises when the two elements (the common intention and detrimental conduct) occur, i.e. before the court case.	Proprietary estoppel is essentially a remedy declared by the court.

Proprietary estoppel – examples of remedies	Outline of the relevant case
Transfer of the legal title to the home to the claimant	*Pascoe v Turner* [1979] 1 WLR 431 – When the cohabitants split up, the defendant told the claimant that the house was hers. In reliance on this assurance, the claimant expended money on improvements, decoration and repairs. Subsequently, the defendant gave the claimant two months' notice to leave the house. The Court of Appeal awarded a transfer of the legal title to the claimant.
Grant of the right of occupancy of the home for life	*Greasley v Cooke* [1980] 1 WLR 1306 – Doris Cooke was the family maid who later cohabited in the property with the legal owner's son. She was assured by the son (later deceased) and his brother (the claimant) that she could occupy the property for the rest of her life. She looked after the Greasley family, including a mentally ill daughter, acting as housekeeper without payment. The Court of Appeal granted her an irrevocable licence to occupy the property for the rest of her life.

Proprietary estoppel – examples of remedies	Outline of the relevant case
Sum of £200,000 representing the detriment suffered by the claimant (as opposed to his expectation of the home worth £435,000)	*Jennings v Rice* [2002] NPC 28 – Mrs Royle (deceased) had told the claimant (a part-time gardener) that her house would be his one day. For the last three years of Mrs Royle's life, and following a burglary, the claimant slept on a sofa in Mrs Royle's sitting room almost every night to provide her with some security. Despite her assurances, Mrs Royle in fact died intestate. Robert Walker J stated 'the most essential requirement is that there must be proportionality between the expectation and the detriment'. Accordingly, the Court of Appeal awarded the claimant £200,000 although he had expected to inherit the house worth £435,000.

The home is bought in the joint names of the cohabitants

Since April 1998, where the home is bought in the name of joint legal owners, Land Registry form TR1 enables joint legal owners to make a declaration of trust regarding their **beneficial** interest in the home. We are now concerned with the legal situation when there is no such express declaration.

First – the presumption	In *Jones v Kernott* [2011], Lord Walker and Lady Hale stated that the starting point is that equity follows the law, i.e. there is a presumption that the parties are joint tenants both in law and equity *Fowler v Barron* [2008].
Second – displacing the presumption	Lord Walker and Lady Hale stated that the presumption could be displaced by showing that the parties had a different common intention when they acquired the home, or that they had later formed a common intention that their respective shares would change.
Third – deducing the common intention	Lord Walker and Lady Hale stated that the common intention was to be deduced objectively from the parties' conduct. Examples of the sort of evidence that might be relevant to drawing such an inference were given in paragraph 69 *Stack v Dowden* [2007] – listed above in this chapter.
Fourth – if this was not possible	The court would impute an intention to the parties that their shares should be such as the court 'considers fair having regard to the whole course of dealing of the parties ... enabling a similar range of factors to be taken into account' as in the third stage above.

In *Jones v Kernott,* a property was purchased for £30,000 in 1985 in joint names with Ms Jones paying the deposit of £6,000 and the balance raised by a mortgage in joint names. When Mr Kernott moved out of the property in 1993, Ms Jones continued to live in the home with their two children and took over responsibility for all outgoings and the maintenance of the two children. Mr Kernott subsequently acquired a place of his own but, in 2006, claimed his half share in the property on severing the joint tenancy. The Supreme Court held that when Mr Kernott moved out of the property in 1993, any common intention regarding the parties' beneficial interest had changed (i.e. the presumption that equity follows the law was displaced) and awarded Ms Jones a 90% interest in the property, and Mr Kernott a 10% interest.

Finally – improvements to property made by married couples or civil partners

The following Act has limited application. It applies to spouses and was extended to civil partners by the Civil Partnership Act 2004.

Section 37 Matrimonial Proceedings and Property Act 1970

It is hereby declared that where a husband or wife contributes in money or money's worth to the improvement of real or personal property ... the husband or wife so contributing shall ... be treated as having then acquired by virtue of his or her contribution a share or enlarged share.

Thus, in *Re Nicholson* [1974], the wife acquired a larger share in the home on account of her expenditure of £189 on installing central heating.

A final word on the family home:

Aim Higher

As you revise this subject and consider how a cohabitant may claim a beneficial interest in the family home and how that interest may be quantified, make a note of the limitations of each type of trust and proprietary estoppel so that you can criticise the current law if need be.

You should also be aware of the Law Commission's recommendations for reform set out in their 2007 Report No 307 entitled *Cohabitation: The Financial Consequences of Relationship Breakdown*. This is available on the Law Commission website where there is also an outline Executive Summary. Briefly, the Law Commission recommends an 'opt-out scheme' for cohabitants who had a child together or who had lived together for a specified number of years. The Law Commission suggests a period between 2 and 5 years. To quote the Law Commission, 'the scheme would seek to ensure that the pluses and minuses of the relationship were fairly shared between the couple. The applicant would have to show that the respondent retained a benefit or that the applicant had a continuing economic disadvantage. The value of any award would depend on the extent of the retained benefit or continuing economic disadvantage'.

Putting it into practice

When Sarah met Philip, she was living in a rented flat. Philip persuaded her to give it up and come and live with him in a cottage that he was thinking of buying in Fletford. Sarah was very nervous of giving up her flat but Philip said, 'The cottage will be as much yours as mine'. She asked him if he would be putting it into their joint names but he said that as the mortgage was going to be in his name, it would be better if legal title was in his name. He reassured Sarah again that it was 'their cottage' and she decided to live with him.

Over the next five years, Sarah did a lot of redecorating work on the cottage. She used her salary to pay the utility bills and frequently helped Philip with the mortgage repayments.

For the last six months, Philip and Sarah have been quarrelling and, last week, Philip told Sarah that he had met someone else and he wanted Sarah to move out of the cottage. Sarah is shocked and seeks your advice as to whether she has any beneficial interest in the cottage. Advise Sarah.

Feedback on putting it into practice

One way of answering this question is to consider each type of trust in turn to see whether Sarah could claim a beneficial interest.

Although Philip orally declared that the cottage was 'as much yours as mine', you will remember that a declaration of an **express trust** of land must be evidenced in writing and signed by the settlor in accordance with s 53(1)(b) Law of Property Act 1925. As Sarah has no written evidence of Philip's declaration, any claim that she had an equal share in the beneficial interest under an express trust would be unenforceable.

Regarding a **resulting trust**, you should mention that following *Stack v Dowden* [2007], the resulting trust is out of favour when claiming a beneficial interest in the family home. In any event, Sarah has not made a direct contribution to the purchase price. The parties' rights crystallise at the time of purchase and as Sarah did not accept legal liability for the mortgage, her assistance with the mortgage repayments would not count – *Curley v Parkes* [2004].

You should then explain the elements required to claim a beneficial interest under the **express common intention constructive trust** in accordance with Lord Bridge's statements in *Lloyds Bank v Rosset* [1991]. Philip's oral declaration and his excuse could be regarded as evidence of a common intention that Sarah had a beneficial interest in the cottage. There is no need for evidence in writing as s 53(2) Law of Property Act 1925 exempts constructive trusts from the formalities in s 53(1) of the Act. However, Sarah would have to provide evidence that she acted to her detriment in reliance upon the understanding that she had a beneficial interest in the cottage. Her financial contributions and her redecoration of the cottage would satisfy this requirement. Relevant cases should be cited, e.g. *Grant v Edwards* [1986].

You could also mention the **inferred common intention constructive trust** as described in *Lloyds Bank v Rosset*. The common intention would be inferred from Sarah's direct contributions (i.e. her assistance with the mortgage repayments) and her indirect financial contributions (i.e. payment of the utility bills) as in *Le Foe v Le Foe* [2001]. You could refer to Baroness Hale's statement in *Stack v Dowden* [2007] that the law has moved on since Lord Bridge's comment that only direct contributions will raise the inference of the common intention.

You should then refer to the *dicta* in *Jones v Kernott* [2011] to the effect that the parties' common intention is deduced objectively from their conduct. Examples of relevant conduct are the factors listed in paragraph 69 of *Stack v Dowden*. You should refer to those factors that are relevant to the problem, e.g. discussions between the parties at the time of transfer, how the property was financed, both initially and subsequently.

Finally, you should mention **proprietary estoppel**, identifying the three key elements, and noting that the court does the minimum to satisfy equity, balancing the claimant's expectation against the detriment suffered. Relevant cases should be cited to illustrate the type of remedies that may be granted by the court.

Table of key cases referred to in this chapter

Case name	Area of law	Principle
Burns v Burns [1984]	Inferred common intention constructive trust	Domestic contributions did not give rise to an inferred common intention constructive trust.
Curley v Parkes [2004]	Resulting trust	Mortgage payments are not direct contributions unless by the party who has accepted legal liability for the mortgage.

Eves v Eves [1975]	Express common intention constructive trust	An excuse may be evidence of a common intention.
Fowler v Barron [2008]	Joint legal owners	Presumption that equity follows the law was not rebutted.
Gissing v Gissing [1971]	Inferred common intention constructive trust	Dicta that indirect financial contributions should give rise to a beneficial interest.
Grant v Edwards [1986]	Express common intention constructive trust	An excuse may be evidence of a common intention.
Greasley v Cooke [1900]	Proprietary estoppel	Claimant awarded right of occupation in home for her life.
Hammond v Mitchell [1992]	Express common intention constructive trust	An excuse may be evidence of a common intention.
Jennings v Rice [2002]	Proprietary estoppel	Court balances expectation of the claimant against the detriment suffered.
Jones v Kernott [2011]	Common intention constructive trust	Joint legal owners – principles to be applied when presumption that equity follows the law is displaced.
Laskar v Laskar [2008]	Resulting trust	Resulting trust still relevant when claiming a beneficial interest in investment property.
Le Foe v Le Foe [2001]	Inferred common intention constructive trust	Indirect financial contributions may give rise to an inferred common intention constructive trust.
Lloyds Bank v Rosset [1991]	Common intention constructive trust	Established elements necessary for the express and the inferred common intention constructive trusts.
Midland Bank v Cooke [1995]	Inferred common intention constructive trust	Direct contribution gave rise to an inferred common intention constructive trust.

Case name	Area of law	Principle
Nicholson [1974]	Matrimonial Proceedings and Property Act 1970	Application of Act to enlarge share of wife's beneficial interest in the property on account of improvements.
Oxley v Hiscock [2004]	Express common intention constructive trust	Court had regard to the 'whole course of dealing' between the parties when quantifying the beneficial interest.
Pascoe v Turner [1979]	Proprietary estoppel	Court ordered the transfer of the legal title to the property to the claimant.
Springette v Defoe [1992]	Resulting trust	Qualification for a discount was a direct contribution to the purchase price of the property.
Stack v Dowden [2007]	Common intention constructive trust	Joint legal owners – principles to be applied when presumption that equity follows the law is displaced.
Tinker v Tinker [1970]	Presumption of advancement	Presumption of advancement was not rebutted as claimant did not intend to retain a beneficial interest.

@ **Visit the book's companion website to test your knowledge**

❖ Resources include a subject map, revision tip podcasts, downloadable diagrams, MCQ quizzes for each chapter, and a flashcard glossary

❖ www.routledge.com/cw/optimizelawrevision

9

Private Purpose Trusts

Revision objectives

Understand the law
- Can you explain the objections to a private purpose trust?
- Are you able to describe the three types of unenforceable trust?

Remember the details
- Do you remember the different ways in which gifts to unincorporated associations may take effect?
- Are you able to explain the limitations of each of these methods?

Reflect critically on areas of debate
- Why is the contractual basis for the distribution of surplus funds on the dissolution of an unincorporated association preferred to the resulting trust approach?

Contextualise
- Can you explain the rule against remoteness of vesting?
- What is meant by the rule against inalienability?

Apply your skills and knowledge
- Can you answer the problem question concerning the dissolution of an unincorporated association with surplus funds?

Chapter Map

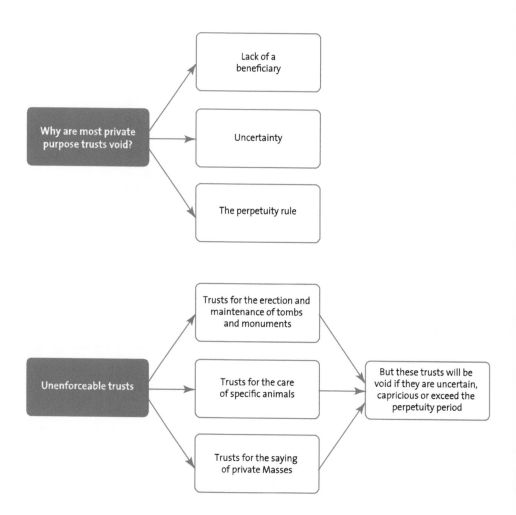

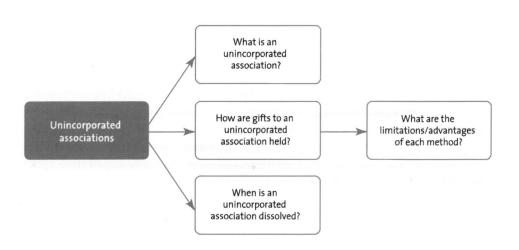

Introduction to private purpose trusts

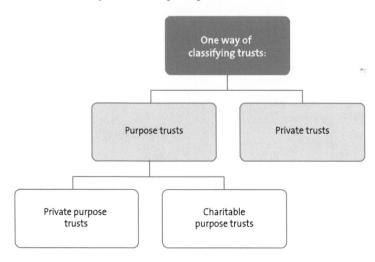

So far in this book, we have been looking at private trusts, i.e. trusts for ascertainable individuals. Express trusts, resulting trusts and constructive trusts are all types of private trust. We come to charitable purpose trusts (also called public trusts) in the next chapter. This chapter is concerned with private purpose trusts, sometimes referred to as non-charitable purpose trusts. With a few exceptions, private purpose trusts are void and we need to know why.

Why are most private purpose trusts void?

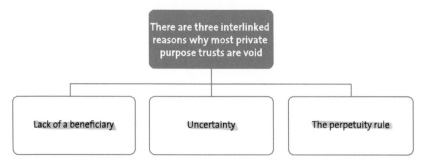

Two of these reasons were explained by William Grant MR in *Morice v Bishop of Durham* [1804] as follows:

'There can be no trust over the exercise of which this Court will not assume a control; for an uncontrollable power of disposition would be ownership and not trust. If there be a clear trust, but for uncertain objects, the property, that is the subject of the trust, is indisposed of and the benefit of such trust must result to those to whom the law gives the ownership in default of disposition by the former owner. But this doctrine does not hold good with regard to trusts for charity. Every other trust must have a definite object. There must be somebody, in whose favour the Court can decree performance.'

This is a common assessment area, so with the above statement in mind, let us look in detail at the three reasons why most private purpose trusts are void.

Lack of a beneficiary

There must be a beneficiary who can enforce the trust, i.e. a beneficiary who can go to court if the trustees do not fulfil their obligation to carry out the trust. Only a person with a proprietary interest in the trust property, i.e. a beneficiary, has the *locus standi* to bring proceedings against the trustee. This rule that there must be a beneficiary in whose favour the court can decree performance of the trust is called **the beneficiary principle**.

Private trusts have ascertainable beneficiaries who could enforce the trust but purpose trusts do not, i.e. they are for a purpose. Whilst charitable purpose trusts (i.e. public trusts) are enforced by the Attorney General on behalf of the Crown, there is no one appointed to enforce private purpose trusts and, for that reason, they are void. On failure of the private purpose trust, as the above extract from *Morice v Bishop of Durham* indicates, the property will result back to the settlor/testator. When it results back to the deceased testator, it will be held for the residuary beneficiary under the testator's will or, if there is no residuary beneficiary, for the testator's next of kin under the intestacy rules.

Aim Higher

When discussing this subject in an answer, you could mention that the distinction between private purpose trusts and private trusts is not always clear cut. For example, in Chapter 6, in *Re Abbott Fund Trusts* [1900], there was a trust for the maintenance of two deaf and dumb sisters. It could be argued that this was for a purpose. In other words, many purposes are for the benefit of persons (unless they are abstract purposes). For more on this topic, see *Re Denley* [1969] below.

As we shall see later, there are three exceptions when, despite the lack of a beneficiary, the purpose trust will not be void. These exceptions are known as **unenforceable trusts** or **trusts of imperfect obligation** – these names reflecting that there is no beneficiary to enforce the trustee's obligation.

Uncertainty

How can a court supervise or enforce a trust if its terms/objects are uncertain? Lack of a beneficiary and uncertainty were the reasons why the trusts failed in the following case.

Case precedent – *Re Astor's Settlement Trusts* [1952] Ch 534

Facts: In a settlement expressly limited to the perpetuity period, Lord Astor declared that most of the shares of the Observer Ltd were to be held by trustees to apply the income for purposes that included the 'maintenance of good understanding, sympathy and co-operation between nations' and 'the preservation of the independence and integrity of newspapers'.

Roxburgh J held that the trusts were void primarily because there was no beneficiary to enforce the trusts. He said, 'A court of equity does not recognise as valid a trust which it cannot both enforce or control'. A secondary reason for failure was that the objects of the trusts (including those mentioned above) were conceptually uncertain.

Principle: A trust will fail if there is no beneficiary to enforce the trust or its terms are uncertain.

Application: When you apply this decision, you should mention that Roxburgh J stated that the three exceptions to the beneficiary principle (i.e. unenforceable trusts) would not be extended.

The perpetuity rule

The rule needs to be explained before we look at its application to the topic of private purpose trusts. There are two parts to the rule, as the following diagram illustrates.

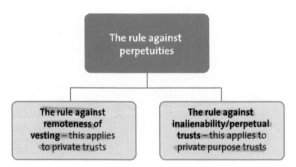

The rule against remoteness of vesting

This rule requires a future interest to be vested in a beneficiary within a certain time limit. This ensures that property is not tied up indefinitely in a long-term trust. Long-term trusts would not only be disadvantageous to future beneficiaries who would be restricted in their ability to deal with the property held in trust, but would also be stifling to the national economy. Under the Perpetuities and Accumulations Act 2009, the perpetuity period is 125 years, i.e. property must vest in the ascertainable beneficiary within 125 years. It should be stressed that the rule against remoteness of vesting applies to **private trusts**, i.e. where there are future interests in property for **people**.

The rule against inalienability/perpetual trusts

This rule brings us to the **third objection** to private purpose trusts and again it is linked to the lack of a beneficiary. If private purpose trusts were permitted, then because the trust property would not be vested in a beneficiary with a limited lifespan, there would be the possibility that the trust could last for ever. Endowments (i.e. the provision of a permanent source of income for the trust's purposes) would be inalienable (i.e. non-transferable), which runs counter to public policy that property/capital should be capable of circulating freely in the economy – hence the rule against inalienability. (Note that the rule against inalienability does not apply to charitable purpose trusts where capital and property can be retained in a trust indefinitely.)

As mentioned earlier, there are three exceptions to the rule that private purpose trusts are void. These exceptions are called **unenforceable trusts** but even they cannot last indefinitely and are subject to the above rule against inalienability. Unlike the rule against remoteness of vesting, the rule against inalienability is **not** governed by the Perpetuities and Accumulations Act 2009 and therefore the perpetuity period (i.e. the period for which the trust may last) remains subject to the **common law**.

Common Pitfall

A common pitfall is to think that the statutory perpetuity period of 125 years applies to unenforceable trusts and therefore it is stressed that the **Perpetuities and Accumulations Act 2009** does not apply to the rule against inalienability. The common law perpetuity period for unenforceable trusts is usually taken to be 21 years.

However, it may well be that the other two common law perpetuity periods also apply, i.e. a life in being, or a life in being plus 21 years – for example, the testator could stipulate that the unenforceable trust is to last for his son's life plus 21 years. This doubt regarding the perpetuity period arises because there have been a few cases where these two other common law periods have been employed without being challenged, e.g. there was no objection to a royal life clause being used in *Re Astor's Settlement Trusts* although (as we saw earlier) the trusts failed on other grounds.

Unenforceable trusts (or trusts of imperfect obligation)

The possible rationale for upholding these unenforceable testamentary trusts was stated by Roxburgh J in *Re Astor's Settlement Trusts* [1952] as follows: 'Perhaps the late Sir Arthur Underhill was right in suggesting that they may be concessions to human weakness or sentiment, see Underhill A, Law of Trusts, 8th edition.'

Note also Lord Evershed's statement in *Re Endacott* [1960] regarding the three categories of unenforceable trusts: '... in my judgment, the scope of these cases ... ought not to be extended ... No principle perhaps has greater sanction of authority behind it than the general proposition that a trust by English law, not being a charitable trust, in order to be effective, must have ascertained or ascertainable beneficiaries. These cases constitute an exception to that general rule'.

These three exceptions often arise in mixed-topic problem questions and we will consider each head as follows:

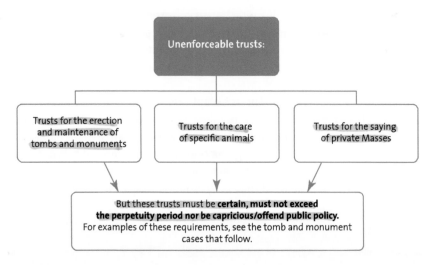

Key tomb and monument cases

Case precedent – *Mussett v Bingle* [1876] WN 170

Facts: A testator gave £300 for the erection of a monument to his wife's first husband and £200 to provide income for its maintenance. The Court upheld the first gift but held that the second gift was void as it offended the rule against inalienability/perpetual trusts, i.e. the money was to be held as a permanent source of income.

Case precedent – *Re Endacott* [1960] Ch 232

Facts: The testator left his residuary estate amounting to £20,000 to the North Tawton Devon Parish Council 'for the purpose of providing some useful memorial to myself'. The court held that the purpose of the trust was too uncertain to fall within this group of cases and thus failed.

Case precedent – *Brown v Burdett* [1882] 21 Ch D 667

Facts: The testatrix instructed that a house left on trust should be sealed up for 20 years and subject thereto held upon trust for Mr Burdett for life and thereafter to Mr Baxter absolutely. The court held that the gift served no useful purpose – it was capricious and against public policy – and ordered the house to be unsealed.

Principle: A testamentary gift for the erection or maintenance of a tomb will be upheld provided it is certain, within the perpetuity period, and is not capricious.

Application: You should be aware that if the testator's gift was for the maintenance of a whole graveyard, or for a tablet in a church, this would qualify as a charitable trust under the head of advancement of religion (see Chapter 10).

Notice that the three categories of unenforceable trusts, including those above and below, are **testamentary** trusts not *inter vivos* trusts.

Key animal cases

Case precedent – *Re Dean* [1889] 41 Ch D 552

Facts: William Dean left funds to his trustees for the care of his eight horses and his hounds for up to 50 years. The court upheld the trust but did not address the issue of the perpetuity period.

Case precedent – *Pettingall v Pettingall* [1842] 11 LJ Ch 176

Facts: A testator left £50 for the care of his favourite black mare. The court upheld the trust.

Principle: A trust for the care of specific animals will be upheld (but should not offend the perpetuity period).

Application: Strictly, the perpetuity period in both of the above cases should have been 21 years since no life in being was identified. In neither case was the question of perpetuity addressed. However, the courts do take judicial notice of the normal lifespan of an animal, i.e. that a particular animal will not survive 21 years.

You will have noticed that the above cases concerned the care of specific animals. A trust for the care of animals in general would constitute a charitable purpose trust under the head 'the advancement of animal welfare' – see Chapter 10.

A key case on private Masses

Case precedent – *Bourne v Keane* [1919] AC 815

Facts: The testator left £200 to Westminster Cathedral for the purpose of saying private Masses for the dead. The House of Lords upheld this trust.

Principle: A trust for the saying of private Masses will be upheld provided it is limited to the perpetuity period.

Application: You should be aware that if the trust was for the saying of public Masses, then it would be a valid charitable purpose trust under the head of the advancement of religion. As we shall see in the next chapter, charitable purpose trusts are not subject to the rule against inalienability/perpetual trusts and therefore endowments of capital/property to provide the income for the saying of **public** Masses may be retained intact indefinitely.

Unincorporated associations

This topic will be discussed under the following heads:

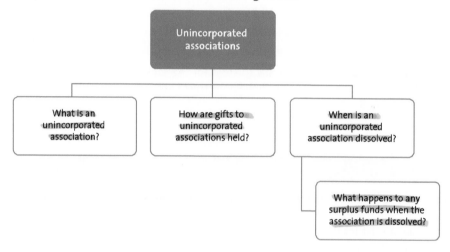

What is an unincorporated association?

An unincorporated association (unlike a corporate body) is not a legal person. This means that it is not a legal entity in itself but is made up of the persons who have grouped together for some common purpose. Clubs, societies, associations are examples of unincorporated associations, whereas limited companies and public limited companies are incorporated bodies.

Question: Is there a definition of an unincorporated association?

❖ **Answer:** In *Conservative and Unionist Central Office v Burrell* [1982], Lawton LJ gave the following definition: 'Two or more persons bound together for one or more common purposes, not being business purposes, by mutual undertakings, each having mutual duties and obligations, in an organisation that has rules which identify in whom control of its funds rests and on what terms, and which can be joined or left at will.'

How are gifts to unincorporated associations held?

As an unincorporated association is not a legal person, it has no legal rights and duties in itself and in particular, it cannot own property. This raises the issue of how a gift to such an association takes effect – an issue that often comes up as an examination question as follows:

| David died a few months ago. In his will, he left £50,000 to the Blackstone Cricket Club | ➡ | The validity of this gift has been challenged by the residuary beneficiary under David's will | ➡ | Advise David's executors of the legal position |

Before we consider the answer, it is interesting to note that although people give to unincorporated associations all the time, e.g. members pay their subscriptions to clubs, it is only when large sums of money are left to an association in a will that the validity of the gift is likely to be challenged by those entitled to the property should the gift fail (usually the residuary beneficiary under the testator's will, or if no such person, the testator's next of kin under the intestacy rules).

Aim Higher

When answering a question such as that above, it would be impressive if you could identify the limitations and advantages (if any) of the various ways in which gifts to unincorporated associations have been construed by the courts. For that reason, the sample question is now considered by examining each interpretation in turn, identifying the limitations/advantages of each interpretation, and studying any relevant precedent. All the diagrams below assume that the unincorporated association is the Blackstone Cricket Club and that David gave £50,000.

The club is a charitable association

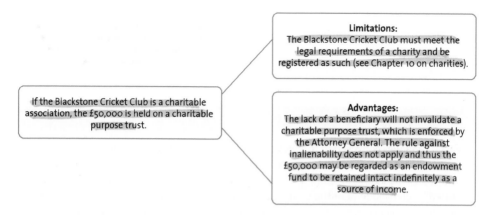

If the Blackstone Cricket Club is a charitable association, the £50,000 is held on a charitable purpose trust.

Limitations:
The Blackstone Cricket Club must meet the legal requirements of a charity and be registered as such (see Chapter 10 on charities).

Advantages:
The lack of a beneficiary will not invalidate a charitable purpose trust, which is enforced by the Attorney General. The rule against inalienability does not apply and thus the £50,000 may be regarded as an endowment fund to be retained intact indefinitely as a source of income.

In all the **following diagrams** it is assumed that the Blackstone Cricket Club (i.e. the unincorporated association) is non-charitable.

The gift is for the club's purposes

The £50,000 is given to the Blackstone Club for its purposes	**Limitations:** A gift for a non-charitable purpose is **void** (see beginning of this chapter) – *Re Grant's Will Trusts* [1990]

An example of this interpretation of the gift is *Re Grant's Will Trusts* [1990] 1 WLR 360, in which the testator gave all his real and personal estate to '. . . the Chertsey and Walton Constituency Labour Party Property Committee'. This local committee did not control the branch's property, which meant that this gift was held on trust for the Labour Party's **purposes** and could not be claimed by the members. The court held that it was a gift for non-charitable purposes and was void because it lacked a beneficiary. Furthermore, the gift was intended as an endowment fund and infringed the rule against inalienability. The gift therefore devolved to the testator's next of kin as on intestacy.

Gift for purposes that directly/indirectly benefit the members of the club

Gift to the Blackstone Cricket Club is for its purposes (which directly or indirectly are for the benefit of its members)	**Limitations:** This interpretation is based on the controversial decision in *Re Denley*. It would only apply where the purpose of the association directly or indirectly benefited the members, i.e. the purpose/object was inward looking as opposed to outward looking or abstract/impersonal. It would be void if it offended the rule against perpetuities.
	Advantages: This interpretation (if correct) would validate gifts for non-charitable purposes that were inward looking, i.e. for the direct/indirect benefit of members.

Case precedent – *Re Denley's Trust Deed* [1969] 1 Ch 373

Facts: Land was conveyed to trustees by Martyn & Co Ltd 'to be maintained and used . . . for the purpose of a recreation or sports ground primarily for the benefit of employees'. The trust was expressly limited to the perpetuity period. Goff J upheld the trust and stated '. . . in my judgment the beneficiary principle of *Re Astor's Settlement Trusts*, which was approved in *Re Endacott* . . . is confined to purpose or object trusts, which are abstract or impersonal. The objection is not that the trust is for a purpose or object *per se*, but that there is no beneficiary . . . Where, then, the trust though expressed as a purpose, is directly or indirectly for the benefit of an individual or individuals, it seems to me that it is in general outside the mischief of the beneficiary principle'.

Principle: A trust that is directly or indirectly for the benefit of individuals is valid even though expressed as for a purpose. It must not offend the rule against perpetuities.

Application: Although *Denley* did not concern a gift to an unincorporated association, the decision was one of the bases on which the trust in *Re Lipinski's Will Trusts* [1976] was upheld. In *Lipinski,* the testator left half his residuary estate to the Hull Judeans (Maccabi) Association to be used in constructing new buildings for the association – a purpose that it was held benefited the Anglo-Jewish members of the association.

Up for Debate

Is the trust in *Re Denley* a private trust or a purpose trust? If it is a purpose trust, then it is an important exception to the rule that private purpose trusts (excluding the three unenforceable trusts) are void. For further reading see L McKay, 'Trusts for Purposes – Another View' [1973] The Conveyancer, page 420.

Outright gift to the members of the club

Presumption that the £50,000 is an outright gift for the members of the Blackstone Cricket Club at the date of the gift, as joint tenants or tenants in common

Limitations:
This presumption may be contrary to the intention of the testator and impractical in terms of numbers of members and the nature of the gift – *Re Leahy.*
This interpretation does not take into account future members of the club.
As this is an outright gift (then as explained in *Neville Estates Ltd v Madden* [1962]), the members, if tenants in common, could simply take their share of the money for their own use – or if joint tenants, could do the same after severing their share – it is unlikely that the testator intended such a result when he gave the £50,000 to the club.

Advantage:
There is no question of this private trust offending the rule against perpetuities .

Gift held on trust for present members of the club

Presumption that the £50,000 is held on trust for the members of the Blackstone Cricket Club from the time of the gift (as joint tenants or tenants in common)

Limitations:
Again, this presumption may be contrary to the intention of the testator and impractical in terms of numbers of members and the nature of the gift – *Re Leahy*.
This interpretation does not take into account future members of the club.
Again, the members as tenants in common/joint tenants could claim their share and if *sui juris* and all in agreement, terminate the trust under the rule in *Saunders v Vautier* (see Chapter 1) and divide the property.

Advantage:
There is no question of this private trust offending the rule against perpetuities as it is for present members only, who have the ability to claim their share.

A case that demonstrates the above interpretation is *Leahy v Attorney General for New South Wales* [1959] AC 457 in which an Australian testator left his homestead with 730 acres of grazing land known as 'Elmslea' on trust for 'such order of nuns of the Catholic Church or the Christian Brothers as my executors and trustees shall select'. Some of the religious orders were purely contemplative and therefore the trust could not be regarded as a charitable purpose trust. The question thus arose as to whether this could be regarded as a private trust for the members of the orders.

The Privy Council held that it was not valid as a private trust – the form of the gift was to benefit selected orders, not existing members, who, in any case, were very numerous and possibly spread over the world. It was also unrealistic to suppose that the members of the orders were intended to become beneficial owners of Elmslea, given the nature of the property. In fact, the trust was saved as a charitable trust under a New South Wales statute.

Gift is held on trust for present and future members

£50,000 on trust for the present and future members of the Blackstone Cricket Club

Limitations:
In accordance with the rule of remoteness of vesting, future interests must vest within the perpetuity period (now 125 years).
Furthermore, there must be nothing in the rules of the club that prevents members at any time from dividing the gift amongst themselves, otherwise the rule against inalienability of capital will be infringed.

Advantage:
The trust takes account of future members. However under s 8 of the Perpetuities and Accumulations Act 2009, members who are not ascertained/identified by the end of the perpetuity period of 125 years will be excluded from the gift.

Gift is to members on a contractual basis

This is the favoured interpretation and is based on *obiter dicta* in *Re Recher's Will Trusts* [1972]. However, it too has limitations as the following diagram indicates.

£50,000 is a gift to members of the Blackstone Cricket Club but subject to their contractual rights. It is regarded as an accretion to the funds of the Club under the control of its committee/trustees.

Limitations:
There has to be a contract between the members. (The constitution/rules of the association may be taken to constitute a contract between members.)
The constitution/rules must enable the members to dissolve the association and divide the proceeds in order to avoid infringement of the rule against perpetuities.

Advantage:
The members cannot sever their share while the association exists. This is likely to be in keeping with the testator's intention when he made the gift. This solution applies whether the association is inward looking or outward looking. This interpretation ties up with the contractual basis for dealing with surplus funds on dissolution (see later – *Re Bucks*).

Case precedent – *Re Recher's Will Trusts* [1972] Ch 526

Facts: A testatrix gave her residuary estate to the London and Provincial Anti-Vivisection Society, a non-charitable unincorporated association that had ordinary and life members. In fact, the society had amalgamated with another society shortly before the will was made and it was held that the testatrix had not intended to leave her estate to the amalgamated body, so the gift failed. However, the case is important for the *obiter dicta* of Brightman J as follows.

Principle: A gift to an unincorporated association may be construed as a gift to existing members of the association at the date of the gift as an accretion to the funds of the society and subject to the contractual rights and duties of the members (as evidenced in the association's rules or constitution). Members' rights terminate on resignation/death. New members acquire the same rights during their membership. In order to adhere to the rule against perpetuities, there must be nothing in the constitution/rules that prevents members from dissolving the association and dividing the assets.

Application: When citing this case, you should mention that this is the favoured solution for how gifts to unincorporated associations take effect, and how such an association holds property. It was applied in *Re Horley Town Football Club* [2006] EWHC 2386 (Ch).

Mandate/authority given to officer of the club

During his life, David gives authority to the Treasurer/other officer of the Blackstone Cricket Club to use the £50,000 for the benefit of the Club.

Limitations:
Whilst this is a suitable solution for an *inter vivos* gift, it cannot apply to a legacy as the authority/mandate given to the Treasurer ceases on the donor's death. The Treasurer is effectively acting as an agent during David's lifetime.

Aim Higher

You could conclude an answer on this topic by explaining that the above difficulties concerning gifts to an unincorporated association for its purposes would be avoided if the organisation were incorporated, i.e. if it was legally registered as a company limited by guarantee. It would then be a legal entity able to hold property in its own name for its objects.

When is an unincorporated association dissolved?

Some questions require you to explain how an unincorporated association is dissolved.

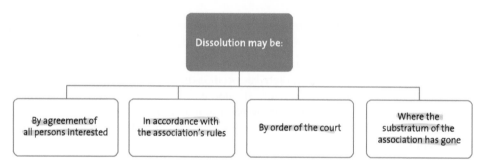

Dissolution may be:

- By agreement of all persons interested
- In accordance with the association's rules
- By order of the court
- Where the substratum of the association has gone

These four ways were recognised by the court in *GKN Bolts and Nuts Sports and Social Club* [1982] and it was added that mere inactivity will not amount to dissolution unless it is coupled with other circumstances which indicate that the purpose or substratum of the association has gone. For example, in *GKN Bolts and Nuts*, there was no active use of the club's sports ground and there was supporting evidence that the club had ceased to exist, including the dismissal of the club's steward, the ending of the club's VAT registration and the sale of the club's stock of drinks.

What happens to any surplus funds when the unincorporated association is dissolved?

As we saw above, an unincorporated association is not a legal person and therefore cannot hold property in its own name. When such an association is dissolved, the question arises regarding the distribution of surplus funds if this has not been expressly stated in the association's rules or constitution.

There are **three** relevant first instance cases.

The first case to note is *Re West Sussex Constabulary's Widows, Children & Benevolent Fund* [1971] Ch 1. This case involved a fund that provided benefits to widows of members of the West Sussex Constabulary, and came to an end when the police force was amalgamated with other forces. There was £35,000 in the fund and the question arose as to its distribution. The fund arose from four sources, which were distributed as follows:

Source:	Recipient:	Reason:
Members' subscriptions	*Bona vacantia* to the Crown	Members had subscribed on the basis of contract and had received what they had bargained for
Legacies and donations	Resulting trust for donors	The legacies and donations were made for a specific purpose, which had failed
Collecting boxes	*Bona vacantia* to the Crown	Donors were anonymous and gave the donation out-and-out
Proceeds of entertainments	*Bona vacantia* to the Crown	Donors had received what they bargained for

This decision in *Re West Sussex* has not been overruled but it is not the favoured solution, the decision in *Re Bucks* below being preferred. See *Horley Town Football Club* [2006].

Case precedent – *Re Bucks Constabulary Widows' and Orphans' Fund Friendly Society* [1979] 1 WLR 936

Facts: The fund of the Friendly Society provided benefits for the widows and orphans of deceased members of Bucks Constabulary and was wound up when the Bucks police force amalgamated with other forces. There was a surplus of £40,000 and, as the issue was not covered in the rules, the question arose as to its distribution. The court held that the funds should pass as follows:

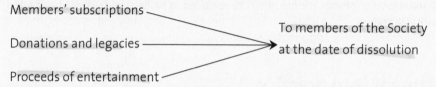

Members' subscriptions

Donations and legacies ——→ To members of the Society at the date of dissolution

Proceeds of entertainment

Principle: Walton J held that on the basis of a term implied into the contract that existed between all the members of the Society, the surplus funds should, on dissolution, be divided equally amongst all who were members of the Society at that time (unless the rules of the Society indicated a different form of division).

Application: You could mention the often cited *obiter dicta* of Walton J that 'if a society is reduced to a single member neither he, nor still less his personal representatives … can say he is or was the society and therefore entitled solely to its fund … and so indeed the assets have become ownerless'.

It is important to note that Walton J's *dicta* that the fund should pass as *bona vacantia* to the Crown when only a single member remained was not followed in the more recent case – *Hanchett-Stamford v Attorney General* [2008] below.

Case precedent – *Hanchett-Stamford v Attorney General* [2008] EWHC 330 (Ch)

Facts: The Performing and Captive Animals Defence League was an unincorporated association founded in 1914. Finally, however, there was only one surviving member left, the claimant, Mrs Hanchett-Stamford, who wished to transfer the assets of the League, worth over £2 million, to Born Free, an active charity that supported animal welfare. The issues for the court were firstly whether the objects of the League were charitable, in which case the fund could be applied cy-près and pass to Born Free, and secondly, if the objects were not charitable, then to whom the fund should pass.

Lewison J held that the objects of the league were not charitable as one of its main objects was political, i.e. to change the law in order to stop (amongst other things) the use of performing animals in circuses. Regarding the second issue, Lewison J followed the general principle in *Re Bucks* that the assets of the league vested in the members subject to their contractual rights. Mrs Hanchett-Stamford was therefore entitled to the assets and was free to dispose of them as she wished, i.e. the *dicta* of Walton J, regarding a single member remaining, was not followed.

Principle: To deprive a member of the League of her share of the League's assets when becoming the sole surviving member would be in breach of Article 1 of Protocol 1 of the European Convention on Human Rights and Fundamental Freedoms, which protects the right of an individual to peaceful enjoyment of possession.

Application: This decision is also useful to illustrate that if the main object of an organisation is to change the law, it will be regarded as political and will not be granted charitable status.

Putting it into practice

Last year, John Summers and eight of his friends formed a non-charitable unincorporated association called The Society Against Performing Dolphins.

Over the following 10 months, they were able to raise a considerable amount of money from different sources: members' subscriptions, donations from relatives, the proceeds of two car-boot sales and six film evenings showing dolphins in the wild. Then, three months ago, John's uncle died and left a legacy of £12,000 to the Society.

Last month, John, who is a freelance underwater cameraman, was filming dolphins in the sea near Madagascar when he was attacked by a shark. His friends and family in England rallied round to raise a fund for emergency medical treatment in Madagascar and the flight home to England. Over £16,000 was raised. As it transpired, John's insurance policy covered both the medical treatment and the flight back to England so there was no need to use the £16,000.

In the meantime, a Private Member's Bill has successfully passed through Parliament banning performing dolphins and The Society Against Performing Dolphins is to be dissolved next week. The constitution of the Society contains no provision regarding dissolution or the disposal of surplus assets, which in this case amount to £63,000.

Advise John and his friends how the Society may be dissolved and what should happen to the £16,000 raised for John and the surplus assets of the Society.

Feedback on putting it into practice

Problem questions on the dissolution of unincorporated associations with surplus funds are often combined with the topic of surplus funds in a trust set up to help a beneficiary, which we covered in Chapter 6 on resulting trusts. You will notice that the above problem question contains both these topics, which need to be dealt with separately. The answer outlined in the diagram below begins with how this particular Society may be dissolved and goes on to consider the distribution of surplus assets of the Society, before turning to the fund set up to help John.

<table>
<tr><td>Explain how an unincorporated association may be dissolved, citing *GKN Bolts & Nuts Sports & Social Club*, and identify the methods that are relevant to the problem</td><td></td><td>In the present case, the most likely methods of dissolution would be by agreement of the members of the Society, or on the basis that the substratum upon which the Society was founded has gone</td></tr>
<tr><td>Regarding distribution of the Society's surplus funds, note that the Society is a non-charitable unincorporated association, and discuss the two approaches, citing *Re West Sussex* and *Re Bucks*</td><td></td><td>When applying *Re West Sussex*, identify the sources of the fund and the courts' decision in respect of each source. When applying the contractual approach in *Re Bucks*, mention that it is the favoured decision, citing more recent cases, e.g. *Horley Town Football Club*</td></tr>
</table>

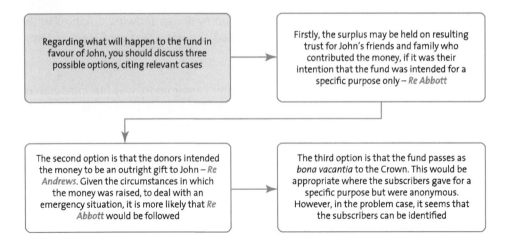

Regarding what will happen to the fund in favour of John, you should discuss three possible options, citing relevant cases

Firstly, the surplus may be held on resulting trust for John's friends and family who contributed the money, if it was their intention that the fund was intended for a specific purpose only – *Re Abbott*

The second option is that the donors intended the money to be an outright gift to John – *Re Andrews*. Given the circumstances in which the money was raised, to deal with an emergency situation, it is more likely that *Re Abbott* would be followed

The third option is that the fund passes as *bona vacantia* to the Crown. This would be appropriate where the subscribers gave for a specific purpose but were anonymous. However, in the problem case, it seems that the subscribers can be identified

Table of key cases referred to in this chapter

Case name	Area of law	Principle
Astor's Settlement Trusts, Re [1952]	Private purpose trust	Trusts were void for lack of a beneficiary and uncertainty of terms
Bourne v Keane [1919]	Unenforceable trust	Upheld as an unenforceable trust for the saying of private Masses
Brown v Burdett [1882]	Unenforceable trust	Failed as an unenforceable trust as capricious and against public policy
Bucks Constabulary Widows' and Orphans' Fund Friendly Society [1979]	Unincorporated association	Surplus funds distributed to members of the association at the date of dissolution
Conservative & Unionist Central Office v Burrell [1982]	Unincorporated association	Provided definition of an unincorporated association
Dean, Re [1889]	Unenforceable trust	Upheld as an unenforceable trust for the care of specific animals
Denley's Trust Deed, Re [1969]	Private purpose trust	Trust for a purpose that directly/indirectly benefited individuals upheld
Endacott, Re [1960]	Unenforceable trust	Failed as an unenforceable trust as terms uncertain
GKN Bolts & Nuts Sports & Social Club [1982]	Unincorporated association	Lists the ways in which an unincorporated association may be dissolved

Grant's Will Trusts, Re [1990]	Private purpose trust	Gift for purpose failed as private purpose trust void
Hanchett-Stamford v Attorney General [2008]	Unincorporated association	Single member of League entitled to surplus funds on dissolution
Horley Town Football Club [2006]	Unincorporated association	Ownership of assets by members of association on a contractual basis
Leahy v Attorney General for New South Wales [1959]	Unincorporated association	Presumption that gift held for members of the religious orders displaced as contrary to testator's intention and impractical given numbers
Lipinski's Will Trusts, Re [1976]	Private purpose trust	Trust for purposes that directly benefited members of association upheld
Morice v Bishop of Durham [1804]	Private purpose trust	Beneficiary principle explained
Mussett v Bingle [1876]	Unenforceable trust	Trust for erection of monument upheld; trust for maintenance of tomb void as perpetual
Pettingall v Pettingall [1842]	Unenforceable trust	Trust for care of specific animal upheld as an unenforceable trust
Recher's Will Trusts, Re [1972]	Unincorporated association	*Dicta* that gift to association held by members subject to contract *inter se*
West Sussex Constabulary's Widows, Children and Benevolent Fund [1971]	Unincorporated association	Surplus funds held on resulting trust basis regarding legacies and donations given for specific purposes of association

---

@ Visit the book's companion website to test your knowledge

❖ Resources include a subject map, revision tip podcasts, downloadable diagrams, MCQ quizzes for each chapter, and a flashcard glossary

❖ www.routledge.com/cw/optimizelawrevision

10 Charitable Trusts

Revision objectives

Understand the law

- Can you identify the requirements for the creation of a valid charity?
- What are the fiscal privileges enjoyed by charities?

Remember the details

- Are you able to give examples of each of the 13 heads of charitable purposes listed in s 3(1) of the Charities Act 2011?

Reflect critically on areas of debate

- Can you explain and criticise the personal nexus test?
- Can you outline the poverty exception to the public benefit requirement?

Contextualise

- Are you able to explain the legal advantages enjoyed by a charitable trust when compared with a private trust?
- In the context of the cy-près doctrine, can you distinguish between initial failure and subsequent failure of a charity?

Apply your skills and knowledge

- Can you answer the problem question at the end of this chapter?

Chapter Map

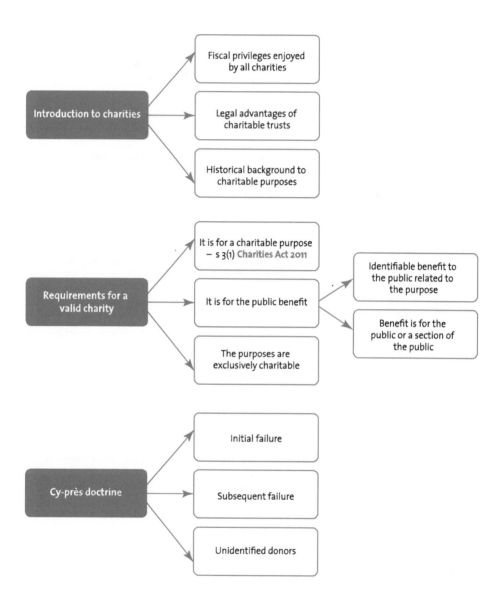

Introduction to charities

Charities may operate under different legal forms: not only as charitable trusts, but as charitable corporations, unincorporated associations and charitable incorporated organisations (CIOs). CIOs are a new legal form for a charity, introduced by the Charities Act 2011, and intended to meet the particular administrative needs of charities.

Whatever legal form the charity takes, it has to be:

❖ established for a charitable purpose, and
❖ established for the public benefit, and
❖ exclusively charitable.

These three requirements will be considered later in this chapter but first you should be aware of the privileges/advantages enjoyed by charitable trusts.

All charities enjoy fiscal privileges, which is why most organisations seek to be registered as charities. It also explains why so many cases involve the Inland Revenue Commissioners (IRC) in which the IRC questions the organisation's charitable status.

The Charity Commission, which is a corporate body, maintains the register of charities and decides whether charitable status should be granted or taken away. There are 'excepted' charities, so called because they are excepted from registration, e.g. charities with an annual income of less than £100,000. The Charity Commission also investigates and deals with maladministration of charities. Appeals from the Charity Commission's decisions are heard by the recently formed First-Tier Tribunal (Charity) and Upper Tribunal.

The main fiscal privileges, some of which are enjoyed by those giving to the charity as opposed to the charity itself, are listed in the following box.

Main fiscal privileges enjoyed by charities

Exemption from income tax provided that the income is used for charitable purposes only
Exemption from income tax on profits of trade provided the profits are used for purpose of the charity and either the trade relates to the primary purpose of the charity or is carried out by beneficiaries of the charity
Exemption from corporation tax provided profits used for charitable purposes only
Exemption from capital gains tax provided gain is used for charitable purposes only
Buildings used for religious purposes are exempt from rates on those buildings
Buildings used for other charitable purposes are exempt for 80% of rates on those buildings
Relief from stamp duty
Gifts to charities are exempt from inheritance tax
Relief from income tax is available on gift aid donations

If the charity operates as a charitable trust (also known as a charitable purpose trust or a public trust) then it enjoys legal advantages when compared with private trusts. These legal advantages are listed in the next box.

Legal advantages enjoyed by charitable trusts

Charitable trusts are for a purpose but, unlike non-charitable purpose trusts, they are valid even though there is no identifiable beneficiary. They are enforced by the Attorney General.
There is no need for certainty of objects. For example, a trust 'for charitable purposes' would be valid. The Charity Commission would draw up a scheme for the application of the funds.
Charitable trusts may be perpetual. Endowment capital may be held in trust indefinitely.
Where property is given for charitable purposes that cannot be carried out, the cy-près doctrine may apply, under which the Charity Commission or the court may draw up a scheme so that the property can be applied for similar charitable purposes.

Historical background of charitable purposes

Aim Higher

It is recommended that you know something about the historical background of charitable purposes because this has a bearing on the current law.

The Statute of Charitable Uses 1601

This Elizabethan statute was important for its preamble, which listed charitable purposes as follows: 'the relief of aged, impotent and poor people, the maintenance of sick and maimed soldiers and mariners, schools of learning, free schools and scholars of universities, the repair of bridges, ports, havens, causeways, churches, sea banks and highways, the education and preferment of orphans, the relief, stock or maintenance of houses of correction; the marriages of poor maids; the supportation, aid and help of young tradesmen, handicapped men and persons decayed; the relief or redemption of prisoners or captives; and the aid or care of any poor inhabitants concerning the payment of fifteens, setting out of soldiers and other taxes'.

Until the Charities Act 2006, the courts still referred to the preamble to decide whether a new purpose before the court was 'within the spirit and intendment of the preamble'.

IRC v Pemsel [1891]

In this House of Lords case, Lord Macnaghten grouped the charitable purposes in the above preamble under the following four heads:

❖ For the relief of poverty
❖ For the advancement of education

- ❖ For the advancement of religion
- ❖ For other purposes beneficial to the community

There was a presumption of public benefit with the first three heads of this classification.

Over the next century, a large body of case law developed regarding these four heads of charitable purposes and this case law is still relevant today.

Charities Act 2006

This Act provided the first statutory definition of a charitable purpose as one that fell within the charitable purposes listed in the Act and that was for the public benefit. The list contained 13 charitable purposes – the first three being the same as the first three identified by Lord Macnaghten and most of the new purposes being based on purposes that had been recognised by the courts as charitable under Lord Macnaghten's fourth group. These purposes have been re-enacted in the Charities Act 2011.

Charities Act 2011

This Act consolidates the various statutes on charities, e.g. the Charities Act 2006, the Charities Act 1993, the Recreational Charities Act 1958. The first two sections of the Act contain key definitions.

Section 1(1) For the purposes of the law of England and Wales, 'charity' means an institution which:

(a) is established for charitable purposes only, and
(b) falls to be subject to the control of the High Court in the exercise of its jurisdiction with respect to charities.

Section 2(1) For the purposes of the law of England and Wales, a charitable purpose is a purpose which:

(a) falls within s 3(1), and
(b) is for the public benefit (see section 4).

Public benefit is no longer presumed for the prevention or relief of poverty, the advancement of education and the advancement of religion. In this respect, all charities are now treated equally and **public benefit** must be proved in each case – see later in this chapter.

We now consider the three requirements for a valid charity – two of these were referred to in the definitions in the Charities Act 2011 above; the third, that a charity must be exclusively charitable, is found in case law. It is essential when answering a problem or essay question on charitable trusts to know about these three requirements as follows.

Requirements for a valid charity

There are three requirements for a valid charity, regardless of whether it is a charitable trust or operates under a different form, e.g. as a corporation.

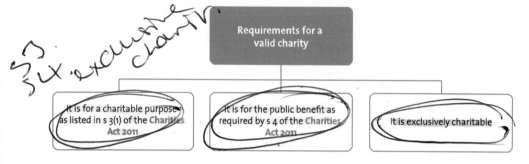

Charitable purposes listed in the Charities Act 2011

The 13 charitable purposes are listed in s 3(1) of the **Charities Act 2011**. To help you answer questions on this topic, these purposes are dealt with in turn, together with short examples or extracts from relevant cases. The more examples and cases you know, the better, and it is suggested that you add your own examples of familiar charities as we go through this list.

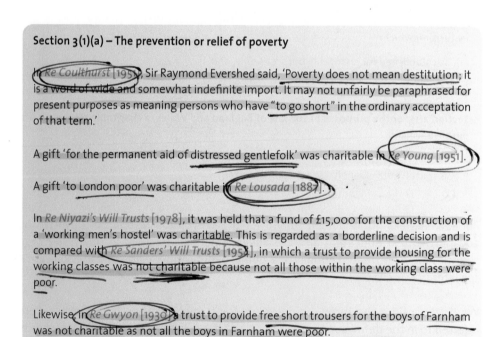

Section 3(1)(a) – The prevention or relief of poverty

In *Re Coulthurst* [1951], Sir Raymond Evershed said, 'Poverty does not mean destitution; it is a word of wide and somewhat indefinite import. It may not unfairly be paraphrased for present purposes as meaning persons who have "to go short" in the ordinary acceptation of that term.'

A gift 'for the permanent aid of distressed gentlefolk' was charitable in *Re Young* [1951].

A gift 'to London poor' was charitable in *Re Lousada* [1887].

In *Re Niyazi's Will Trusts* [1978], it was held that a fund of £15,000 for the construction of a 'working men's hostel' was charitable. This is regarded as a borderline decision and is compared with *Re Sanders' Will Trusts* [1954], in which a trust to provide housing for the working classes was not charitable because not all those within the working class were poor.

Likewise, in *Re Gwyon* [1930] a trust to provide free short trousers for the boys of Farnham was not charitable as not all the boys in Farnham were poor.

Section 3(1)(b) – The advancement of education

This head covers a very wide range of educational and cultural activities such as:

❖ **Public schools, nursery schools, universities.**
❖ **Zoos and museums.**

The Incorporated Council of Law Reporting was held to be charitable in 1972. The fact that the law reports helped lawyers to earn money was incidental to the main function of advancement of education.

It was held in *Re Delius* [1957] that a trust set up by Delius' widow for the advancement of his compositions and performance of his work was a charitable trust for cultural advancement.

The Royal Choral Society was held to be charitable in *Royal Choral Society v IRC* [1943] under this head.

Regarding research, the general rule is that the learning must be imparted, not simply accumulated – see *Re Hopkins* [1965], in which a trust to find evidence that Shakespeare's plays were in fact written by Bacon was granted charitable status, and compare *Re Shaw* [1957], in which a trust to research the benefits of a 40-letter alphabet was held not to be charitable.

In *Re Mariette* [1915], with respect to a gift to provide squash and Eton fives courts, Eve J said that 'learning to play games at a boarding school was as important as learning from books'.

In *IRC v McMullen* [1981], a trust established by the Football Association to provide sports facilities at school and universities was charitable under this head.

In *Re Pinion* [1965], it was held that the views of the donor regarding the educational benefit of his collection described by the judge as 'this mass of junk' were not conclusive of the matter and the collection was not granted charitable status.

In *Re Hopkinson* [1949] Vaisey J said that 'political propaganda masquerading ... as education ... is not charitable'.

Section 3(1)(c) – The advancement of religion
Section 3(2)(a) – Religion includes (i) a religion which involves belief in more than one god and (ii) a religion which does not involve belief in a god.

Section 3(2)(a) makes it clear that a polytheistic religion such as Hinduism and a religion which does not believe in a god, such as Buddhism, are religions within the law on charitable purposes.

However, a trust for the study and dissemination of **ethical** principles was held not to be charitable under this head in *South Place Ethical Society* [1980] although it was charitable under the advancement of education. Similarly, in *United Grand Lodge of Freemasons* [1957] freemasonry was held not to be charitable.

The law is tolerant as to which religions are charitable, as was clear from *Thornton v Howe* [1862] in which a trust, established for the publication of the sacred writings of Joanna Southcott, who claimed that she was with child by the Holy Ghost, was held to be charitable.

A large number of purposes are included under this head although they are only indirectly connected with the advancement of religion, for example: trusts for the maintenance and erection of religious buildings, trusts for the maintenance of a graveyard – *Re Manser* [1905], trusts for the support of the clergy – *Re Forster* [1939], trusts for a church choir, and trusts for the saying of public Masses – *Re Hetherington* [1990].

Section 3(1)(d) – The advancement of health or saving lives
Section 3(2)(b) – The advancement of health includes the prevention or relief of sickness, disease or human suffering

Hospitals which are run on voluntary contributions are charitable, as is medical research. Faith healing is included – *Funnell v Stewart* [1996].

A trust to provide accommodation for nurses was held to be charitable – *London Hospital Medical College v IRC* [1976].

Regarding saving lives – the Royal National Lifeboat Association is charitable, so too is mountain rescue and St John's Ambulance, and the fire services – see *Re Wokingham Fire Brigade Trusts* [1951].

Section 3(1)(e) – The advancement of citizenship or community development
Section 3(2)(c) – The above includes: rural or urban regeneration, the promotion of civic responsibility, volunteering, the voluntary sector or the effectiveness or efficiency of charities

The Charity Commission's guidance on charitable purposes includes the following examples: the Scout and Girl Guide groups, the promotion of Good Citizenship Award schemes, and promotion of community capacity building.

Section 3(1)(f) – The advancement of the arts, culture, heritage or science

The Charity Commission's guidance on charitable purposes includes the following examples: promoting art at a national, professional, local or amateur level; the provision of arts facilities; the promotion of crafts; charities which preserve ancient sites; preservation of historical traditions, e.g. carnivals, country dancing; local or national history/archaeology societies; local arts societies; charities concerned with various learned societies or institutions, e.g. the Royal College of Nursing, the Royal Geographical Society.

See *Re Pinion* [1965] and *Re Delius Will Trust* [1957] considered under Advancement of Education, which could also apply under this head.

Section 3(1)(g) – The advancement of amateur sport
Section 3(2)(d) – 'Sport' means sports or games which promote health by involving physical or mental skill or exertion

The Charity Commission's guidance includes the following examples: charities advancing sport at a local club, e.g. local football, rugby, tennis, multisport centres.

See also *Re Mariette* [1915] and *IRC v McMullen* [1981], considered under Advancement of Education.

See also provision of recreational facilities considered under s 3(1)(m) below.

Section 3(1)(h) – The advancement of human rights, conflict resolution or reconciliation or the promotion of religious or racial harmony or equality and diversity

Charity Commission guidance includes the following examples: charities concerned with the protection of human rights at home or abroad, such as relieving victims of human rights abuse, raising awareness of human rights issues; mediation charities; charities promoting equality and diversity by the elimination of discrimination on grounds of age, sex or sexual orientation; charities enabling people of one faith to understand the religious beliefs of others.

In *McGovern v Attorney General* [1981] it was held that Amnesty International was not charitable because some of its objects were political since they were aimed at changing the law.

Section 3(1)(i) – The advancement of environmental protection or improvement

Charity Commission guidance includes the following examples: charities concerned with the conservation of flora, fauna or the environment generally; zoos; promotion of sustainable development and biodiversity; promotion of recycling and sustainable waste management; research projects into the use of renewable energy sources.

Section 3(1)(j) – The relief of those in need by reason of youth, age, ill-health, disability, financial hardship or other disadvantage
Section 3(2)(e) – The above includes relief given by the provision of accommodation or care to the persons mentioned

Charity Commission guidance includes the following examples: charities concerned with the care, upbringing or establishment in life of children or young people, e.g. children's care homes, apprenticing; charities concerned with the relief of the effects of old age, such as those providing specialist advice, equipment or accommodation, drop-in centres; charities concerned with the relief of disability, such as those providing specialist advice, equipment or accommodation or providing access for disabled persons; charities concerned with the provision of housing, such as alms houses, housing associations.

Section 3(1)(k) – The advancement of animal welfare

Charity Commission guidance includes the following examples: charities promoting kindness and to prevent or suppress cruelty to animals; animal sanctuaries; charities concerned with the care and re-homing of animals that are abandoned, mistreated or lost; feral animal control, e.g. neutering.

Examples include the RSPCA and the Royal Society for the Protection of Birds.

In Re Wedgwood [1915], it was said that such trusts benefit humanity by promoting public morality and curbing an inborn tendency to cruelty.

Section 3(1)(l) – The promotion of the efficiency of the armed forces of the Crown or of the efficiency of the police, fire and rescue services or ambulance service

Charity Commission guidance includes the following: increasing the physical fitness of members of the services through the provision of sporting facilities, equipment and competitions; providing memorials to commemorate the fallen or victories; providing facilities for military training, e.g. drill halls; providing and maintaining band instruments and equipment; encouraging recruitment to the services, e.g. through exhibitions; provision of emergency air or rescue services and equipment.

Section 3(1)(m) – Any other purposes

Section 3(1)(m) of the Charities Act 2011 states that these are purposes recognised as charitable purposes under existing charity law or by virtue of s 5 (recreational and similar trusts). Also included are purposes that may reasonably be regarded as analogous to, or within the spirit of any of the purposes in s 3(1)(a)–(l) above.

The Charity Commission guidelines include: the provision of public works, e.g. repair of bridges, ports; the promotion of agriculture and horticulture; the preservation of public order.

Regarding s 5 Charities Act 2011, this replaces the Recreational Charities Act 1958 and covers the provision of facilities for recreation and other leisure time occupation in the interests of social welfare with the object of improving the conditions of life of persons for whom they are intended and those persons have need of the facilities because of their youth, age, infirmity or disability, poverty, or social and economic circumstances **or** the facilities are available to members of the public at large or to male, or to female, members of the public at large. Examples would include: youth clubs, women's institutes, swimming pools, riding for the disabled.

NO POLITICS 4 CHARITY

Before we leave charitable purposes, it is essential to know that a trust with a political purpose is not charitable, e.g. a charity may not support a political party – *Bonar Law Memorial Trust v IRC* [1933]. A trust whose main object is to change the law of the United Kingdom or of a foreign country is regarded as political – see *McGovern v Attorney General* under s 3(1)(h) Charities Act 2011 above. This was one of the reasons why charitable status was not granted in *National Anti-Vivisection Society v IRC* [1948]. The Charity Commission has published useful guidance (available on its website) to explain what sort of political activity may be undertaken by charities and it is recommended that you look at this.

The public benefit requirement

Introduction

This is the second requirement that you need to be able to discuss. In return for the fiscal privileges enjoyed by charities, a charity must be for the public benefit. There is an implied covenant between charities and society to this effect. The requirement is now stated in the Charities Act 2011 as follows:

Section 2(1) For the purposes of the law of England and Wales, a charitable purpose is a purpose which:

(a) falls within s 3(1), and
(b) is for the public benefit (see s 4).

Section 4(2) In determining whether the public benefit requirement is satisfied in relation to any purpose falling within s 3(1), it is not to be presumed that a purpose of a particular description is for the public benefit.

(3) . . . any reference to the public benefit is a reference to the public benefit as that term is understood for the purposes of the law relating to charities in England and Wales.

Until the **Charities Act 2006**, it was presumed that charities for the relief of poverty, for the advancement of education and for the advancement of religion were for the public benefit. Section 4(2) above makes it clear that the presumption no longer applies. This means that in their Annual Report to the Charity Commission, **all** charities will have to show that they satisfy the public benefit requirement.

Two aspects to public benefit

Notice that s 4(3) **Charities Act 2011**, cited above, indicates that past case law on public benefit still stands. This past case law reveals two aspects to the public benefit requirement (which are also reflected in the Charity Commission's guidance on their website). The content of these two aspects is set out in the diagram below and then the relevant past cases are considered.

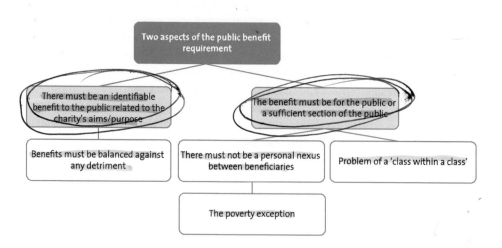

First aspect of the public benefit requirement

There must be an identifiable benefit to the public related to its aims/purposes

As mentioned earlier, there is no longer a presumption that the first three heads of charity are for the public benefit. For example, a trust for the advancement of education that seeks to be registered as charitable must prove that its purpose is beneficial to the public.

NUNS – PRAYING NOT BENEFIT

The controversial House of Lords case *Gilmour v Coates* [1949] concerned the charitable status of a trust for a community of contemplative nuns, who devoted their lives to prayer. Lord Simonds dismissed the submissions that the nuns' prayers conferred a benefit on the public because it was 'not susceptible of proof' and that the public benefited from observing the community's way of life because that was 'too vague and intangible', i.e. there was **no identifiable benefit to the public related to its aims**.

Benefits must be balanced against any detriment or harm

In *National Anti-Vivisection Society v IRC* [1948], the House of Lords rejected the Society's appeal for charitable status and held that any 'public benefit in the direction of the advancement of morals and education was far outweighed by the detriment to medical science and research … which would result if the society succeeded in achieving its object'.

Second aspect of the public benefit requirement

Benefit must be for the public or a sufficient section of the public

Regarding the issue of the benefit being for a sufficient section of the public, you should know about the personal nexus test. This relates to whether there is some personal connection (nexus) between the beneficiaries. If there is, then they do not constitute a sufficient section of the public.

The personal nexus test

CONTRACT – NEXUS

Case precedent – *Oppenheim v Tobacco Securities Trust Co Ltd* [1951] AC 297

Facts: Income from a trust was to be applied to provide 'for the education of children of employees of the British American Tobacco Co Ltd or any subsidiary or allied company'. It was argued that this was a charitable trust for the advancement of education and therefore was not caught by the rule against perpetuities. The House of Lords held in accordance with the principle below that the trust did not benefit a section of the public and that charitable status would not be granted.

ALL KNEW ANOTHER

Principle: In order to benefit a section of the public, the beneficiaries must not be numerically negligible nor may there be a personal nexus or link between the beneficiaries, e.g. by blood or by contract.

Application: In the above case, the beneficiaries were not negligible as there were over 100,000 employees but the beneficiaries were all linked by contract. When you apply this decision, it is recommended that you mention the dissenting judgment of Lord MacDermott – see 'Up for Debate' box below.

Up for Debate

Extracts from Lord MacDermott's dissenting judgment in *Oppenheim v Tobacco Securities Co Ltd* [1951] regarding the personal nexus test: '. . . with the great respect due to those who have formulated this test, I find myself unable to regard it as a criterion of general applicability and conclusiveness. In the first place, I see much difficulty in dividing the qualities or attributes, which may serve to bind human beings into classes, into two mutually exclusive groups, the one involving individual status and purely personal, the other disregarding such status and quite impersonal'.

'. . . Is a distinction to be drawn in this respect between those who are employed in a particular industry before it is nationalised and those who are employed therein after that process has been completed and one employer has taken the place of many? . . . Is the relationship between those in the service of the Crown to be distinguished from that obtaining between those in the service of some other employer? Or, if not, are the children of, say, soldiers or civil servants to be regarded as not constituting a sufficient section of the public to make a trust for their education charitable?'

Notice that there is a possible way round the personal nexus test, which is to create a trust for a wide class of beneficiaries but direct the trustees to give **preference** to a limited class who might be connected by blood or contract. In *Re Koettgen's Will Trusts* [1954], an educational trust was available to the public at large subject to a direction that trustees should give preference up to 75% of the income to the families of employees of a company. The trust was held to be charitable. However, this may be compared with the trust that failed in *IRC v Educational Grants Association Ltd* [1967] concerning a larger preference of 76–80% of the income for the education of children of those connected with the Metal Box Company.

The poverty exception

For more than 200 years, provided the beneficiaries are not identified by name, a gift to 'poor relations' has been upheld as charitable although the beneficiaries are clearly connected by blood. This is called the 'poverty exception' to the public benefit requirement and has been extended to 'poor employees' as recognised in the House of Lords case *Dingle v Turner* [1972] and to poor members of a society in *Spiller v Maude* [1886].

There was doubt whether the poverty exception had survived the Charities Act 2006 requirement on public benefit and therefore a reference was made in *Attorney General v Charity Commission* [2012] to the Upper Tribunal, which held that a trust for the relief of poverty in which there was a personal connection between the beneficiaries was capable of being charitable. It said that the public benefit requirement in the Charities Act related to the meaning of the term in the first sense (see diagram above) as opposed to the second limb that it should benefit a section of the public. The poverty exception related to the second limb.

Problem of a class within a class ~ NO

Whilst it is reasonable to restrict a charity's purposes, for example to a particular geographical area, a problem may arise when there is a further restriction, as occurred in the following case.

> **Case precedent – *IRC v Baddeley* [1955] AC 572**   METODIST CLASSINC
>
> **Facts:** The object of the trust was to provide social and recreational facilities for Methodists in West Ham and Leyton. The House of Lords held that the trust was not for a sufficient section of the public as it was restricted to a class of beneficiaries (Methodists) within a class (in West Ham and Leyton).
>
> **Principle:** The public benefit requirement may not be satisfied if it is to benefit a class within a class.
>
> **Application:** This principle should be applied with caution as it depends on whether the restriction is unreasonable or arbitrary. In any event, it has not been applied consistently by the courts – see *Re Faraker* [1912] in which the trust 'for the poor widows of Rotherhithe' was upheld as charitable, although there were three restrictions.

Exclusively charitable purposes

This is the third requirement for a valid charity and is established by case law. Examples of key points are given in the following boxes.

Case where 'OR' was used	*Chichester Diocesan Fund and Board of Finance v Simpson* [1944] – Gift for 'charitable or benevolent' purposes failed because benevolent purposes were not necessarily charitable in law.
Cases where 'AND' was used	*Re Sutton* [1885] – A gift for 'charitable and deserving' objects was upheld as it was possible to construe the phrase conjunctively as opposed to disjunctively. However, in *Attorney General of the Bahamas v Royal Trust Co* [1986], a gift 'for education and welfare' was too wide a concept to enable the court to read the two words in conjunction.

| Incidental non-charitable purposes | Whilst incidental non-charitable purposes will not cause charitable status to be refused – see *Incorporated Council of Law Reporting in England and Wales v Attorney General* [1948] under Advancement of Education above, subsidiary non-charitable purposes will lead to failure – see *Oxford Group v IRC* [1949]. |

Cy-près doctrine

Introduction

Examination questions on charitable trusts, whether they are problem or essay questions, usually contain some element relating to this doctrine.

We saw in Chapter 6 that when an express trust fails, the property is held on resulting trust for the settlor. One of the legal advantages of a charity is that when a charitable trust fails, the property/funds is applied cy-près. The cy-près doctrine enables the court or the Charity Commission to draw up a scheme so that the property/funds can be applied for charitable purposes as close as possible (cy-près) to the purpose intended by the donor.

When the charitable trust fails from the start, this is known as **initial failure** and, in order to apply the cy-près doctrine, it is necessary to find a general charitable intention on the part of the settlor/donor. When an existing charitable trust becomes impossible or impractical to carry out, this is known as **subsequent failure**. It is not necessary to find a general charitable intention in this case and, provided the charitable purpose has become impossible or impractical to carry out, the cy-près doctrine will be applied. These principles are illustrated in the following diagram and considered in greater detail below.

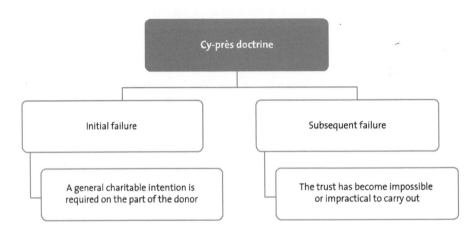

Initial failure

DONOR (handwritten)

When a charitable trust fails at the date of the gift, it must be shown that the donor had a **general charitable intent** as opposed to an intention that the property should be applied for a **specific** purpose or a **specific** institution. In the former case, the property will be applied cy-près. In the latter case, the gift will lapse. The following diagrams consider initial failure of a gift for a **purpose** and then initial failure of a gift to an **institution**.

Initial failure

Gift was intended for a charitable purpose, which failed. But was there a general charitable intention?

Yes, if the gift was for a particular purpose, but taking the trust instrument as a whole, it was possible to find a general charitable intention – see *Biscoe v Jackson* [1887] concerning a gift for the establishment of a soup kitchen in Shoreditch. A general charitable intention was found to benefit the poor of Shoreditch and the gift was applied cy-près.

No, if the gift was for a particular purpose, both in form and substance – see *Re Good* [1950] concerning a gift to provide rest homes in Hull. A very detailed scheme was laid down by the donor regarding the type of homes and persons who could reside there. No general charitable intention was found and the gift lapsed.

Initial failure

Gift was intended for a charitable institution, which failed. But was there a general charitable intention?

Yes, if the gift was for a non-existent charitable institution, it is easier to find a general charitable intention. In *Re Harwood* [1936], a gift of £300 was made to the Peace Society of Belfast. This society had never existed but the court found a general charitable intention to benefit societies whose purpose was the promotion of peace. See also *Re Satterthwaite's Will Trusts* [1966].

No, if the gift was for an institution that had ceased to exist at the time of the gift, but the wording made it clear that it was for a specific institution only. In *Re Harwood*, a gift of £200 was made to the Wisbech Peace Society, which had ceased to exist. The gift failed as the wording was regarded as specific. See also *Re Rymer* [1895] where a gift failed because it was made to a particular seminary that had ceased to exist.

HARWOOD = PEASE!! LOL (handwritten)

The following diagram is concerned firstly with whether there is initial failure when a charity has amalgamated with another, and secondly, with the distinction made between incorporated and unincorporated institutions in the context of the cy-près doctrine.

Is there initial failure when the charity continues in a different form?

If the named charity was amalgamated with others, then the gift will not lapse – see *Re Faraker* [1912] in which a gift to Mrs Bayley's Charity in Rotherhithe had been amalgamated with a number of other charities for the poor in Rotherhithe.
See also *Re Lucas* [1948].

In *Re Vernon's Will Trusts* [1972], Buckley J said 'every bequest to an unincorporated charity by name ... must take effect as a gift for a **charitable purpose**...' Conversely, a gift to an incorporated body takes effect as a gift to that body. See *Re Finger's Will Trusts* [1972] below for an illustration of these principles.

Case precedent – *Re Finger's Will Trusts* [1972] Ch 286

Facts: The testatrix left her residuary estate on trust to 11 charitable institutions. One of these was an unincorporated body called the National Radium Commission and another was an incorporated body called the National Council for Maternity and Child Welfare. Both bodies had ceased to exist when the testatrix died.

Regarding the unincorporated body, it was held that there was **no** initial failure as it was regarded that the gift had been made for a charitable purpose and did not depend upon the continued existence of the Commission. Conversely, the gift to the incorporated body was regarded as a gift to a legal entity that had ceased to exist. However, in this instance, the testatrix had shown a general charitable intention; the gift was applied cy-près.

Principle: A gift to an unincorporated association prima facie takes effect as a gift for purposes and a gift to a corporate body prima facie takes effect as a gift to the particular legal entity.

Application: It may help to remember Chapter 9, in which we saw that an unincorporated association is not a legal entity so any gift to it is prima facie for a purpose.

Subsequent failure

If the gift to a charity takes effect, then the property is charitable from that point onwards and even if the charity body ceases to operate, or the charitable purpose becomes impossible or impractical, that property will remain charitable and will be applied cy-près. This is known as subsequent failure.

Section 62 Charities Act 2011 (which replaces s 13 Charities Act 1993) sets out the circumstances when it is regarded that the purposes of a charity have become impossible or impractical to carry out. These circumstances are as follows:

Section 62(1)(a) Where the original purposes in whole or in part –

  (i) have been as far as may be fulfilled, or
  (ii) cannot be carried out, or not according to the directions given and to the spirit of the gift, or

(b) Where the original purposes provide a use for part only of the property available by virtue of the gift, or

(c) Where:

  (i) the property available by virtue of the gift, and
  (ii) other property applicable for similar purposes, can be more effectively used in conjunction, and to that end can suitably, regard being had to the appropriate considerations, be made applicable to common purposes, or

(d) Where the original purposes were laid down by reference to:

  (i) an area which then was but has since ceased to be a unit for some other purpose, or
  (ii) a class of persons or an area which has for any reason since ceased to be suitable, regard being had to appropriate considerations, or to be practical in administering the gift, or

(e) Where the original purposes, in whole or in part, have, since they were laid down –

  (i) been adequately provided by other means,
  (ii) ceased, as being useless or harmful to the community or for other reasons, to be in law charitable, or
  (iii) ceased in any other way to provide a suitable and effective method of using the property available by virtue of the gift, regard being had to the appropriate considerations.

An example of s 62(1)(a) **Charities Act 2011** is *Re Lepton's Charity* [1972] where a testator, who died in 1716, devised property on trust and directed his trustees to pay an annual sum of £3 to a Protestant Minister in Pudsey, and to apply the surplus income from the property to the poor and aged of Pudsey. By the date of the court case, the total income of the trust was £790 and the court, having regard to the spirit of the gift, approved a cy-près scheme increasing the Minister's entitlement to £100 per annum.

In *Re North Devon and West Somerset Relief Fund* [1953], a surplus remained after a generous response from the public following a flood disaster at Lynton. This part of the charitable fund was applied cy-près for a similar charitable purpose in accordance with s 62(1)(b).

We have seen an example of s 62(1)(c) in *Re Faraker* [1912] regarding a gift to Mrs Bayley's Charity, Rotherhithe, which had been amalgamated with a number of other charities for the benefit of the poor in Rotherhithe.

Peggs v Lamb [1994] provides an example of s 62(1)(d). This concerned land held for the charitable purpose of providing an income for poor and needy freemen and their widows in the Borough of Huntingdon. By 1992, the income had risen to £550,000, whilst the number of beneficiaries had gone down to 15. Having regard to s 62(1)(d) and the spirit of the gift, the court approved the enlargement of the class of beneficiaries to include all the inhabitants of Huntingdon and not just the freemen and their widows.

Section 62(1)(e)(iii) was applied in *Varsani v Jesani* [1999], which concerned a charitable trust for a particular Hindu sect. The sect had split into two parts and the court approved a scheme dividing the assets of the charity between the two groups. A similar decision was recently reached in *White v Williams* [2010] in which the Bibleway Trust, which owned four church buildings, split into three congregations. Briggs J said, 'A scheme or schemes whereby each place of worship is transferred to separate trustees whose role is directed to the fulfilment of purposes specific to the congregation or locality associated with it, seems to me to be plainly the best solution'.

Unidentified donors and anonymous donations to charity collections

These two situations concern initial failure and are dealt with by s 63 and s 64 Charities Act 2011 as follows.

The first situation occurs when property was given for a specific charitable purpose that failed from the start, and advertisements and inquiries have been made but the donor cannot be identified or found, or where the donor disclaimed the right to have the property returned. In both these cases, s 63 of the Charities Act 2011 provides that the property will be applied cy-près as if given for charitable purposes generally.

Section 64 Charities Act 2011 is concerned with proceeds of cash collections, e.g. from collecting boxes and lotteries, which will be conclusively presumed to belong to unidentified persons. The same will apply when it would not be reasonable having regard to the amounts or the lapse of time to return the donations. In both cases, the property will be applied cy-près.

Cy-près scheme

Both the Charity Commission and the court have the power to set up a cy-près scheme. In so doing, they are required by s 67 of the Charities Act 2011 to have regard to the spirit of the original gift and to apply the property for charitable purposes as close as possible to the original purposes, if these are appropriate in the light of current social and economic circumstances.

Putting it into practice

In his will, David Davies, a retired Head of Department at Aberworth University, endeavoured to set up the following trusts:

(a) £60,000 to the registrar of Aberworth University to distribute amongst such charitable or benevolent objects as he shall select;
(b) £200,000 to be applied for the promotion of the education of children of staff of Aberworth University;
(c) £200,000 to be applied for research to demonstrate the benefits to society of the abolition of the National Health Service;
(d) £20,000 to the Sedley Home for Horses;
(e) £10,000 for the provision of some useful memorial to myself in Aberworth park.

David Davies has just died. His executors have discovered that the Sedley Home for Horses has never existed and seek your advice regarding the validity of the above trusts.

Feedback on putting it into practice

Questions on charitable purpose trusts sometimes include an element of non-charitable purpose trusts. Therefore, a short introduction should be given regarding the requirements for the validity of charitable purpose trusts and it should be explained that, with a few exceptions, non-charitable trusts are void. Outline answers for (a) to (e) are as follows.

(a) Whilst a gift to the registrar of Aberworth University would be deemed for the advancement of education, the trust must be exclusively charitable. Benevolent objects are not necessarily charitable and, as the objects will be read disjunctively, the gift will fail – *Chichester Diocesan Fund & Board of Finance v Simpson*.
(b) Whilst the trust is for the advancement of education and the number of potential beneficiaries is unlikely to be negligible, there is a personal nexus between the beneficiaries – *Oppenheim v Tobacco Securities Trust Co Ltd*, which will cause the trust to fail on the public benefit requirement. Ideally, you should mention Lord MacDermott's dissenting judgment on the personal nexus test.
(c) Whilst research may succeed as a charitable object under the advancement of education, provided it is disseminated and not merely accumulated – *Re Hopkins Will Trusts*, it must satisfy the public benefit aspect, and despite the wording of the gift, this might be questionable as any benefits are outweighed by the harm caused by the aim of the trust – *National Anti-Vivisection Society v IRC*. Furthermore, citing the same case, the trust may be regarded as political.
(d) This is a case of initial failure as the Sedley Home for Horses has never existed. Following *Re Harwood*, a general charitable intention on the part of the testator may be found, and the fund may be applied cy-près.
(e) This is a non-charitable purpose trust. Such trusts are void largely because of the beneficiary principle, and those exceptions permitted, which include trusts for tombs or monuments, are unenforceable trusts. Such unenforceable trusts must be certain, and it was this requirement that led the trust in *Re Endacott* to fail. The same would apply in the problem case.

Table of key cases referred to in this chapter

Case name	Area of law	Principle
Biscoe v Jackson [1887]	Cy-près	General charitable intention found
Chichester Diocesan Fund & Board of Finance v Simpson [1944]	Exclusively charitable purposes	Gift for charitable or benevolent purposes failed
Coulthurst, Re [1951]	Prevention or relief of poverty	Poverty – persons who have 'to go short'
Dingle v Turner [1972]	Public benefit	Poverty exception
Finger's Will Trust, Re [1972]	Cy-près	Gift to an unincorporated association takes effect prima facie as a gift for a purpose
Gilmour v Coates [1949]	Advancement of religion	No identifiable benefit to the public
Good, Re [1950]	Cy-près	No general charitable intention found
Harwood, Re [1936]	Cy-près	Institution never existed – general charitable intention found
Hopkins, Re [1965]	Advancement of education	Research – learning must be imparted not simply accumulated
IRC v Baddeley [1955]	Public benefit	Class within a class
IRC v McMullen [1981]	Advancement of education	Provision of sports facilities at schools and universities was charitable
IRC v Pemsel [1891]	Charitable purposes	Lord Macnaghten classified charitable purposes into four heads
Lepton's Charity, Re [1972]	Cy-près	Original purpose impractical so cy-près doctrine applied
McGovern v Attorney General [1981]	Political purpose	A political purpose is not a charitable purpose
National Anti-Vivisection Society v IRC [1948]	Public benefit	Benefit must be balanced against any detriment
Niyazi's Will Trusts, Re [1978]	Prevention or relief of poverty	'Working men's hostel' charitable under this head
Oppenheim v Tobacco Securities Co Ltd [1951]	Public benefit	Personal nexus test
Pinion, Re [1965]	Advancement of education	Donor's view of educational benefit not conclusive
Sutton, Re [1887]	Exclusively charitable purposes	Gift for charitable and deserving objects upheld

@ Visit the book's companion website to test your knowledge

❖ Resources include a subject map, revision tip podcasts, downloadable diagrams, MCQ quizzes for each chapter, and a flashcard glossary

❖ www.routledge.com/cw/optimizelawrevision

11

Trusteeship

Revision objectives

Understand the law

- Can you explain when a replacement trustee may be appointed under s 36(1) Trustee Act 1925?
- How may a trustee be removed from office?

Remember the details

- Do you remember a trustee's duties when he is exercising his power of investment under the Trustee Act 2000?
- When can a trustee invest in land under the Trustee Act 2000?

Reflect critically on areas of debate

- In private trusts for beneficiaries entitled in succession, should trustees select investments in terms of capital and income or should they be able to adopt total return investment?

Contextualise

- Are purchases of trust property by trustees always voidable?
- If a trustee purchases a beneficiary's equitable interest, why is s 53(1)(c) Law of Property Act 1925 relevant?

Apply your skills and knowledge

- Can you answer the problem question at the end of this chapter?

Chapter Map

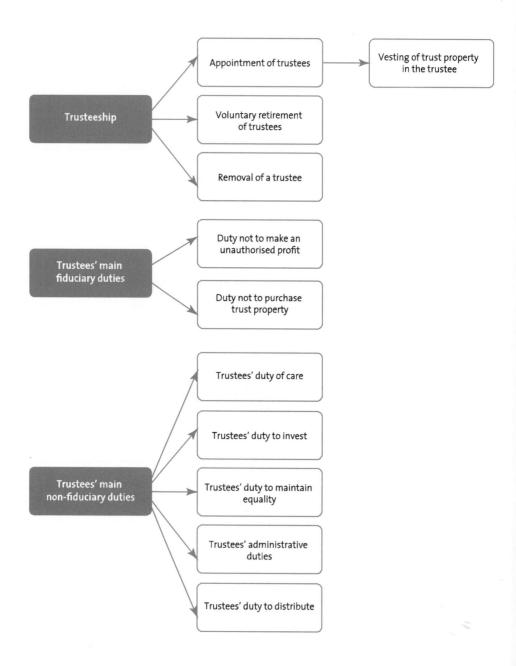

Trusteeship

Examination questions on trusteeship relate to the appointment, retirement and removal of trustees and the main duties of a trustee, all of which are considered below. However, the questions may also refer to trustees' powers, which are dealt with in the next chapter.

Appointment of trustees

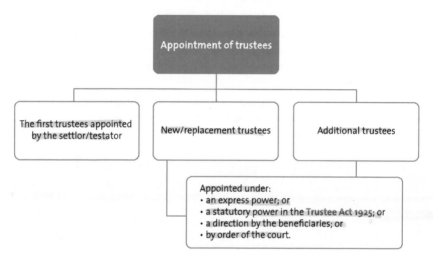

As you can see from the above diagram, the appointment of trustees may arise in three situations, dealt with in turn below.

The first trustees

The settlor of an *inter vivos* trust normally appoints the first trustees and, if it is a testamentary trust, the testator will usually have nominated the trustees in his will (very often the same people who are acting as his executors).

Any legal person having legal capacity, whether an individual or a trust corporation (e.g. the trustee department of a bank) may be appointed as a trustee of an **express trust.** An infant does not have legal capacity and s 20 of the Law of Property Act 1925 states 'the appointment of an infant to be a trustee in relation to any settlement or trust shall be void'.

However, we saw in Chapter 6 in *Re Vinogradoff* [1935] that an infant was a trustee under a **resulting trust** of personal property. This would not apply to a resulting trust of real property because an infant cannot hold a legal estate in land.

Regarding numbers of trustees, it is unwise to appoint just one trustee (other than a trust corporation) because of the risk of fraud or maladministration. In any event, in the case of land, a sole trustee (other than a trust corporation) cannot give a valid receipt for capital money, which means that there have to be at least two trustees when trust land is sold. As for the maximum number of trustees, in respect of a trust of land, s 34 of the Trustee Act 1925 provides that there may be no more than four trustees and, although there is no maximum for trusts of personal property, it is unusual to have more than four trustees. It follows from the above that, in most trusts, there are normally between two and four trustees.

A trust will not fail for want of a trustee

If the trustee appointed by the settlor or testator disclaims or has already died, then the property reverts to the settlor or the personal representatives of the testator to be held upon trust, i.e. the trust will not fail. The authority is *Mallot v Wilson* [1903], which was approved recently by the Court of Appeal in *Harris v Sharp* [2003].

If a sole trustee dies while in office, again the trust will not fail because the property will vest in his personal representatives to be held upon the trusts of the settlement.

Common Pitfall

It is a common mistake to think that the new trustees are the original trustees appointed by the settlor. As we have seen, the original trustees are called the first trustees. New trustees are, in effect, replacement trustees and are considered next.

New trustees/replacement trustees

If you look back at the diagram, you will notice that new trustees may be appointed under an express power in the trust instrument. These express powers are rare because the statutory power in s 36(1) of the Trustee Act 1925 is so wide. So, we will pass to the statutory power. As you read s 36(1) below, note that it not only states when new trustees may be appointed, it also states who has the power to appoint those new trustees.

Trustee Act 1925

Section 36(1) Where a trustee, either original or substituted, and whether appointed by a court or otherwise, is dead, or remains out of the United Kingdom for more than 12 months, or desires to be discharged from all or any of the trusts ... or refuses or is unfit to act therein, or is incapable of acting therein, or is an infant, then subject to the restrictions imposed by this Act on the number of trustees –

(a) the person or persons nominated for the purpose of appointing new trustees by the instrument, if any, creating the trust; or
(b) if there is no such person, or no such person able and willing to act, then the surviving or continuing trustees or trustee for the time being, or the personal representatives of the last surviving or continuing trustee;

may, by writing, appoint one or more other persons (whether or not being the persons exercising the power) to be a trustee or trustees . . .

Points to notice about s 36(1) Trustee Act 1925

First, notice that there are **seven** situations when a new trustee may be appointed. Three of these need some explanation, as follows.

'remains out of the United Kingdom for more than 12 months'	This relates to a continuous period of 12 months. In *Re Walker* [1901], the provision could not be used in respect of a trustee who had returned to the United Kingdom for just one week in the year.
'is unfit to act therein'	This relates to some defect in character – and applied in *Re Wheeler and De Rochow* [1896] to a trustee who was bankrupt and absconded.
'is incapable of acting therein'	This relates to physical or mental incapacity and was used in *Re East* [1873] regarding a trustee of unsound mind.

Second, notice that there are **three** groups of people, in a particular order, who may exercise the statutory power to appoint new trustees. These three groups are discussed below.

'person or persons nominated . . . by the trust instrument'	It is normal for someone to be nominated to exercise the statutory power. If two persons are nominated to exercise it jointly, then it is not exercisable by just one of those persons.
'the surviving or continuing trustees'	Section 36(8) of the Act states that a continuing trustee includes 'a refusing or retiring trustee'. However, a trustee who is being **removed** from the trust is not a retiring trustee – *Re Stoneham's Settlement Trusts* [1953].
'the personal representatives of the last surviving/ continuing trustee'	This is the last group that can exercise the statutory power. If there is no one in this group, then the court has the power to appoint new trustees under s 41 Trustee Act 1925 and the beneficiaries have the right of direction to appoint (for both of these, see later).

Appointment of additional trustees

Looking back at the diagram, you will see that an additional trustee may be appointed by an express power in the trust instrument but, again, such express powers are unusual because the statutory power in s 36(6) Trustee Act 1925 is very wide. It authorises the appointment of additional trustees where no trustee is being replaced (i.e. where s 36(1) is not being used). Section 36(6) reads as follows:

> **Trustee Act 1925**
>
> **Section 36(6)** Where, in the case of any trust, there are not more than three trustees:
>
> (a) The person or persons nominated for the purpose of appointing new trustees by the instrument, if any, creating the trust; or
> (b) If there is no such person, or no such person able and willing to act, then the trustee or trustees for the time being;
>
> may, by writing, appoint another person or other persons to be an additional trustee or additional trustees . . .

Note the restriction that an additional trustee cannot be appointed under the statutory power if there are already four trustees. Also note that the person nominated to appoint the additional trustee cannot appoint himself because the Act refers to appointing 'another person'.

Appointment of new or additional trustees by direction of the beneficiaries

This power was given to beneficiaries by s 19 of the Trusts of Land and Appointment of Trustees Act 1996, which reads as follows:

> **Trusts of Land and Appointment of Trustees Act 1996**
>
> **Section 19(1)** This section applies in the case of a trust where:
>
> (a) there is no person nominated for the purpose of appointing new trustees by the instrument, if any, creating the trust; and
> (b) the beneficiaries under the trust are of full age and capacity and (taken together) are absolutely entitled to the property subject to the trust;
>
> **Section 91(2)** The beneficiaries may give . . .
>
> (a) a written direction to a trustee or trustees to retire from the trust; and
> (b) a written direction to a trustee . . . (or if there are none, to the personal representative of the last person who was a trustee) to appoint by writing to be a trustee . . . the person specified in the direction.

Points to notice about the above section. First, the beneficiaries cannot enjoy this right to appoint new trustees if there is someone else who has been nominated in the trust instrument to appoint. Next, see the following:

'beneficiaries ... are of full age and capacity ... and absolutely entitled ...'	If the beneficiaries satisfy these requirements, it is in fact a bare trust and, **in practice**, the beneficiaries are more likely to exercise their rights under the rule in *Saunders v Vautier* and bring the trust to an end than appoint a new trustee under s 19.
'a written direction to a trustee ... to retire from the trust'	This extract shows that the beneficiaries may use s 19 to require a trustee to retire although they can also use it simply to appoint a new trustee. In either case, the wording of s 19 reveals that they do not actually appoint the person themselves but direct a trustee to do so.

Appointment of new or additional trustees by the court

The court has **inherent** jurisdiction to appoint trustees but this is rarely used because it has a wide **statutory** power to appoint new or additional trustees under s 41 Trustee Act 1925 as follows:

Trustee Act 1925

Section 41(1) The court, may, whenever it is expedient to appoint a new trustee or new trustees, and it is found inexpedient, difficult or impracticable so to do without the assistance of the court, make an order appointing a new trustee or trustees either in substitution for or in addition to any existing trustee or trustees, or although there is no existing trustee.

In particular and without prejudice to the generality of the foregoing provision, the court may make an order appointing a new trustee in substitution for a trustee who lacks capacity to exercise his functions as trustee, or is a bankrupt, or is a corporation which is in liquidation or has been dissolved.

Three criteria were identified in *Re Tempest* providing guidance when the court appoints trustees under this provision.

The court will have regard to three criteria when exercising its discretion under s 41 Trustee Act 1925	In *Re Tempest* [1866] Turner LJ said that the court would have regard to (a) the wishes of the settlor; (b) the interests of the beneficiaries; and (c) the effective administration of the trust. Accordingly, the court held that the beneficiary's nominee for trustee, a Mr Petre, should not be appointed as this would be in opposition to the specific wishes of the testator.

When exercising its power under s 41 Trustee Act 1925, the court is very reluctant to appoint a beneficiary or a beneficiary's spouse as trustee because of the potential for a conflict of interest – *Re Coode* [1913].

Vesting of trust property in the trustee

In Chapter 4, we saw that legal title to the trust property must be vested in the trustee by the settlor in order for the trust to be completely constituted. How this is done depends on the subject matter of the property. In the case of the first trustees, it will still be necessary to vest legal title in the trustees.

However, when new/replacement trustees are appointed, s 40 Trustee Act 1925 provides that vesting of the trust property will be **automatic**, provided the trustees are appointed by deed. There are exceptions to this automatic vesting and the important ones to note are stocks and shares because the transfer must still be registered by the relevant company, and registered land where the change of legal proprietor must still be registered by the Land Registry.

Voluntary retirement of trustees

There is no fixed retirement age for trustees. However, should a trustee wish to retire, there are three ways in which this may be achieved.

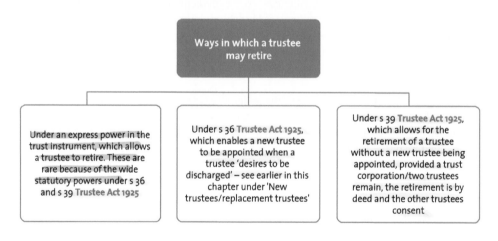

Example: Tim and Toby are trustees. If Toby wishes to retire and there is no express power in the trust instrument, he would have to retire under s 36 Trustee Act 1925 with a new trustee being appointed in his place. He could not use s 39 Trustee Act 1925 as that only applies when at least two trustees/a trust corporation remain.

As we shall see in Chapter 13, Toby would remain liable for breaches of trust committed during his time as a trustee – he cannot hope to escape liability by retiring.

Removal of a trustee

We are now concerned with removing a trustee against his wishes. Note that there are four ways this could be achieved.

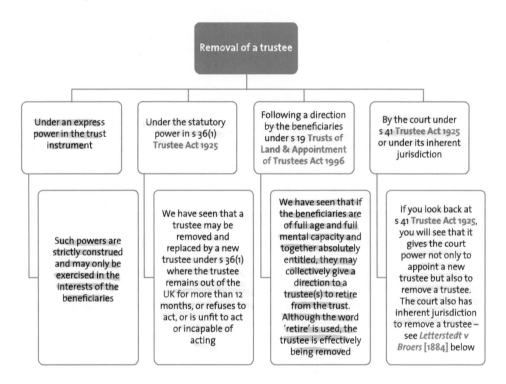

The court's inherent jurisdiction to remove a trustee is exercised primarily to protect the interests of the beneficiaries. Lord Blackburn provided some guidance in *Letterstedt v Broers* [1884], stating 'if it appears clear that the continuance of the trustee would be detrimental to the execution of the trusts, even if for no other reason than that human infirmity would prevent those beneficially interested, or those who act for them, from working in harmony with the trustee ... the trustee is always advised ... to resign ... if, without reasonable ground, he refused to do so , it seems to their Lordships that the court might think it proper to remove him'.

The duties of trustees

The duties of trustees depend on the type of trust but examination questions are concerned only with those key duties that are common to all trustees. These duties may be divided into two groups, which are subdivided as shown in the following diagram.

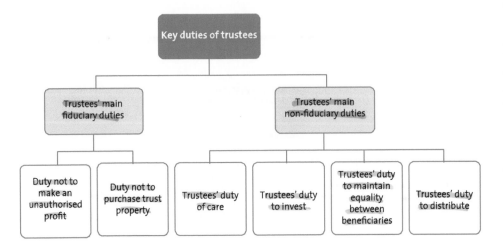

Trustees' main fiduciary duties

In Chapter 7 on constructive trusts, we saw that trustees are fiduciaries and that they, and other fiduciaries such as solicitors and company directors, must act in good faith towards their principal and must not place themselves in a position where their duty to their principal and their personal interests conflict.

Duty not to make an unauthorised profit

The cases that we studied in Chapter 7 under the above heading apply equally here and there is no point repeating them, so long as you are aware that they are part of a trustee's fiduciary duties. Instead, other aspects of the duty, which apply specifically to trustees, are now considered.

Can a trustee keep his director's fees?

If the trust instrument authorises the trustee to keep any director's fees, then he may do so. Otherwise, the answer to the question depends on whether the trustee used his position as trustee to obtain the directorship. The following diagram reflects the facts in *Re Francis* [1905].

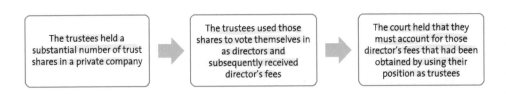

Re Francis can be usefully compared with *Re Dover Coalfield Extension Ltd* [1908] in which a director of Dover Coalfield was appointed a director of Kent Collieries Corporation. He was required to hold 1,000 shares in Kent Collieries and these were provided for him by Dover Coalfield on the condition that he was holding them on trust for Dover Coalfield. The Court of Appeal held that he could keep his director's fees from Kent Collieries because he was a director before he was a trustee, i.e. the directorship did not flow from his trusteeship. In *Re Gee* [1948], a trustee who was elected as director could keep his director's fees because he would have been so elected even if the votes attached to the trust shares had been disregarded.

Is a trustee entitled to remuneration?

The basic rule is that a trustee is not entitled to remuneration but notice that this is subject to a number of exceptions, as shown in the following diagram.

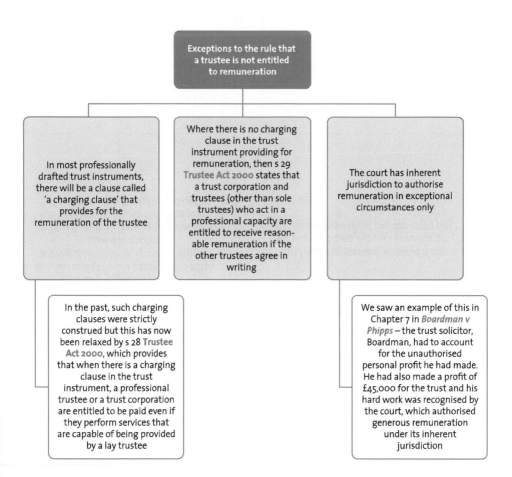

Exceptions to the rule that a trustee is not entitled to remuneration

In most professionally drafted trust instruments, there will be a clause called 'a charging clause' that provides for the remuneration of the trustee

In the past, such charging clauses were strictly construed but this has now been relaxed by s 28 **Trustee Act 2000**, which provides that when there is a charging clause in the trust instrument, a professional trustee or a trust corporation are entitled to be paid even if they perform services that are capable of being provided by a lay trustee

Where there is no charging clause in the trust instrument providing for remuneration, then s 29 **Trustee Act 2000** states that a trust corporation and trustees (other than sole trustees) who act in a professional capacity are entitled to receive reasonable remuneration if the other trustees agree in writing

The court has inherent jurisdiction to authorise remuneration in exceptional circumstances only

We saw an example of this in Chapter 7 in *Boardman v Phipps* – the trust solicitor, Boardman, had to account for the unauthorised personal profit he had made. He had also made a profit of £45,000 for the trust and his hard work was recognised by the court, which authorised generous remuneration under its inherent jurisdiction

As for **expenses** incurred by a trustee, s 31 of the Trustee Act 2000 gives the right to reimbursement of these but without interest.

Duty not to purchase trust property

This duty is found in two rules (the self-dealing rule and the fair-dealing rule), which are explained in the following diagram.

The self-dealing rule – this applies when the trustee purchases trust property for himself	The fair-dealing rule – this applies when the trustee purchases the beneficial interest of the beneficiary
Example: A racehorse owned by the trust is to be sold by the trustees. Tim, one of the trustees, decides to buy the racehorse	Example: A racehorse is held on trust for four beneficiaries. Ben, one of the beneficiaries, wants to sell his equitable interest and Tim, the trustee, decides to buy Ben's equitable interest in the horse
Tim has a conflict of interest. He should sell the horse for the best price but he has a personal interest in a low price	Notice that Ben is disposing of his subsisting equitable interest and, you may remember from Chapter 3 that, in accordance with s 53(1)(c) Law of Property Act 1925, the disposition would have to be in writing and signed by Ben

Under the **self-dealing rule**, the sale to Tim would be voidable, i.e. the beneficiaries may, if they wish, ask the court to set the sale aside provided they act within a reasonable time.

Under the **fair-dealing rule**, the sale is not voidable as such, provided it was fair and honest, i.e. it can be shown that the beneficiary was not subject to undue influence by the trustee, that full disclosure was made to the beneficiary and that the trustee paid an adequate price – *Thomson v Eastwood* [1877].

Trustees' main non-fiduciary duties

These are duties imposed on trustees in relation to the management of the trust.

Trustees' duty of care

Before the Trustee Act 2000, the trustees' duty of care was that laid down in *Speight v Gaunt* [1883], which required a trustee to act as an ordinary prudent man of business would act in managing his own affairs. The weakness of this common law duty was that it did not differentiate between the professional trustee and the lay trustee.

Section 1 of the Trustee Act 2000 replaces the common law duty of care with a statutory duty, which sets down a variable standard that takes into account the knowledge and experience of the trustee.

It reads as follows:

Trustee Act 2000

Section 1(1)   Whenever the duty under this subsection applies to a trustee, he must exercise such care and skill as is reasonable in the circumstances, having regard in particular –

(a)   to any special knowledge or experience that he has or holds himself out as having, and
(b)   if he acts as trustee in the course of a business or profession, to any special knowledge or experience that it is reasonable to expect of a person acting in the course of that kind of business or profession.

Section 2   Schedule 1 makes provision about when the duty of care applies to a trustee.

Points to notice about this duty of care are that it contains an objective element in s 1(1)(b) (for example, an accountant who acts as trustee in the course of his profession would be judged according to how a reasonable person in that profession would act), but it also contains a subjective element in s 1(1)(a) in that his particular knowledge or experience would be taken into account by the court. The duty applies to the long list in Schedule 1 of all the key functions carried out by trustees. However, the duty of care can be excluded by the trust instrument and it is assumed that, in such a case, the common law duty of care would still apply.

Duty to invest

Within a reasonable time after the creation of the trust, trustees have a duty to invest the trust fund. When doing so, they must bear in mind the different interests of the beneficiaries. For example, if £500,000 is held on trust for Anne for life, remainder to her children, Jack and John, then the trustees must ensure that the investments yield a reasonable income for Anne, and do not diminish the capital to which Jack and John will eventually be entitled.

The following diagram illustrates the source of the trustees' power to invest.

Trustees' power to invest derives from:

An express power of investment in the trust instrument

The express power prevails over the statutory power – it may be narrower than the statutory power, e.g. the settlor might state that investments should not be made in tobacco companies or, conversely, the express power could be wider than the statutory power, e.g. authorising the acquisition of freehold and leasehold land outside the United Kingdom

A statutory power of investment in the Trustee Act 2000

The Trustee Act 2000 repeals the far more restrictive Trustee Investments Act 1961 and grants a general power of investment – see below.
The Trustee Act 2000 came into force on 1 February 2001 and what is important to note is that s 7 states that it is retrospective, i.e. it applies to trusts created before that date

The general power of investment in s 3(1) of the Act provides that: 'a trustee may make any kind of investment that he could make if he were absolutely entitled to the assets of the trust'.

Exception: s 3(3) of the Act states that **the general power of investment** does not permit a trustee to make investments in land other than lending money by way of mortgage. However, investment in land is specifically dealt with in s 8 of the Act, as we shall see below.

You may have noticed how wide the general power of investment is. However, it is **essential** to know that the trustees are subject to a number of duties when exercising this general power of investment. These duties are set out in the following diagram.

Trustees' duties when exercising the statutory power of investment in the Trustee Act 2000

Section 1 Trustee Act 2000 – trustees must abide by the general duty of care in s 1 and already considered in this chapter

Section 4(1) Trustee Act 2000 – 'when exercising any power of investment...a trustee must have regard to the standard investment criteria' – see s 4(3) below

Section 4(2) Trustee Act 2000 – 'A trustee must from time to time review the investments of the trust and consider whether, having regard to the standard investment criteria, they should be varied'

Section 5(1)(2) Trustee Act 2000 – 'Before exercising the power of investment ...and when reviewing the investments ...a trustee must obtain and consider proper advice' about whether, having regard to the standard investment criteria, the power that should be exercised, or the investments varied

Section 4(3) Trustee Act 2000 defines the standard investment criteria as 'the suitability to the trust of investments' and 'the need for diversification of investments'

In *Jeffrey v Gretton* [2011] the trust acquired a dilapidated house from the deceased in 2001. The trustees were held to be in breach of their duty to review when they decided to renovate the house, taking six years to do so. If they had reviewed the investment and taken professional advice, it would have been sold immediately in its dilapidated state

Section 5(3) Trustee Act 2000 – 'a trustee need not obtain such advice if he reasonably concludes that in all the circumstances, it is unnecessary or inappropriate to do so'

Section 5(4) Trustee Act 2000 – 'proper advice is the advice of a person who is reasonably believed by the trustee to be qualified to give it by his ability in and practical experience of financial and other matters relating to the proposed investment'

If a trustee does **not** carry out his investment duties above, he may be liable for breach of trust – as we shall see in Chapter 13 under 'Breach of trust'.

Mortgages of land as an investment

Such an investment is permitted by s 3(3) of the Trustee Act 2000 but it is s 8 of the

Trustee Act 1925 that provides **guidance** as to the amount of the loan that should be made, as illustrated in the following diagram.

When making the loan, the trustee should act upon a report as to the value of the property made by a person whom he reasonably believed was a qualified surveyor/valuer	This surveyor/valuer should be employed independently of the owner of the property	The amount of the loan should not exceed two-thirds of the value of the property

If the trustee follows this guidance, he will be protected should the valuation of the property be wrong. However, if he lends more than two-thirds of the value of the property and loss occurs, he will be liable to make good the excess. Thus, in *Shaw v Cates* [1909], the trustee should have lent only £3,400. Instead, he lent £4,400 and accordingly was liable for £1,000 with interest.

Purchasing land as an investment

This is governed specifically by s 8 of the Trustee Act 2000, which provides as follows:

> **Trustee Act 2000**
>
> **Section 8(1)**   A trustee may acquire freehold or leasehold land in the United Kingdom –
>
> (a)   as an investment;
> (b)   for occupation by a beneficiary; or
> (c)   for any other reason.

Two points to note – firstly, under s 10 of the Act, this power is retrospective so it applies to trusts that were created before the Act came into force, and secondly, it is confined to land in the United Kingdom.

Two general principles regarding investment derived from case law

Suppose that the trustees have strong ethical or political views regarding certain investments, e.g. in alcohol, armaments. Can the trustees refrain from making such investments?	In *Cowan v Scargill* [1985], Megarry VC said, 'In the conduct of their own affairs, of course, they are free to abstain from making such investments. Yet under a trust, if investment of this type would be more beneficial to the beneficiaries than other investments, the trustees must not refrain from making the investments by reason of the view they hold'.

| Suppose that the trustees invest over-cautiously although in accordance with the **portfolio theory of the period:** should they be liable for the potential loss of profit to the beneficiary? | In *Nestle v National Westminster Bank Plc* [2000], the remainderman claimed that if the bank had properly reviewed the trust investments and invested a higher proportion in ordinary shares, the fund of £269,203 would be worth over £1 million. The bank was held not to be in breach of its investment duty. Staughton J stated: 'Here one must take care to avoid two errors. First, the trustees' performance must not be judged with hindsight ... Second ... one must bear in mind that investment philosophy was very different in the early years of this trust from what it became later ...' |

Duty to maintain equality between beneficiaries

This duty is particularly relevant in trusts for beneficiaries entitled in succession, e.g. in his will, Sam sets up a trust of his residuary estate for his widow for life, remainder to his children. The widow will be entitled to the income from the trust and the children will be entitled to the capital on the widow's death. In order to manage such trusts, the trustees clearly have to distinguish between capital and income receipts. Let us suppose that when Sam died, most of his residuary personal estate was non-income producing (and therefore unavailable to the widow) or of a wasting nature (and therefore unavailable to the children). There are rules of conversion and apportionment to deal with this problem (e.g. the rule in *Howe v Earl of Dartmouth*), described by the Law Commission as archaic and overly complex, and which it recommends should be abolished for future trusts). In this connection, see the Law Commission's proposals in the 'Up for Debate' box below.

Up for Debate

In Law Commission Report 315 (2009) *Capital and Income in Trusts: Classification and Apportionment*, the Law Commission stated 'selecting investments with a view to the likely returns (in terms of capital or income) rather than the overall value of returns ... constrains investment choice. ... Many trustees would prefer to invest without such restrictions, concentrating instead on the total return to the trust'.

'Total return investment is possible if trustees have a power to allocate the global investment return received by the trust to the income and capital beneficiaries according to what the beneficiaries might expect to enjoy in the light of their respective interests in the fund.'

'We recommend that HMRC and HM Treasury enter into discussions with the trust industry as to the feasibility and mechanics for total return investment for trusts within the parameters of current tax policy.'

The trustees' administrative duties

When a trustee is appointed, he has certain duties as indicated in the first column below. Apart from the first two, these duties continue throughout his trusteeship, together with his duty to provide accounts and information to the beneficiaries, and his duty to act jointly with his co-trustees.

Trustee's duties on appointment (and thereafter)	Trustee's duty to provide accounts and information	Trustee's duty to act jointly with co-trustees
On appointment, a trustee should familiarise himself with the terms of the trust.	Trustees have a duty to prepare and maintain proper accounts (although this is usually carried out by a qualified accountant acting as the trustees' agent).	Where there is more than one trustee of a trust, the trustees must act jointly when making a decision as there is no ability to reach a majority decision unless this is authorised by the trust instrument or the court.
Having done so, he should check that neither retiring trustees not continuing trustees have committed a breach of trust. To this end, he may require such trustees to provide him with relevant information.

He should ensure that the trust property is invested in accordance with the trust instrument and the Trustee Act 2000.

He should also ensure that all chattels and securities held in trust are in proper custody. | Every beneficiary under the trust has the right to inspect these accounts and may, if necessary, challenge the accounts.

A beneficiary is entitled to see trust documents but this is subject to certain limitations set out in the Privy Council case *Schmidt v Rosewood Trust Ltd* [2003]. Firstly, documents that state the reason why trustees made particular decisions when exercising their discretionary powers do not have to be disclosed unless the court orders disclosure; secondly, documents where there are issues of commercial or personal confidentiality do not have to be disclosed to the beneficiary. | This duty to act collectively is relevant with regard to the trustees' liability for breach of trust as we shall see in Chapter 13. |

Duty to distribute

If the trustee fails to distribute the trust fund, be it income or capital, to the correct beneficiary, he will be in breach of trust and personally liable to make good any loss.

A trustee can protect himself in several ways, for example:

❖ Under s 27 Trustee Act 1925, the trustee can **advertise for claimants** or creditors and, after complying with the formalities, distribute the trust assets without fear of liability.
❖ In Chapter 2, we saw that if a trustee does not know the whereabouts of a beneficiary, or whether he is dead or alive, the trustee may apply to court for **a Benjamin order**, which enables him to distribute the trust property and escape liability should the missing beneficiary turn up.
❖ In Chapter 2, we noted that the trustee might prefer to take out **missing beneficiary insurance**.
❖ As a last resort, there is the unsatisfactory solution that we saw in *Re Gillingham Bus Disaster Fund* [1959] in Chapter 6 regarding surplus trust assets, which were **paid into court** to await possible claimants.

A final word regarding the office of trustee

As we have seen in this chapter, the office of trustee is very demanding. In its 1982 report on the *Powers and Duties of Trustees*, the Law Reform Committee stated 'there is much to be said about the duties and obligations of a trustee and little of his rights'.

Aim Higher

It is important to remember that duties must be carried out by the trustee, and to make the connection with the trustee's personal liability for breach of trust (see Chapter 13).

Putting it into practice

By his will, Horace, a wealthy bachelor who died six months ago, gave £1 million to his friends, Graham and Stewart, to hold on trust for his niece, Jane, for life, remainder to her children.

Graham and Stewart have discovered that Jane is in financial difficulty and has nowhere to live. She has two daughters, Amy and Anna. They would like to be able to use some of the money to buy her a house and, as they are very keen on renewable energy, they wish to invest the rest of the money in Gales plc, a company involved in building wind farms.

Advise Graham and Stewart concerning their investment powers and duties, having regard to the above circumstances.

Feedback on putting it into practice

The following diagram gives a suggested answer plan.

First – Where beneficiaries are entitled in succession, the trustees must try to maintain equality. So, Graham and Stewart should choose investments that yield income but also maintain capital. Could mention Law Commission's proposals regarding total returns investment.

Second – Graham and Stewart have wide powers of investment under the **Trustee Act 2000**. Section 3(1) provides trustees with a general power of investment (but this section does not include land).

Third – Graham and Stewart have the power to invest in land under the **Trustee Act 2000**. Section 8 provides trustees with the power to purchase land as an investment or for occupation. Jane and her children could occupy the house and it would also be a capital investment.

Fourth – When selecting investments, Graham and Stewart must have regard to their duties under the **Trustee Act 2000**. Explain trustees' duty of care under s 1, and their duty to have regard to standard investment criteria under s 4. Also mention trustees' duty to seek advice under s 5, and to review the investments.

Fifth – When selecting investments, Graham and Stewart's main consideration is the financial interest of the beneficiaries Cite *Cowan v Scargill* to the effect that trustees should not pursue a policy of ethical investment if this is based on their own views.

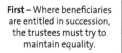

Table of key cases referred to in this chapter

Case name	Area of law	Principle
Cowan v Scargill [1985]	Duty to invest	Trustee's duty when selecting investments is the beneficiaries' financial interests
Dover Coalfield Extension, Re [1908]	Director's fees	Trustee could keep fees as he was appointed director before he became a trustee

East, Re [1873]	Replacement of trustee	Trustee of unsound mind and incapable of acting as trustee
Francis, Re [1905]	Director's fees	Trustee cannot retain fees if he used his position as trustee to be elected as director
Gee, Re [1948]	Director's fees	Trustee elected as director even if trust share votes ignored
Letterstedt v Broers [1884]	Inherent jurisdiction of court to remove a trustee	Guidance regarding court's power to remove trustee
Nestle v National Westminster Bank plc, Re [2000]	Duty to invest	Trustees' performance must not be judged with hindsight
Schmidt v Rosewood Trust [2005]	Trustees' duty to provide information	Beneficiaries' right to see trust documents is subject to limitations
Stoneham's Settlement Trusts, Re [1953]	Removal of trustee	A trustee who is being removed is not a retiring trustee
Tempest, Re [1866]	Appointment of trustee by the court	Criteria for court when exercising its jurisdiction under s 41 Trustee Act 1925
Walker, Re [1901]	Replacement of trustee	Trustee has to be out of the UK for a continuous period of 12 months
Wheeler and De Rochow, Re [1896]	Replacement of trustee	Trustee morally unfit to act as trustee

---

@ Visit the book's companion website to test your knowledge

❖ Resources include a subject map, revision tip podcasts, downloadable diagrams, MCQ quizzes for each chapter, and a flashcard glossary

❖ www.routledge.com/cw/optimizelawrevision

12

Trustees' Powers

Revision objectives

Understand the law	• Can you describe the trustees' power of collective delegation? • Are you able to describe a trustee's power of individual delegation?
Remember the details	• Which gifts carry the intermediate income and are therefore available for the maintenance of an infant beneficiary?
Reflect critically on areas of debate	• Do you consider that the power of advancement should be reformed?
Contextualise	• Can you compare the statutory power of maintenance with the statutory power of advancement? • Are you able to distinguish between a trustee's distributive and administrative functions?
Apply your skills and knowledge	• Can you answer the problem question at the end of the chapter?

Chapter Map

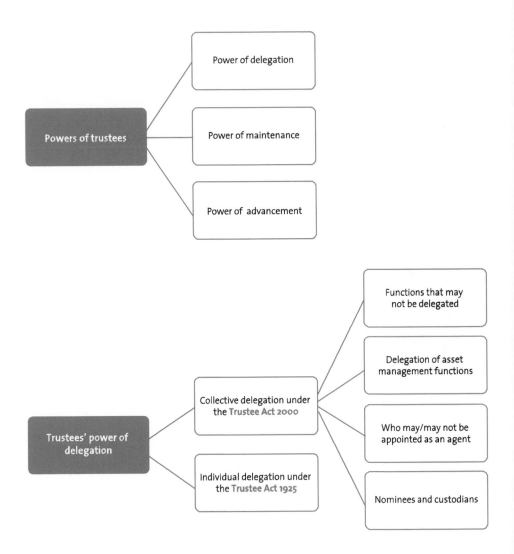

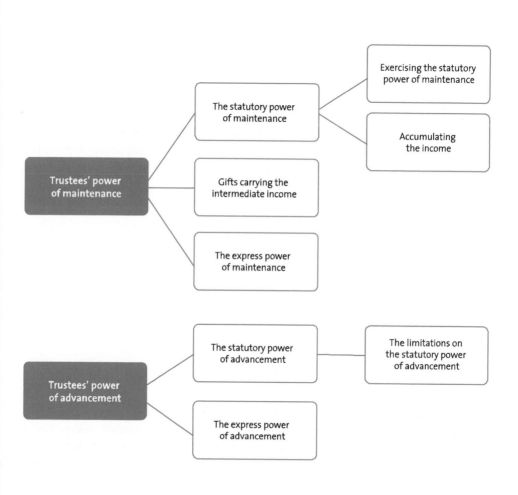

Trustees' powers

Introduction

Examination questions on trustees' powers usually relate to one or all of the following powers:

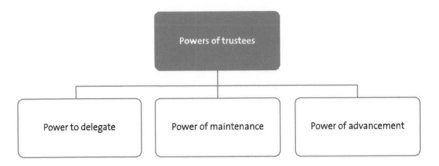

Remember that powers are different to duties in that whereas there is a mandatory obligation to perform a duty, the exercise of a power is discretionary. Although a trustee does not have to carry out a power, he must consider its exercise if the circumstances are such that it could be exercised.

The power to delegate

The law's attitude to delegation has changed over the last 200 years. Originally, the principle was that a delegate was not able to delegate (*delegatus non potest delegare*). However, as the world of business has become increasingly sophisticated, it is recognised that a trustee may not have the expertise to perform certain duties and, since the Trustee Act 1925, it is no longer necessary for the trustee to justify delegation.

Collective delegation under the Trustee Act 2000
Functions that cannot be delegated

The law regarding delegation is now found in the Trustee Act 2000. The Act is concerned with collective delegation by the trustees. Individual delegation is considered at the end of this section. The Trustee Act 2000 does not state which functions may be delegated by the trustees of a private trust. Instead, s 11(2) of the Act lists those functions that **cannot be delegated**. It reads as follows:

> **Section 11(2)** Trustee Act 2000
>
> In the case of a trust other than a charitable trust, the trustees' delegable functions consist of any function other than:
>
> (a) any function relating to whether or in what way any assets of the trust should be distributed,

(b) any power to decide whether any fees or other payment due to be made out of the trust funds should be made out of income or capital,

(c) any power to appoint a person to be a trustee of the trust, or

(d) any power conferred by any other enactment or the trust instrument which permits the trustees to delegate any of their functions or to appoint a person to act as a nominee or custodian.

You will notice from the above that trustees cannot delegate their **distributive** functions, e.g. they cannot delegate their function to distribute the trust fund amongst selected beneficiaries of a discretionary trust.

Delegation of asset management functions

It follows from the wording of s 11(2) of the Act that trustees have very wide powers of delegation. However, should they seek to delegate what is called an asset management function – for example, an investment decision, or the acquisition of property for the trust, or the disposal of property that is subject to the trust – then they must comply with s 15 of the Trustee Act 2000, which reads as follows.

Section 15 Trustee Act 2000

(1) The trustees may not authorise a person to exercise any of their asset management functions as their agent except by an agreement which is in or evidenced in writing.

(2) The trustees may not authorise a person to exercise any of their asset management functions as their agent unless –

(a) they have prepared a statement that gives guidance as to how the functions should be exercised ('a policy statement') . . . . .

(3) The trustees must formulate any guidance given in the policy statement with a view to ensuring that the functions will be exercised in the best interests of the trust.

(4) The policy statement must be in or evidenced in writing.

For example, if the trustees employed an estate agent to sell a property subject to the trust, this would be an asset management function and it would therefore be necessary to have an agreement and policy statement requiring the estate agent to act in the best interests of the trust.

Who may/may not be appointed as an agent

Section 12 of the Act states that trustees may appoint one of the other trustees as an agent but cannot appoint a beneficiary (even if he is a trustee). The reason is that the beneficiary might take advantage of his position as agent to prefer himself over other beneficiaries. If the trustees appoint more than one person to exercise the same function, those delegates must act jointly. Also relevant is s 13 of the Act, which allows trustees to decide on the amount of remuneration of the agent.

Nominees and custodians

Sections 16, 17 and 18 of the Act enable trustees to appoint nominees (e.g. to hold legal title in the name of the trustee) or to appoint custodians (i.e. to hold trust assets). These appointments must be evidenced in writing. An example of a situation when a nominee or custodian would be appointed as a matter of commercial convenience would be when trust shares are transferred electronically using the CREST system.

Liability for agents, nominees and custodians

Section 22 of the Act requires trustees 'to keep under review the arrangements' under which agents, nominees or custodians act, and to intervene (e.g. revoke the delegate's authority) if the trustees consider a need for such intervention has arisen. Section 23 of the Act states that a trustee will not be liable for the acts of his agents, nominees or custodians, provided that he has complied with his general duty of care laid down in s 1 of the Act regarding the initial appointment and subsequent supervision of the agent, nominee or custodian. Section 1 of the Trustee Act 2000 (referred to and discussed in Chapter 11) is reproduced below.

> **Section 1** Trustee Act 2000
>
> (1) Whenever the duty under this subsection applies to a trustee, he must exercise such care and skill as is reasonable in the circumstances, having regard in particular –
>
>   (a) To any special knowledge or experience that he has or holds himself out as having, and
>   (b) If he acts as trustee in the course of a business or profession, to any special knowledge or experience that it is reasonable to expect of a person acting in the course of that kind of business or profession.
>
> (2) In this Act the duty under subsection (1) is called 'the duty of care'.

Individual delegation

Section 25 of the Trustee Act 1925 allows an individual trustee to delegate by power of attorney all his functions (i.e. distributive or administrative) for up to 12 months, e.g. if he was going to be out of the country. The trustee (the donor of the power) would be liable for the acts and defaults of the donee of the power, as if they were his own.

The power of maintenance

Trustees have a discretionary power to make payments out of income from a trust fund to provide for the maintenance of a beneficiary, provided the gift to the beneficiary carries the available income (referred to as the 'intermediate income'). The diagram below illustrates how this power arises.

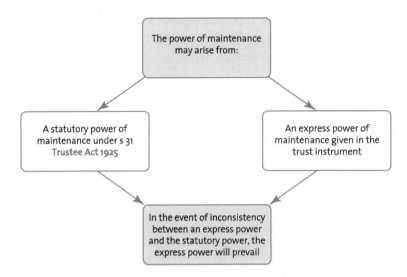

Similarly, if there is inconsistency between the statutory power and a direction in the trust instrument (e.g. the trust instrument directs that all income must be accumulated), this will prevail and the trustees would be unable to use their statutory power to pay the income to the infant beneficiary for his maintenance.

The statutory power of maintenance

Examination questions on maintenance are usually concerned with the statutory power in s 31 Trustee Act 1925, which relates to the maintenance of **infant** beneficiaries. It is set out below.

Section 31 Trustee Act 1925

Subsection (1) provides:

'Where any property is held by trustees in trust for any person for any interest whatsoever, whether vested or contingent, then subject to any prior interests or charges affecting that property:

(i) During the infancy of any such person, if his interest so long continues, the trustees may, at their sole discretion, pay to his parent or guardian, if any, or otherwise apply for or towards his maintenance, education, or benefit, the whole or such part, if any, of the income of that property as may, in all the circumstances, be reasonable, whether or not there is –
   (a) Any other fund applicable to the same purpose; or
   (b) Any person bound by law to provide for his maintenance or education; and

(ii) If such person attaining the age of 18 years has not a vested interest in such income, the trustees shall thenceforth pay the income of that property and of any accretion thereto under subsection (2) of this section to him, until he either attains a vested interest therein or dies, or until failure of his interest.

Some of the concepts in this statutory power are difficult to understand and, therefore, they are explained by reference to the types of scenario that you may encounter in an examination question.

Example 1 – an infant beneficiary with a vested interest
Samuel's will provides '£800,000 on trust for my son, Peter, for life, remainder to David'. Peter is 10 years old when Samuel dies.

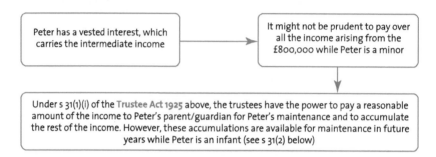

Note that the gift to David does **not** carry the intermediate income because there is a prior interest, i.e. the life interest of Peter. The trustees could not exercise the power of maintenance in favour of David. However, on Peter's death, David will become entitled to the capital.

Example 2 – beneficiary with a vested interest attains 18 years of age
Following on with the above example, when Peter attains 18, he is entitled to all the income and the trustee's statutory power of maintenance comes to an end.

Example 3 – infant beneficiary with a contingent interest
Samuel's will provides '£800,000 for my daughter, Penelope, on attaining 25 years of age'. Penelope is currently 16 years old.

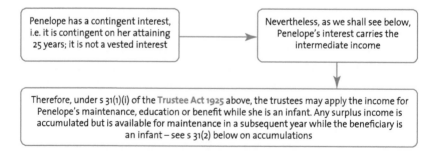

Example 4 – beneficiary with a contingent interest attains 18 years of age
The effect of s 31(1)(ii) is that, on attaining 18 years of age, Penelope's interest is accelerated and the trustees are required to pay her all the income from the fund

until she attains 25 years of age or dies before that age. However, during this period (i.e. between 18 and 25 years of age), Penelope is not entitled to income that may have been accumulated during her infancy, under Example 3. This is now regarded as capital and will be paid only when Penelope attains 25 years and the trust comes to an end.

Gifts carrying the intermediate income

Remember that the statutory power of maintenance applies only when the gift carries what is called the intermediate income. Vested interests (such as Peter's interest in Example 1) always carry the intermediate income.

The general rule is that contingent gifts carry the intermediate income, although there are complex rules (largely found in s 175 Law of Property Act 1925) regarding contingent gifts arising under a will and these are set out in the following diagrams.

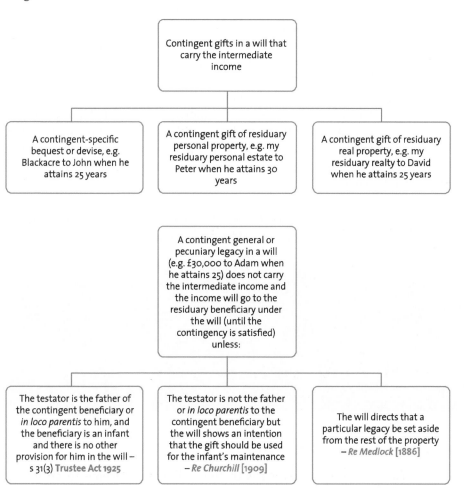

In our example of a contingent pecuniary legacy to Penelope, the testator was Penelope's father and if there was no other provision for Penelope in his will, the gift would have carried the intermediate income.

Exercising the statutory power of maintenance

When deciding whether to use the income for the infant's maintenance, education or benefit, the trustees are required by s 31(1) Trustee Act 1925 to consider 'the age of the infant, and his requirements and generally to the circumstances of the case, and in particular to what other income, if any, is applicable for the same purposes'.

In *Wilson v Turner* [1883] the trustees paid the income over automatically to the infant's father without consciously exercising their discretion and were liable for breach of trust when the father used the money for his own benefit.

Accumulating the income

Section 31(2) Trustee Act 1925 provides that any income not applied for the infant's maintenance, education or benefit shall be accumulated. We saw in Examples 1 and 3 above that such accumulated income may be used in subsequent years for the maintenance of the beneficiary, provided he is still an infant.

In Peter's case, we saw that as he has a life interest, once he attains 18 years he becomes entitled to all the income. Furthermore, under s 31(2)(i)(a), upon his majority (or his marriage under that age), he is entitled to the accumulated income that was not used for his maintenance while he was an infant (after all, having a life interest, strictly he was entitled to that income all along). Therefore, this accumulated income will not go to David.

In Penelope's case, she will only receive the accumulated income when she satisfies the contingency of attaining 25 years and the trust comes to an end.

Common Pitfall

A final word on maintenance – it is important to remember that the trustees' statutory power of maintenance applies only to **infant** beneficiaries.

However, a settlor may give trustees an **express power** in the trust instrument under which the settlor may authorise trustees to maintain **adult** beneficiaries. Furthermore, the court has inherent jurisdiction to authorise the trustees to maintain beneficiaries who may include adult beneficiaries.

The power of advancement

Whereas maintenance is concerned with the payment of income to an infant beneficiary, advancement is concerned with the payment of capital to any beneficiary before the time when he is entitled to the trust fund. The details of advancement are explained by examples based on the type of scenario often encountered in examination questions, as follows:

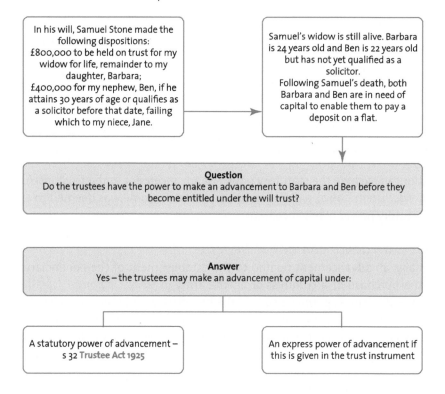

The statutory power of advancement

This statutory power applies to all trusts unless a contrary intention is expressed in the trust instrument.

Who can ask for an advancement under the statutory power?

The answer is provided in s 32(1) Trustee Act 1925, which reads as follows:

Section 32(1) Trustee Act 1925

Trustees may at any time or times pay or apply any capital money subject to a trust for the advancement or benefit, in such manner as they may, in their absolute discretion, think fit, of any person entitled to the capital of the trust property or of any share thereof, whether absolutely or contingently on his attaining any specified age or on the occurrence of any other event, or subject to a gift over on his death under any specified age or on the occurrence of any other event, and whether in possession or in remainder or reversion, and such payment or application may be made notwithstanding that the interest of such person is liable to be defeated by the exercise of a power of appointment or revocation, or to be diminished by the increase of the class to which he belongs.

Let us apply s 32 Trustee Act 1925 to our scenario regarding Barbara and Ben on the previous page.

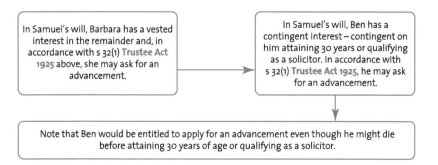

In Samuel's will, Barbara has a vested interest in the remainder and, in accordance with s 32(1) Trustee Act 1925 above, she may ask for an advancement.

In Samuel's will, Ben has a contingent interest – contingent on him attaining 30 years or qualifying as a solicitor. In accordance with s 32(1) Trustee Act 1925, he may ask for an advancement.

Note that Ben would be entitled to apply for an advancement even though he might die before attaining 30 years of age or qualifying as a solicitor.

A settlor can exclude the statutory power of advancement in the trust instrument. In *IRC v Bernstein* [1960], a direction to accumulate income was deemed to exclude the statutory power of advancement.

What is an advancement or benefit?

Originally, an advancement related to the establishment of the beneficiary in life (e.g. the purchase of a commission in the army in *Lawrie v Bankes* [1858] or the purchase of business premises so that the beneficiary could set up as a doctor in *Re Williams Will Trust* [1953]), but the addition of the word 'benefit' to the statutory power has enabled the trustees to make the payment for any form of material benefit of the beneficiary.

Clearly, the trustees cannot make an advancement that benefits the trustees or that benefits a person other than the beneficiary. In *Molyneux v Fletcher* [1898], the trustees advanced money to a beneficiary so that she could pay her father's debt to one of the trustees. This was clearly an improper use of the power of advancement. See also *Re Pauling's Settlement Trusts* below.

Case precedent – *Re Pauling's Settlement Trusts* [1964] Ch 303

Facts: The bank, Coutts & Co, was the trustee of a marriage settlement for Mrs Younghusband (née Pauling) for life with remainder on her death to her children.

Mrs Younghusband and her husband, Commander Younghusband, lived beyond their means and when the trustees made a number of advancements, ostensibly to the children (who were all adults in their twenties) so that they could make improvements to their homes and buy furniture, the advancements were used to purchase a house for Commander Younghusband on the Isle of Man and to pay off Mrs Younghusband's overdraft.

The children later complained that these advancements had been made in breach of trust. The Court of Appeal held that what the trustee 'cannot do is to prescribe a particular purpose, and then raise and pay the money over to the advancee leaving him or her entirely free, legally and morally, to apply it for that purpose or to spend it any way he or she chooses without any responsibility on the trustees even to inquire as to its application'.

Principle: Trustees have a duty to see that the advancement is used for the stated purpose.

Application: When applying this decision, it might be appropriate to mention that the trustees pleaded a number of defences (which we will consider in Chapter 13 in 'Breach of trust').

In *Pilkington v IRC* [1964] AC 612, the House of Lords approved an advancement to a beneficiary with a contingent interest, for the purpose of settling the money on new trusts in her favour in order to avoid death duties. Lord Radcliffe said that advancement or benefit meant 'any use of the money which will improve the **material** situation of the beneficiary'.

However, 'benefit' was taken to include 'moral benefit' in *Re Clore's Settlement Trusts* [1966] when an advancement was made to a beneficiary with a contingent interest as he felt a genuine moral obligation to make payments to charity.

The limitations on the statutory power of advancement
There are three limitations on the use of the statutory power. These are stated in s 32 Trustee Act 1925 and are identified in the following diagram.

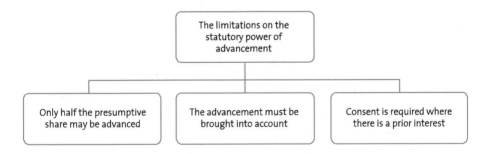

The practical effect of these three limitations is illustrated in the next diagram.

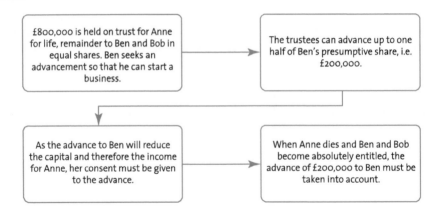

Express power of advancement

If an express power is given in the trust instrument, it is usually to enable the trustees to advance more than one half of the beneficiary's presumptive share.

Aim Higher

When a person dies intestate, the intestacy rules establish statutory trusts to safeguard property when those entitled to inherit are under 18. The Law Commission has proposed amending the power of advancement relating to these statutory trusts to enable the trustees to apply the whole of the capital rather than half the beneficiary's presumptive share. It subsequently proposed that this reform of s 32 **Trustee Act 1925** should apply to all trusts. It is useful to look at the publication on the Law Commission's website, not only for its proposals regarding this reform but because it also contains examples of the current law. See 'Intestacy and Family Provision Claims on Death: Sections 31 and 32 of the **Trustee Act 1925** – A Supplementary Consultation Paper No 191 (Supplementary), 26 May 2011'.

Putting it into practice

By her will, Felicity, after appointing Horace and Oswald to be her executors and trustees, left £900,000 to them upon trust to divide into three equal parts and to hold the three parts upon the following trusts:

(i) as to one third part, to accumulate the income until the year 2023 and thereupon all capital and accumulated income to my dear son, John, absolutely;

(ii) as to another third part, upon trust in equal shares for such of my three dear daughters, Anne, Brenda and Celia, until Anne attains 18, when they may take absolutely;

(iii) as to the final third part thereof upon trust to pay the income to my dear husband, David, for life, remainder between my four children equally.

Felicity has just died leaving John, aged 22, her three daughters, Anne, Brenda and Celia aged 13, 16 and 17, and her husband, David.

Advise Horace and Oswald regarding the following:

(a) Whether they may apply the trust income in parts (ii) and/or (iii) to pay the private school fees of Anne and Brenda?
(b) What they should do with any surplus income in part (ii)?
(c) Whether they may apply trust capital from parts (i) and/or (iii) to enable John to qualify as a solicitor?

Feedback on putting it into practice

This question concerns the statutory power of maintenance and the statutory power of advancement.

(a) The issue is whether the trustees may exercise the statutory power of maintenance in the girls' favour by using the income from the second or third part of the trust to pay their school fees. Explain that the statutory power of maintenance in s 31 Trustee Act 1925 applies to infant beneficiaries with a vested interest and infant beneficiaries with a contingent interest. The main problem is whether the income is available for their use, i.e. does it carry the intermediate income?
   The income from the third part of the trust is not available as there is a prior interest – David's life interest – and the income will be paid to him for his lifetime. The income from the second part of the trust may carry the intermediate income as a contingent pecuniary interest if it was the testatrix's intention that it should be available for maintenance. If not, then the income will go to the residuary beneficiary under Felicity's will.

(b) Pending Anne's attainment of the age of 18, at which date the trust property can be distributed, s 31(2) of the Trustee Act directs that the income not used for maintenance can be accumulated. However, s 31(1) provides that when a beneficiary attains 18 (and Brenda and Celia will be 18 soon) but still does not have a vested interest under the trust fund, the beneficiary will nevertheless become entitled to her share of the income as it arises, i.e. her interest is accelerated regarding the right to income.

(c) The issue is whether the trustees may exercise their power of advancement under s 32 Trustee Act. Explain that advancement is potentially available to the extent of half of John's presumptive share. Regarding an advancement from the first fund, a direction to accumulate income may be inconsistent with the statutory power of advancement if *IRC v Bernstein* [1960] is followed. In the case of the third fund, advancement will only be possible if David, the life tenant, consents. The advancement will be for John's material benefit but the trustees must ensure that the advance is used for the purpose stipulated – *Re Pauling's Settlement Trusts* [1964].

Table of key cases referred to in this chapter

Case name	Area of law	Principle
Clore's Settlement Trusts, Re [1966]	Power of advancement	Advancement may be made for the moral benefit of the advancee
IRC v Bernstein [1960]	Power of advancement	Direction in trust instrument to accumulate may exclude power of advancement
Lawrie v Bankes [1858]	Power of advancement	Advancement to purchase a commission in the army
Molyneux v Fletcher [1858]	Power of advancement	Advancement to beneficiary's father in order to pay a debt was an improper use of the power
Pauling's Settlement Trusts, Re [1964]	Power of advancement	Trustees have a duty to see that the advancement is used for the stated purpose
Pilkington v IRC, Re [1964]	Power of advancement	Advancement to avoid death duties was of material benefit to the advance
Williams Will Trust, Re [1953]	Power of advancement	Advancement to enable the advancee to buy business premises from where to practise as a doctor
Wilson v Turner [1885]	Power of maintenance	Trustees must not exercise power of maintenance automatically but consciously exercise discretion

---

@ **Visit the book's companion website to test your knowledge**

❖ Resources include a subject map, revision tip podcasts, downloadable diagrams, MCQ quizzes for each chapter, and a flashcard glossary

❖ www.routledge.com/cw/optimizelawrevision

13

Breach of Trust

Revision objectives

Understand the law	• Can you explain when a retired trustee will be liable for breach of trust? • Are you able to describe the type of personal actions that may be brought against a trustee who is in breach of trust?
Remember the details	• Can you give details of the defences available to a trustee who is sued for breach of trust? • Can you remember the rules regarding tracing in equity?
Reflect critically on areas of debate	• Should trustee exemption clauses be more strictly controlled? • Should the qualifying conditions for tracing in equity be abolished?
Contextualise	• Do the common law rules of causation and remoteness of loss apply to compensatory claims against a trustee?
Apply your skills and knowledge	• Can you answer the problem question at the end of this chapter?

Chapter Map

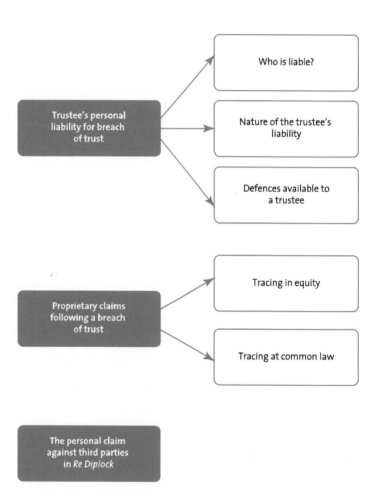

Trustee's personal liability for breach of trust

Who is liable?

Nature of the trustee's liability

Defences available to a trustee

Proprietary claims following a breach of trust

Tracing in equity

Tracing at common law

The personal claim against third parties in *Re Diplock*

Introduction to breach of trust

A breach of trust may occur in many different ways. To take three examples encountered in Chapter 11 regarding a trustee's **duties**: a trustee makes an unauthorised profit in breach of his fiduciary duty; a trustee does not carry out his duties relating to investment; a trustee purchases trust property. Similarly, in Chapter 12, regarding a trustee's powers, we saw that if a trustee exercises a **power** improperly, he may be in breach of trust.

The consequences of the breach of trust may also be different; for example, if the trustee has caused loss to the trust, he may be liable to compensate the trust. However, in Chapter 7, we saw that if a trustee wrongly disposed of trust property, the beneficiary might have a proprietary interest that would enable him to trace the proceeds of that disposal from the trustee, or where appropriate enable him to trace the property into the hands of a third party.

To cover all these possibilities, the topic of breach of trust will be considered under the following headings.

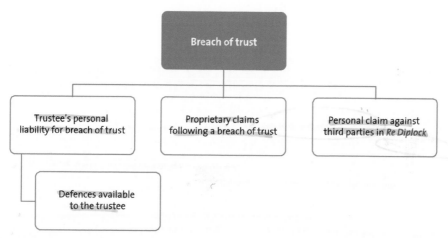

Trustee's personal liability for breach of trust

If a question requires you to discuss the personal liability of the trustees, first you may need to work out who is liable (e.g. whether a retiring trustee is liable or whether a trustee is liable for his co-trustee's actions); second, you will need to discuss the nature of the trustee's liability; and third, consider whether the trustee has any defence. These three aspects are considered below.

Who is liable?

In Chapter 11 we saw that, on appointment, a trustee is required to familiarise himself with the terms of the trust and, having done so, must check whether a retiring trustee or the continuing trustees are in breach of trust. A retiring trustee remains liable for breaches that he committed while in office and will also be liable if he retired so as to enable a breach of trust to take place.

A trustee's liability is personal, which means that he is not normally liable for a breach of trust by a co-trustee unless he was also at fault; for example, if he stood by without acting when he knew that a breach was taking place, or if he permitted trust funds to remain in the sole control of a co-trustee.

However, where he is liable together with a co-trustee, then liability is joint and several, which means that the beneficiary could recover his loss from both trustees or from just one of the trustees. If the beneficiary chose to sue just one of the trustees, then that trustee might be able to recover a contribution to the compensation he has to pay from his co-trustees under the Civil Liability (Contribution) Act 1978.

Nature of the trustee's liability

To answer a question on this subject, you need to be aware of the terminology as the following diagram explains.

Common Pitfall

The difficulty with the topic of the nature of the trustee's liability is the terminology.

The term equitable compensation is used rather than the common law term of damages.

Another problem is that, traditionally, the courts have referred to claims against the trustee in terms of the 'trustee's liability to account'. This relates to the trustee's duty to keep accounts of his management of the trust and the beneficiary's right to challenge these accounts. Where trust property is misapplied by the trustee, the beneficiary is entitled to 'falsify the account'. Where a trustee is negligent and causes loss to the trust, the beneficiary is entitled to 'surcharge the account'.

The next diagram illustrates the three different types of claim that may be brought against the trustee personally. In order to clarify the subject, the various alternative terms used by the courts are stated.

The different claims that may be brought against the trustee personally

Breaches of trust by trustee that involve misapplication of trust property, i.e. acts that are not authorised by the trust instrument	Other types of breaches of trust by trustee that are not concerned with the trust instrument but that cause loss	Trustee makes an unauthorised profit in breach of his fiduciary duty
Examples of these breaches: unauthorised investment is made; unauthorised distribution is made	Example: breach of trustee's duty of care, i.e. trustee acts negligently and causes loss	For examples, see Chapter 7 under 'Unauthorised profits made by a fiduciary'
Beneficiary can require the account 'to be falsified', i.e. in effect, the beneficiary asks for the disbursement to be disallowed	Beneficiary is entitled 'to surcharge the account' – meaning there is an omission in the accounts for which the trustee is liable	Sometimes referred to as a disgorgement claim or restitutionary response to unjust enrichment
Primary duty of the trustee is to restore the original trust property to the trust, sometimes called 'specific restitution'	Trustee is required to compensate the beneficiary for the loss	Trustee liable to account for the profit he has made (this is a personal remedy – as opposed to the proprietary remedy of a constructive trust), see Chapter 7
If specific restitution of the original trust property is not possible, the trustee is personally liable to pay money compensation equal to the value of the property lost to the trust – variously called substitutive compensation and equitable compensation	This is equitable compensation: it is sometimes called compensatory damages	

Up for Debate

The next confusing topic relates to the two **compensatory claims** in the above diagram and the question of measure of liability and whether the common law rules of causation and remoteness of loss apply, e.g. does the beneficiary have to prove that the breach caused the loss and the loss was reasonably foreseeable? This is not entirely clear cut. It seems (see selected extracts below) that in breaches involving misapplication of trust property, compensation is based on equitable principles only, but in other types of breach (e.g. a breach of a duty of care that causes loss), the common law rules of causation and remoteness would apply.

Do the common law rules of causation and remoteness of loss apply to the compensatory claims?

Breaches of trust that involve misapplication of trust property

Other types of breach that cause loss, e.g. breach of trustee's duty of care

Target Holdings Ltd v Redferns [1996] Lord Browne-Wilkinson said, 'The basic rule is that a trustee in breach of trust must restore or pay to the trust estate either the assets which have been lost to the estate by reason of the breach, or compensation for such loss. Courts of equity did not award damages, but, acting *in personam*, ordered the defaulting trustee to restore the trust estate ... thus the common law rules of remoteness of damage and causation do not apply. However, there has to be some causal connection between the breach of trust and the loss to the trust estate for which compensation is recoverable, viz. the fact that the loss would not have occurred but for the breach'.

Bristol & West Building Society v Mothew [1998] Millett LJ said, 'Although the remedy which equity makes available for breach of the equitable duty of skill and care is equitable compensation rather than damages, this is merely the product of history and in this context is in my opinion a distinction without a difference. Equitable compensation for breach of the duty of skill and care resembles common law damages in that it is awarded by way of compensation to the plaintiff for his loss. There is no reason in principle why the common law rules of causation, remoteness of damage and measure of damages should not be applied by analogy in such a case'.

Aim Higher

There are two more matters regarding a trustee's personal liability of which you should be aware.

First – where a trustee is liable to compensate the trust for his misapplication of trust property, the trust is also entitled to recover interest on the sum that was misapplied.

Second – the amount of equitable compensation payable is assessed at the date of the court's judgment, i.e. not at the date when the breach occurred.

Defences available to a trustee

Having established that a trustee is personally liable for breach of trust, an assessment question may require you to consider whether the trustee has any defence. These are listed below and then considered briefly in turn.

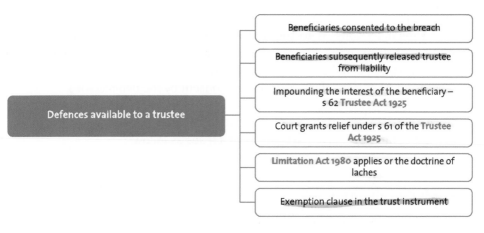

Beneficiaries consented to the breach

If a beneficiary consented to the trustee's breach of trust, the trustees may have a good defence. A useful case with respect to a number of defences is *Re Pauling's Settlement Trusts* [1963], which was considered in Chapter 12. The key facts were as follows:

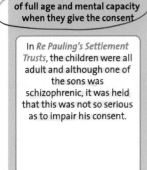

In the early 1950s, a number of advancements were made to the children (all adults), ostensibly so that they could make improvements to their homes but, in reality, used to pay off their mother's overdraft and to buy their father a house on the Isle of Man.

The trustees (Coutts Bank) were in breach of trust as they had failed to check that the advancement was used for the stated purpose. They pleaded the defence that the children had consented to the breach.

There are three conditions for the defence of consent by the beneficiaries to apply as indicated in the following diagram. In respect of some of the advancements made in *Re Pauling's Settlement Trusts*, the conditions were not satisfied and the defence failed.

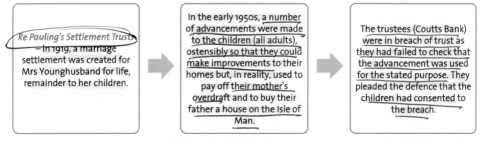

The beneficiaries must be of full age and mental capacity when they give the consent

In *Re Pauling's Settlement Trusts*, the children were all adult and although one of the sons was schizophrenic, it was held that this was not so serious as to impair his consent.

The consent was freely given by the beneficiaries

In the same case, the Court of Appeal rejected the trustees' argument in respect of some of the advancements that consent was freely given and held that the presumption of undue influence between parent and child could continue beyond the age of majority.

The beneficiaries must give informed consent

The beneficiaries must consent with full knowledge of the facts. In *Re Pauling's*, the children were not always fully aware of the nature of their rights when they consented.

Subsequent release of trustee from liability

This is similar to 'consent to the breach by the beneficiaries' in that the same conditions as those in the diagram above apply. However, the timing is different. In this situation, the beneficiaries release the trustees from liability after the breach has occurred, i.e. it is in effect retrospective consent by the beneficiaries.

Impounding the interest of the beneficiary

This is set out in s 62 Trustee Act 1925, which reads as follows:

> **Section 62(1)** Trustee Act 1925
>
> Where a trustee commits a breach of trust at the instigation or request or with the consent in writing of a beneficiary, the court may, if it thinks fit, make such order as to the court seems just, for impounding all or any part of the interest of the beneficiary in the trust estate by way of indemnity to the trustee or persons claiming through him.

Where a beneficiary has requested the breach of trust, s 62 Trustee Act 1925 gives the court the discretion as to whether it should deprive the beneficiary of his equitable interest in order to indemnify (i.e. make good) the loss that the trustee may have incurred as a result, e.g. to other beneficiaries of the trust. In *Re Pauling's Settlement Trusts*, the trustees successfully claimed an indemnity out of the life interest of Mrs Younghusband.

Court grants relief under s 61 Trustee Act 1925

The court has a discretion to relieve a trustee from liability for breach of trust under s 61 Trustee Act 1925, extracts from which read as follows:

> **Section 61** Trustee Act 1925
>
> If it appears to the court that a trustee . . . is or may be personally liable for any breach of trust . . . but has acted **honestly** and **reasonably**, and **ought fairly to be excused** for the breach of trust and for omitting to obtain the directions of the court in the matter in which he committed such breach, then the court may relieve him either wholly or partly from personal liability for the same.

The three conditions in bold, which must be proved by the trustee, are expanded upon in the following diagram.

Honestly	Reasonably	Ought fairly to be excused
Clearly, a trustee must act in good faith and will not be granted relief under s 61 when he has acted dishonestly. In *Pauling's Settlement Trusts*, the trustees had acted honestly but had they acted reasonably?	It seems that the general standard required of a trustee is that of a prudent man of business managing his own affairs. In *Pauling's Settlement Trusts*, it was held that a higher standard was expected of professional trustees.	This emphasises the discretion given to the court in cases where the trustees have satisfied the first two conditions. The question of fairness should be considered in relation to the trustees, beneficiaries and any other relevant parties, e.g. creditors.

You may have noticed that the section allows the court to grant relief either wholly or partly. In *Re Pauling's Settlement Trusts*, following one advancement to pay off the mother's overdraft, Mrs Younghusband had in fact assigned certain life policies in return to the children, and in respect of that particular transaction, the court did exercise its discretion under s 61 and grant the trustees partial relief from personal liability.

The Limitation Act 1980

Under s 21(3) of the Limitation Act 1980, a beneficiary cannot bring an action against the trustees for breach of trust if the breach occurred more than six years before. The sub-section states that 'the right of action shall not be treated as having accrued to any beneficiary entitled to a future interest in the trust property until the interest fell into possession'. This is explained in the example below.

> **Example**
>
> A trust is created for Adam for life, remainder to Ben. A breach of trust occurs during Adam's lifetime. The six-year limitation period does not begin so far as Ben, the remainderman, is concerned until Adam dies and Ben's interest falls into possession.

In *Re Pauling's Settlement Trusts*, the bank claimed that the limitation period had passed when the beneficiaries brought their action. This defence failed because the mother was still alive and time had not begun to run for the children who were the remaindermen under the trust.

Two main exceptions to the six-year limitation period

These two exceptions are self-explanatory and are set out in s 21(1) of the Act as follows:

> **Section 21(1)** Limitation Act 1980
>
> No period of limitation prescribed by this Act shall apply to an action by a beneficiary under a trust, being an action –

(a) In respect of any fraud or fraudulent breach of trust to which the trustee was a party or privy; or

(b) To recover from the trustee trust property or the proceeds of trust property in the possession of the trustee, or previously received by the trustee and converted to his use.

The doctrine of laches

Where there is no limitation period, for example, in cases falling under s 21(1) Limitation Act 1980 above, or where equitable relief is sought, such as the setting aside of a purchase of trust property by a trustee (see Chapter 11), then the defendant may, at the discretion of the court, rely on the doctrine of laches, i.e. that the beneficiary's claim is barred because it would be unconscionable for him to assert his rights after an unreasonable delay in bringing the action – *Patel v Shah* [2005].

Exemption clause in the trust instrument

There are a number of separate points to note:

In *Armitage v Nurse* [1998], the Court of Appeal considered a trust instrument in which clause 15 provided that 'no trustee shall be liable for any loss or damage … unless such loss or damage shall be caused by his own actual fraud'. Millett LJ rejected the argument that such a clause, which excluded all liability except fraud, was void because it was repugnant or against public policy.

However, Millett LJ said that there was a core of minimum obligations owed by a trustee, but added, 'I do not accept … that these core obligations include the duties of skill and care, prudence and diligence. The duty of the trustees to perform the trusts honestly and in good faith for the benefit of the beneficiaries is the minimum necessary to give substance to the trusts'.

Millett LJ added, 'it must be acknowledged that the view is widely held that these clauses have gone too far … and if clauses such as clause 15 of the settlement are to be denied effect, then in my opinion this should be done by Parliament'.

However, the subsequent Trustee Act 2000 did not deal with trustee exemption clauses and, in fact, by paragraph 7 of Schedule 1 to the Act, the statutory duty of care in s 1 of the Act may be expressly excluded in the trust instrument.

settlor is aware of the meaning and effect of the clause ... and that regulatory and professional bodies should make regulation to such effect ... and enforce such regulation in accordance with their codes of conduct.'

Up for Debate

The Law Commission's recommendations, which have been accepted by the Government, have been criticised as not going far enough to control trustee exemption clauses.

The Commission's justification is that if such clauses were restricted by statute, the effect might be that professional trustees would charge much higher fees to cover their exposure to greater risk, or to cover their insurance premiums, or alternatively might be overly cautious in the management/investment of trust funds to the detriment of beneficiaries, or might even refuse to accept the role of trustee if the risks attaching to trusteeship were too high.

Proprietary claims

Introduction

We are now concerned with the situation where the beneficiary makes a proprietary claim – for example, where the trustee, Tim, has wrongly disposed of trust property to the defendant, David, and the beneficiary claims to have a proprietary interest in the asset in David's hands or claims to have a proprietary interest in the substitute asset that Tim acquired when he disposed of the trust property. The process by which the beneficiary asserts his rights to that asset is called 'tracing' or 'following'.

Aim Higher

Aim higher by using the correct terminology.

'Following' – this is the process of following the same asset as it moves from one person to another.

'Tracing' – this is an identification process, i.e. of identifying the new asset that has been substituted for the original asset.

Notice that following and tracing are **not** remedies but processes. We shall see below that there is a distinction between tracing in equity and tracing at common law.

'Claiming' – this is what the claimant does when either process above has been successfully completed, i.e. he has established the basis to claim a remedy (which is usually a proprietary remedy against the trustee/third party).

There are advantages of a proprietary remedy compared with a personal remedy, as we see below.

Advantages of a proprietary remedy compared with a personal remedy

It is recommended that you look back at the diagram on the comparison between the two types of remedy in Chapter 7 and look at the diagram below, as these advantages of a proprietary remedy may be highly relevant when advising a claimant in a problem question.

Key advantages of a proprietary remedy
A proprietary remedy may be claimed whether the defendant is solvent or insolvent
The property claimed may have appreciated in value since the breach of trust
The limitation period of six years does not apply to proprietary claims

Tracing in equity

There is a distinction between tracing in equity and tracing at common law, the former being far more flexible and extensive. When answering a question on tracing in equity, the following issues **must** be considered.

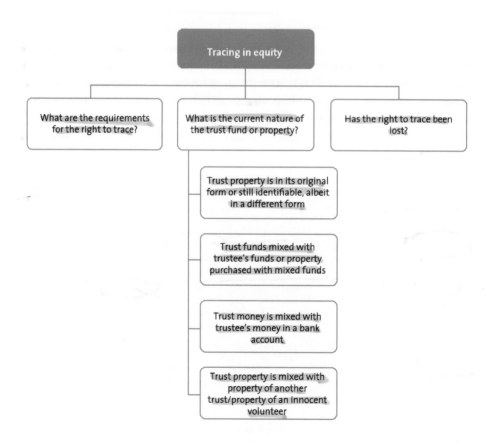

Requirements for right to trace

Traditionally, the right to trace in equity depends on the claimant being within a fiduciary relationship and having an equitable proprietary interest in the property in question.

It follows that the right to trace has not been confined to beneficiaries but exists whenever the claimant is within a fiduciary relationship. This fiduciary relationship has been found very easily by the courts because the relationship need not have existed before the transfer of the claimant's property into the hands of the defendant – the transfer itself may have created the fiduciary relationship. The classic example was stated *obiter* by Lord Browne-Wilkinson in *Westdeutsche Landesbank Girozentrale v Islington Borough Council* [1996] in which he said that if a thief stole money from a victim, then as a result of his fraudulent conduct, the thief would hold the money on constructive trust for the victim, thus providing both the fiduciary relationship and the equitable proprietary interest, and enabling the victim to trace his interest into the proceeds of any sale of the property by the thief.

Up for Debate

The ease with which the two requirements (a fiduciary relationship and equitable proprietary interest) have been found is because the courts have wanted claimants to have the ability to trace in equity. The requirements are therefore considered as artificial and consequently there has been much criticism of the need for these qualifying criteria and for the distinction between tracing in equity and at common law. For more on this, see Lord Millett's *obiter dicta* in *Foskett v McKeown* [2001] 1 AC 102 at 128–129.

The current nature of the trust fund/property

When answering a question on tracing in equity, it is essential to identify what has happened to the trust property, e.g. has it been mixed with the trustee's own property, were trust funds mixed with funds from another trust? In this respect, choose from the appropriate headings below.

Trust property is in its original form or still identifiable, albeit in a different form (i.e. unmixed)

If, for example, the trustee was holding an antique chest on trust and, in breach of that trust, transferred the antique chest to a third party, the claimant could **follow** the property into the hands of the third party, provided the third party was not a bona fide purchaser for value without notice of the trust.

If the trustee, in breach of trust, had sold the antique chest to a bona fide purchaser for value and had kept the proceeds separate from his own money, the claimant would be entitled to those proceeds. If the proceeds had been used to buy a substitute asset (known as 'clean substitution'), e.g. an oil painting, then the claimant would have a choice, as stated by Jessel MR in *Re Hallett's Estate* [1879] as follows:

> Jessel MR: '...the beneficial owner has a right to elect either to take the property purchased, or to hold it as security for the amount of the purchase money or, as we generally express it, he is entitled at his election either to take the property or to have a charge on the property for the amount of the trust money'.

Trust funds mixed with trustee's funds/property purchased with mixed funds

We are now concerned with the situation where the trustee has mixed the trust funds with his own property, or has used mixed funds to purchase property.

According to Ungoed-Thomas J in *Re Tilley's Will Trusts* [1967], it is for the trustee to prove that a particular part of the mixed property is his own. He stated, 'the onus is on the trustee to distinguish the separate assets, and to the extent that he fails to do so, they belong to the trust'.

If the trustee can prove what part of the mixed property was his own, then the claimant has a choice – either he can claim a lien over the mixed property to the value of the trust fund that was wrongly used by the trustee, or he is entitled to a proportional beneficial interest in the mixed property. The first choice would be advisable if the mixed property has depreciated in value, and the second choice would be better if the mixed property has appreciated in value. The following case illustrates this situation.

Case precedent – *Foskett v McKeown* [2001] 1 AC 102

Facts: A trustee, Timothy Murphy, took out a life insurance policy. He paid the first three annual insurance premiums with his own money but the next two annual insurance premiums were paid using trust money. In 1991, Timothy Murphy committed suicide and, under the life insurance policy, £1 million was paid to his children. The beneficiaries of the trust (from which Murphy had taken the money to pay two of the insurance premiums) argued that they were entitled to 40% of policy proceeds, representing a sum in proportion to the premiums they had paid. The children unsuccessfully argued in the House of Lords that the beneficiaries were only entitled to the amount of the premiums.

Principle: Claimants may elect to take a proportional share in the mixed property as opposed to a lien over the mixed property to the value of the trust property that has been wrongly used.

Application: It is relevant to note that the children were volunteers, i.e. they were not bona fide purchasers for value, and could be in no better position than the trustee (i.e. their father).

Trust money is mixed with trustee's money in a bank account

It is more likely that the trustee has mixed the trust funds with his own money in **a bank account.** When this happens, there are special rules.

Regarding a claim by the beneficiary to the balance in the trustee's bank account, it is **presumed** that the trustee withdraws his own money first. For example, if, in breach of trust, a trustee pays in £3,000 of trust money into his bank account, which already contains £3,000 of his own money, and then withdraws £3,000, it is presumed that he has withdrawn his own money, and so the money remaining in the account belongs to the trust – see *Re Hallett's Estate* [1879]. In *Re Hallett*, referring to such a trustee, Jessel MR stated as follows.

> Jessel MR: 'It seems to me perfectly plain that he cannot be heard to say that he took away the trust money when he had the right to take away his own money ... His money was there, and he had a right to draw it out...'

However, this presumption that the trustee withdraws his own money first can work to the claimant's disadvantage, as illustrated in *Re Oatway* below, in which case **an opposite presumption** applies.

Case precedent – *Re Oatway* [1903] 2 Ch 356

Facts: Oatway, a solicitor, misappropriated trust funds of £3,000, which he paid into a bank account that contained his own money. He then withdrew £2,137 from the account and used it to buy shares. He subsequently dissipated the balance in the account. When he died, insolvent, the shares were worth £2,474 and were held to belong to the trust.

Principle: Joyce J said, '...when any of the money drawn out has been invested, and the investment remains in the name or under the control of the trustee, the rest of the balance having been afterwards dissipated by him, he cannot maintain that the investment which remains represents his own money alone'.

Application: Note, however, that such an outcome can operate to the disadvantage of the trustee's creditors and it may be questioned whether this is fair.

So, to recap, if the balance in the trustee's bank account is insufficient to satisfy the trustee's liability to the claimant, then the claimant can trace the trustee's withdrawals into any property purchased with the mixed fund. It may be that, in accordance with the general principle in *Foskett v McKeown,* such a claimant now has a choice – he may elect to take a lien on the property to the amount of the trust funds that were used, or claim a proportionate share of the asset (which, as mentioned earlier, would be the better choice if the asset has appreciated in value). Against this, it should be noted that *Foskett v McKeown* was not concerned with money in a bank account, and it could be argued that if the claimant could choose the second option and thereby recover more than he had actually lost, this would be unfair if the trustee was insolvent and had general creditors who were looking to be paid from the trustee's assets.

Be aware that there is another rule called 'lowest intermediate balance'. This applies when trust funds are mixed with the trustee's money in a bank account, all or part of the money in the account is then dissipated, and later further money belonging to the trustee is paid into the account. Can the claimant assert that he is entitled to that later, further money? The answer provided by *Roscoe v Winder* [1915] 1 Ch 62 is 'no' – the lowest intermediate balance principle will apply, i.e. tracing can only relate to the lowest balance before the later payment in. This is illustrated in the following diagram.

Trustee has a bank account containing £3,000 of his own money. He then misappropriates £3,000 of trust money, which he puts into the account. He then withdraws £5,000 thus leaving £1,000 in the account. The £5,000 is dissipated. According to *Re Hallett*, the £1,000 in the account belongs to the trust. *Re Oatway* would not apply because the money withdrawn was dissipated.	The trustee subsequently pays in £4,000. The account now contains £5,000. Can the claimant argue that he is entitled to claim £3,000 of the money in the account?	The answer is no. Later payments into the account are not treated as repayments of the trust fund unless it can be shown that the trustee intended to replenish the trust fund. The claimant is only entitled to £1,000, i.e. the lowest intermediate balance.

Trust property is mixed with property of another trust/property of an innocent volunteer

The point to notice from this heading is that we are concerned here with competing claims. Firstly, competing claims between two claimants who have the right to trace, and secondly, competing claims between a claimant who has the right to trace and an innocent volunteer.

The general rule is that no one has priority and the claimants share equally, i.e. they rank *pari passu.* A useful case in this respect is *Re Diplock's Estate* [1948], which is the sequel to *Chichester Diocesan Fund and Board of Finance v Simpson* [1944].

Case precedent – *Re Diplock* [1948] Ch 465

Facts: Caleb Diplock directed his executors to apply his residuary estate '. . .for charitable or benevolent object or objects in England'. The executors distributed £203,000 amongst 139 charities. The gift was successfully challenged by Caleb Diplock's next of kin on the ground that it was invalid because it was not exclusively charitable. This action was concerned with the next of kin's attempt to trace the property in the hands of the charities, i.e. a competing claim between beneficiaries (the next of kin) and innocent volunteers (the charities).

Principle: Where trust money is mixed with money of an innocent volunteer, no one has priority and the beneficiaries take rateably with the innocent volunteers.

Application: This principle that the parties take rateably applies whether the mixed property has decreased or increased in value.

Note that special rules apply when the mixing of the funds of two trusts or the funds of a trust with funds of an innocent volunteer occurs in **a current bank account**. In this situation, the court may choose one of three possible solutions as follows:

The general rule in *Clayton's Case* – first in, first out	The rolling charge – North American approach	Claimants rank *pari passu*
This rule can be unfair as the following example shows: £2,000 is deposited in the trustee's own current account from Trust A, £2,000 from Trust B and £2,000 from Trust C. Then £3,000 is withdrawn by the trustee and dissipated, leaving £3,000 in the account for the claimants. Under the rule in *Clayton's Case*, Trust A would get nothing, Trust B gets £1,000 and Trust C gets £2,000.	This exception to the general rule in *Clayton's Case* is complicated and therefore expensive to apply. It is based on the principle that each withdrawal from the account is treated in the same proportions as the different interests in the account at the time of the withdrawal. In short, each withdrawal is attributed proportionately.	It was said in *Barlow Clowes v Vaughan* (see below) that the general rule in *Clayton's Case* should not apply if it is contrary to the express or implied intentions of the claimants, or was unjust or impractical. In such cases, the parties should share *pari passu* in the mixed fund in the account.

Case precedent – *Barlow Clowes International Ltd v Vaughan* [1991] 4 All ER 22

Facts: Barlow Clowes investment company collapsed. Investors' money had been dissipated and the question arose whether the rule in *Clayton's Case* applied as some investors alleged, which would mean that those who invested early would lose all their money, while those who invested late would recover their money. The Court of Appeal held that the rule in *Clayton's Case* was displaced because there was a shared misfortune and it was the **intention** of the investors that the remaining funds should be distributed rateably in proportion to their contributions to the fund.

Principle: The general rule in *Clayton's Case* will not be applied if it is contrary to the express or implied intention of the claimants or is impractical or would cause injustice.

Application: Note that, nowadays, the rule in *Clayton's Case* is not generally followed as the outcome would frequently be unjust.

Up for Debate

It is argued that 'backward tracing' should be allowed. This is where the trustee buys property with borrowed money, intending to repay that borrowed money with later, misappropriated trust funds. It is argued that, in these circumstances, the claimant beneficiary under the trust should be able to trace into that property even though it was purchased before the misappropriated trust money was used.

Has the right to trace been lost?

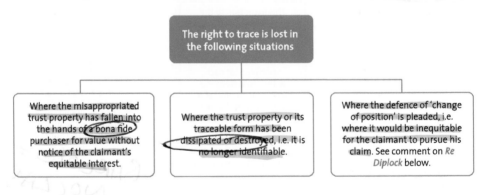

Regarding the above defence of 'change of position' – in *Re Diplock*, some of the charities had used the money they had received from Caleb Diplock's residuary estate to improve their properties. It would have been inequitable to force a sale of those properties in order to satisfy a tracing claim.

Tracing at common law

The right to trace at common law is much more limited than the right to trace in equity.

Original property or clean substitute

The common law allows a **legal owner** to follow/trace his original property or a clean substitute into the hands of the defendant. The authority is *Taylor v Plumer* [1815] below.

> ### Case precedent – *Taylor v Plumer* [1815] 3 M & S 562
>
> **Facts:** Sir Thomas Plumer gave money to a stockbroker, Walsh, to invest in exchequer bills. However, Walsh misappropriated the money and used it to buy bullion and American securities for his own purposes. Sir Thomas Plumer was able to trace his money into the bullion and securities, which were a clean substitute for his money.
>
> **Principle:** Tracing into exchanged property is permitted at common law.
>
> **Application:** Notice that if the substitute property has been used by the defendant and has earned a profit, the claimant is entitled to trace not only the substitute property but also the profit – *Jones (FC) & Sons v Jones* [1996] 3 WLR 703.

Mixed property

Where property is no longer identifiable because it has been mixed with other property or money, it cannot be traced at common law – *Agip (Africa) Ltd v Jackson* [1991] Ch 547.

> ### Common Pitfall
>
> The type of action brought by the claimant at common law can be difficult to understand.
>
> The claimant, who seeks to follow/trace a chattel or a clean substitute at common law, will bring an action for conversion under the **Torts (Interference with Goods) Act 1977**. The successful claimant will not necessarily recover his property or the clean substitute, although the court has a discretion under s 3 of the Act to order delivery instead of damages.
>
> The claimant, who seeks to follow/trace his money at common law, will bring a personal action for 'money had and received'.
>
> Thus, the right to follow/trace (i.e. the proprietary claim) will normally give rise at common law to a **personal remedy**, which is of little use where the defendant is insolvent.

Loss of the right to trace at common law

We have seen that the right to trace at common law will be lost when the claimant's property or money has been mixed with other property or money.

It is clear from *Lipkin Gorman v Karpnale* [1991] that the defence of 'change of position' (see earlier in this chapter) is available as a defence to a **legal** proprietary claim as well as an equitable proprietary claim. Briefly, the facts were that Cass, a solicitor, used money from his firm's client account to gamble at the Playboy Club

(Karpnale). The firm of solicitors, Lipkin Gorman, traced the money at common law and brought an action against the club for 'money had and received' in respect of £222,908. The club was unable to succeed with a defence that they had acted in good faith and given consideration for the money because, at that time, gambling contracts were void. However, they were able to plead the defence of 'change of position', although only in so far as they had paid out winnings to Cass. They were therefore only liable to pay the firm of solicitors £154,695.

The personal claim against third parties in *Re Diplock*

The facts of *Re Diplock* [1948] were given earlier in this chapter regarding the next of kin of Caleb Diplock who sought to recover the money that had been wrongly paid to 139 charities by the executors of Caleb Diplock. They also brought this alternative personal action against the charities, which succeeded in the House of Lords. The action is currently limited in its application to claims regarding the administration of estates, where an underpaid or unpaid legatee, next of kin or creditor sues the recipient who has been wrongly paid by the personal representatives. The action is only available when the sum cannot be recovered from the personal representatives.

Aim Higher

This action against innocent volunteers was mentioned in Chapter 7. We saw that it has been suggested that it should be developed and any innocent third-party volunteers who receive trust property in breach of trust should be similarly strictly liable to make restitution.

Putting it into practice

Toby is a trustee of the Adamson Trust. He has committed a number of breaches of trust over the past year, as follows:

❖ In February, he transferred £10,000 out of the Adamson Trust into his own current account, which contained £6,000.
❖ In March, he withdrew £5,000 from his current account and used it to buy shares in Simmonds Ltd, which are now worth £6,000.
❖ In April, he withdrew another £7,000, which he spent on a holiday in Australia.
❖ In May, he received a legacy of £10,000, which he paid into his current account.

Toby has just been adjudicated bankrupt with debts of £100,000 and the only assets, apart from what is left in his current account, are the shares in Simmonds Ltd.

Advise the beneficiaries of the Adamson Trust regarding their rights as against Toby's trustee in bankruptcy.

Feedback on putting it into practice

Introduction – Toby is clearly in breach of trust but there is no point bringing a personal action against him as he is bankrupt.

↓

Therefore, the beneficiaries should consider a proprietary claim. Explain tracing in equity. Consider whether the beneficiaries have the right to trace.

↓

Beneficiaries are within a fiduciary relationship and have an equitable proprietary interest in the property in question. Therefore, look at each transaction in turn.

↓

Transaction in February constitutes the breach of trust when £10,000 of trust money is misapplied and paid into Toby's current account.

↓

The bank account contains £6,000 of Toby's own money and £10,000 of trust money.

↓

Withdrawal in March of £5,000 to purchase shares. Prima facie, Toby is deemed to have withdrawn his own money first – *Re Hallett's Estate*.

↓

If *Re Hallett* were followed, the account now contains £1,000 of Toby's money and £10,000 of trust money.

↓

However, in April, Toby withdraws another £7,000 and prima facie, Toby is again deemed to have withdrawn his own money first – *Re Hallett's Estate*.

↓

If *Re Hallett* were followed, the account now contains only £4,000 of trust money.

↓

It may be possible to argue that the presumption in *Re Hallett* regarding the March withdrawal should be displaced on the basis that the withdrawal was used to purchase an investment and the balance in the account was subsequently dissipated – *Re Oatway*.

↓

If *Re Oatway* were followed, the shares purchased in March may be traced by the beneficiaries of the Adamson Trust. This would mean that after the withdrawal in March, the account contained £6,000 of Toby's money and £5,000 of the trust money and, following the second withdrawal in April, it contains £4,000 of trust money.

↓

The legacy of £10,000 received by Toby in May cannot be regarded as replacing trust money unless Toby intended this – *Roscoe v Winder* – lowest intermediate balance principle.

↓

Conclusion – there is £10,000 of Toby's money in the account available for his creditors. The remaining £4,000 in the account is trust money. The beneficiaries may claim a charge over the shares of £5,000 (i.e. the amount of trust money used in the purchase) but arguably may claim the increase in value, i.e. £6,000 – *Foskett v McKeown*. Finally, mention that there is no evidence that the right to trace has been lost.

Table of key cases referred to in this chapter

Case name	Area of law	Principle
Armitage v Nurse [1998]	Trustee exemption clause	Clause exempting trustees from all liability except fraud was not void
Barlow Clowes International Ltd v Vaughan [1991]	Tracing in equity	Rule in *Clayton's Case* will not apply if contrary to express/implied intention of claimant
Diplock, Re [1948]	Tracing in equity	Where trust money mixed with money of innocent volunteer, neither has priority
Diplock, Re [1948]	Tracing in equity	Defence of change of position pleaded
Diplock, Re [1948]	Personal claim against third party	Personal claim succeeded against charities
Foskett v McKeown [2001]	Tracing in equity	Claimants may elect to take a lien over mixed property to the value of the misappropriated trust property or a proportional share in the mixed property
Hallett's Estate, Re [1880]	Tracing in equity	Presumption that trustee withdraws own money first from mixed bank account
Lipkin Gorman v Karpnale [1991]	Tracing at common law	Defence of change of position pleaded
Oatway, Re [1903]	Tracing in equity	Claimant may trace into trustee's withdrawal to claim lien in property purchased
Pauling's Settlement Trusts, Re [1963]	Defences available to a trustee	Defences of consent, s 62 Trustee Act 1925 and Limitation Act 1980 pleaded
Roscoe v Winder [1915]	Tracing in equity	Rule regarding lowest intermediate balance applied
Taylor v Plumer [1815]	Tracing at common law	Tracing into exchanged property is permissible at common law

Index